GOD
as
Storyteller

Dedicated to Marmy,
My wife and my soulmate.
Your love and support made these pages possible.

GOD
as
Storyteller

Seeking Meaning in Biblical Narrative

John A. Beck

CHALICE
PRESS

ST. LOUIS, MISSOURI

Scripture quotations marked RSV are from the *Revised Standard Version of the Bible,* copyright 1952 [2nd edition, 1971], by the Division of Christian Education of the National Council of the Churches of Christ in the United States of America. Used by permission. All rights reserved.

Scripture quotations marked (NIV) are taken from the HOLY BIBLE, NEW INTERNATIONAL VERSION®. NIV®. Copyright © 1973, 1978, 1984 by International Bible Society. Used by permission of Zondervan Publishing House. All rights reserved.

Cover art: Jupiterimages/FotoSearch
Cover and interior design: Elizabeth Wright

Visit Chalice Press on the World Wide Web at
www.chalicepress.com

10 9 8 7 6 5 4 3 2 1   08   09   10   11   12

Library of Congress Cataloging–in–Publication Data

Beck, John A., 1956-
    God as storyteller : seeking meaning in biblical narrative / John A. Beck.
        p. cm.
    Includes bibliographical references.
    ISBN 978-0-8272-1254-1
    1. Storytelling–Religious aspects–Christianity. 2. Bible–Criticism,
Narrative. I. Title.

BT83.78.B43 2008
220.6'6–dc22

                                                        2007032276

Printed in the United States of America

Contents

Introduction

If we believe that a divine voice lies behind the pages of our Bible, then we must acknowledge that the God who speaks there is a storyteller. For the Bible is a book filled with captivating and memorable stories. Far from a cold rehearsal of the historical facts, each narrative is an engaging composition that invites the reader to follow, to watch, and to learn as the drama unfolds.

Consider the story from Abraham's life preserved in Genesis 22. In the pages leading up to that chapter, the reader of Genesis has joined Abraham and Sarah waiting for God to make good on the promise to give them a family. Despite their old age, this couple would have a son. Following Isaac's birth, we barely have time to celebrate with the happy couple before we are plunged headlong into the next crisis. Without a word of explanation, God directs Abraham to do the unthinkable. He is to slaughter his son like an animal, and burn his body on an altar! From that point on the storyteller has us. We observe Abraham's quiet preparations. We endure the unsuspecting question of Isaac. "The fire and the wood are here, but where is the lamb for a burnt offering?"(Gen. 22:7). And we shudder to see the knife poised above the heart of Abraham's one and only son.

The facts are engaging on their own, but it is the way the storyteller weaves those details into a narrative that grabs us and will not let us go. So it is, from page to page in our Bible, as God tells us stories from the lives of Joseph, Joshua, Deborah, Hannah, Ruth, Jesus, John, Mary, and Martha.

The notion that God is a storyteller becomes clear not only when we read individual stories like that of Abraham and Isaac, but also when we do the math. Of the sixty-six books in the Bible, twenty-two use story as the primary genre of communication. That is fully one-third of the books in God's inspired Word. But even that statistic undersells the reality. Those twenty-two books, whose primary means of communication is the story, account for nearly half the pages in our Bible. So when God has pulled back the curtain of heaven to speak with those of us who live on this side of that veil, God has spoken in story form more often than in any other way. If we believe that a divine voice lies behind the pages of our Bible, then we must acknowledge that the God who speaks there is a storyteller.

Why Tell a Story?

The fact that God is a storyteller leads quickly to the next question. Why would the eternal God elect to speak to us by using stories? The inspired authors of the Bible do not take the time to discuss or defend this literary choice, much as they do not discuss or defend any of the genre choices deployed throughout our Bible. But given what we know about stories and storytelling, we can reflect for a moment both on why people tell stories in general and why God may have chosen to speak with us in this way.

Some stories are told with the primary intent of entertaining the audience. The sitcoms that reach out to us from our television screens in the evening are an example of this kind of story. We are drawn to them much as crowds may have been drawn to an ancient bard who seized the attention of the audience by telling tales about life and living, heroes and villains. We listen, we laugh, and even cry as the storyteller plays with our thoughts, our fears, and our emotions. In a similar way, the stories told in the Bible draw us to them because they are entertaining. The story of David and Goliath and the story of Jesus' birth in Bethlehem are composed of just those ingredients that make for good entertainment. But at the same moment we acknowledge that Bible stories are entertaining, we must also acknowledge that if an all-powerful God tells a story, that Deity had something more than mere entertainment in mind.

Stories also may function to affirm a personal bond we have with others. My daughter loves to sit at the dinner table and hear the same stories told over and over again about the exploits of our family. One of her favorite stories is about a family camping trip that casts her father as the lead character. After a full day of torrential rain, contending with flooded tents and soaked sleeping bags, Dad made his bid to start a fire with wet wood and wet matches, in a wet fire pit. With the damp and hopeful eyes of the family upon him, he raised the ax above the wood and brought it down with a thud. But instead of connecting with the wood, he connected with the rope holding up the rain tarp, bringing that rain shelter down on the entire family. It is not a moment that sufficiently highlights my outdoor skills, but the story always makes her laugh and reinforces her feeling of connection to everyone caught under that tarp.

In so many ways, our lives are different than those living during the time of the Bible. We live in a location far removed from Israel, we are surrounded by electronic media, and we are employed in very different occupations. But the stories in the Bible build a bridge between the people of God who lived in the past and the people of God who live in the present. We are mothers, sons, and granddaughters. We struggle with temptation. We battle illness. We face financial uncertainty, celebrate at weddings, and mourn at funerals. These very human moments lie at the heart of every single Bible story. We have felt the physical pain of Job, the frustration of Peter, and the grief of Mary. As we read these stories, the differences between God's people of the past and God's people of the present disappear. We become part of a larger family whose members are all looking to the same God for guidance and support. God has prepared heaven to be a place where we will feel this sense of community in its ultimate form. Perhaps God intends for us to feel a modicum of that connection, even this side of heaven, through the stories that God tells.

In addition, these stories that entertain and build community are stories that effectively teach us how to live and how to think. Because we live in a world thoroughly invaded by sin, we are surrounded by lifestyles and worldviews that lead to unhappiness and failure. Since we may easily adopt these ways of thinking and living, God tell us stories designed to shake us to our very core. They challenge us to believe and trust in new and dynamic ways. They give hope to those feeling hopeless. They solicit action from those prone to lethargy in their life of faith. They accomplish this in a way that the declarative sentences in a catechism cannot, since stories touch not only our minds but our hearts as well. God is a storyteller who reaches to us from behind the words and sentences of those stories to grow our faith and to direct our thinking.

Finally, the story has one more quality that makes it such a desirable candidate for divine communication. Storytelling touches our imagination and so makes the lessons taught in the story more memorable.[1] Humans touched by the tragedy of Adam and Eve's fall are prone to forget the words of direction and encouragement that God offers. Like the Israelites in the Wilderness of Zin who hesitated to enter into the promised land, we, too, hesitate to press on in faith. All too quickly, we forget the promises, the words of direction, the sounds of encouragement that allow us to be certain of what we hope for and confident of what we do not see. The men, women, and children whose lives are laid bare in the stories of the Bible touch our imagination and kindle memories that can live on to influence us through the week. Perhaps God also uses stories for this reason, so that God's message might have a longer shelf-life among people who are prone to forget.

This side of heaven, we may never know exactly why God has elected to reveal the divine message and Person to us in stories. One thing is clear. Stories have the power to entertain, to create a sense of community, to effectively teach us, and to endure. Perhaps it is these characteristics of the story that led an all-knowing God to introduce the divine Person to us by using this literary tool.

How Does a Storyteller Make Meaning?

As a storyteller, God imbues the stories in the Bible with meaning. That means we are not done with a story like the one about Cain and Abel

(Gen. 4) until we bid to explain its enduring meaning and its significance for us. When we read the story of the farmer who kills his brother, the herdsman, we need to ask what God is saying to us through this story. Is God urging us to abandon all forms of agriculture because animal husbandry is more pleasing to God? Is he making a statement about the unauthorized taking of human life? Is he making it clear that even the sin of murder will not deter his intentions to bring about salvation through a descendant of Adam and Eve? Is it possible that more than one lesson lies ready to be learned from this story? Those questions lay bear the challenge of interpreting a Bible story. At first glance, stories like those about Jacob and Esau and narratives like Jesus changing water to wine seem better suited for the children's Bible study hour than for sophisticated seminary students or mature church members. But we shall see that investigating the meaning of a story can be a complex task that challenges the most mature of Christian thinkers.

How does a storyteller make meaning? Part of the answer to that question lies in learning as much as we can about the storytelling process. This means thinking about the story in a more careful and intentional way, taking the story apart and assessing how it was assembled from the raw materials available to the storyteller. Perhaps the first thing that stands out, as we begin such an analysis, is that stories are not merely factual accounts of "what happened." Rather they are carefully crafted art forms in which the storyteller selects both what is said (content) and how it is said (form) in a bid both to maintain the focus of the reader and to manipulate the response of the audience. From the start, it is critical to note that a story can be told in more than one way. And the way in which a story is told betrays an agenda.

This becomes clear when we examine some of the stories we have told. Let me share one of my own. When I was about four years old, I was playing in the basement with a small wooden mallet pounding fake nails into a fake board. My younger brother began to tease me mercilessly (as only a younger sibling can). What happened next is a matter of some dispute. But what can be said for sure is that my brother was more successful in ducking the airborne, wooden mallet than was the window behind him. Of course, the shattering of glass was bound to solicit the attention of my parents. So I sped off in the direction of my mother to make sure that she got the "right" story about the broken window. I can tell you that this one event precipitated two very different stories. My brother told a story that was nothing less than a tale of attempted murder by mallet. I told a story of merciless teasing that merited a strong response. As I was gesturing forcefully, the hammer "slipped" from my fingers and drifted in my brother's direction. In the end, both the story I told and the story my brother told agreed on the basic facts; but they were composed with different details, different emphases, and different word choices—all with the intention of leading the listener to two very different conclusions. Thus the same event produced two different stories composed with different content and employing different forms of speech.

Content Selection

One way that a storyteller shades the impact of the story is through the selection of content. Here the storyteller is actively making decisions about what to present to the reader and what to hide. Those decisions will have a clear and vivid impact on the way the listener responds to the story and the meaning drawn from it. Please be careful that you do not misunderstand my point. I am not suggesting that God would in any way misrepresent the facts. But I am suggesting that even God has options in telling a story about something that happened in the past. The biblical authors, under the inspiration of the Holy Spirit, will select certain details of the event for the story while setting aside others. This process of content selection is one of the ways that the storyteller influences our response to the narrative.

This means that the story and the historical event behind the story will not be the same thing. The thought may be disturbing to you at first, but please give it a moment. The event and the story that flows from the event are not the same thing. The event will always be composed of many, many more details than are selected for inclusion in the story. This is partly out of a concern for space, since a story must be told within a reasonable amount of time. If the storyteller were to relate every single detail—such as the temperature, the sky conditions, the time of day, the color of the protagonist's eyes, and so on—then the reader would certainly flounder in a swirling mass of details that would make the point of the story difficult to discern. But good storytellers select carefully from the details of the event so as to keep their story short and focused only on those details that participate in shaping the message the story is intended to deliver. This means that a Bible story will grow from the historical event, but it also means that the story and the event are not exactly the same thing.

A good place to view this selection process at work is those places in the Bible in which a single event is turned into more than one Bible story. For example, the storytellers of both 2 Samuel and 1 Chronicles relate how David defeated the Ammonite city of Rabbah (2 Sam. 11:1–12:31; 1 Chr. 20:1–3). Both stories begin and end with nearly the same details: it is spring time, the time when kings go out to make war; David sends Joab out to attack the Ammonite city of Rabbah while David remains in Jerusalem. Both authors end by saying, "David and all the people returned to Jerusalem following the defeat of Rabbah. In these details, there is symmetry between the two stories.

But did you notice the striking difference in the number of verses between the two accounts? The author of 2 Samuel tells it with fifty-eight verses, while the author of 1 Chronicles recasts the event with only three verses. Obviously there is much more to the story in 2 Samuel. It adds the details about David's sexual affair with Bathsheba, the attempts to cover up this sin, the murder of Uriah, the accusation of David by Nathan, David's repentance, the birth of the child conceived during the affair, and David's reaction to the child's death. Those details included by the divine storyteller in 2 Samuel give this account a very different feeling and impact than the story in 1 Chronicles, although the stories are both based on the same event from David's life.

The process of selection may be as dramatic and obvious as in the story above, or much more subtle–going unnoticed by all but the most careful reader. Consider the story of Matthew's (or Levi's) call to ministry found in the gospels of Matthew, Mark, and Luke. Each writer tells the story with approximately the same number of verses (Mt. 9:9–13; Mk. 2:13–17, and Lk. 5:27–31). If we focus only on the more prominent details, we may assume that the same story has been repeated three times. That story looks something like this. Jesus approaches Matthew while he is at his tax collection station. Jesus invites Matthew to follow him. Matthew follows him. Jesus joins Matthew, other tax collectors, and "sinners" at a dinner. The Pharisees question the disciples about the appropriateness of Jesus' behavior in eating with such people. Then Jesus uses a medical metaphor to respond to the challenge.

But if we read the three accounts more closely, we find subtle differences in the details that are part of the content-selection process involved in telling a story. Mark is the only one who introduces the story by reporting that Jesus was teaching large crowds as he was walking along the lakeshore (Mk. 2:13). The gospel of Matthew identifies the tax collector as "Matthew," both Mark and Luke call him "Levi." Finally, when Matthew quotes Jesus' words that respond to the criticism of the Pharisees, he adds a portion of the quote not cited by Mark and Luke. All three quote Jesus as saying, "Those who are well have no need of a physician, but those who are sick; I have come to call not the righteous but sinners." (Mt. 9:12–13; Mk. 2:17; Lk. 5:31–32). Only Matthew adds a sentence that the other two storytellers leave out. "Go and learn what this means, 'I desire mercy, not sacrifice'" (Mt. 9:13a). So while all three gospel writers relate the same event, that one event has again produced three unique stories. The challenge of the Bible reader is both to notice those small differences and then inquire about how the inclusion or exclusion of content may influence the meaning of the story being told.

Form Selection

The design of a story and its meaning involves more than simply the selection of details that are narrated. Equally important is the artful way in which those details are shaped and shared with the reader. If we were to transcribe and analyze the language used when a wife tells her husband about her day at work, we would likely find her to be using language in a very ordinary way. The vocabulary choices and the sentence structure would be that of ordinary conversation. That is not the way a storyteller relates what happened during the day. The storyteller is a self-conscious composer who selects more elite language forms to tell the story. Robert Alter describes this as "language straining against the decorum of ordinary usage."[2] The use of a more artistic form of language means that we are not viewing the events of the Bible while looking into history through a clear pane of glass, but rather we see the events from the past recast in the soft and contrasting colors of a stained-glass window. This betrays the goal of the artist. The story is not provided as a window that allows us to view the historical events "as they really happened," but to see the events as they have been portrayed by the artist using unique language forms.[3]

Since the stories in the Bible are told with a more distinctive style of language, it becomes necessary to analyze those stories in a more sophisticated way, paying more careful attention to the language choices and patterns employed. When literary scholars are asked what that means for the reader, they have responded with varied and colorful language of their own. For example, Robert Alter encourages Bible readers to pay careful attention to "the artful use of language, to the shifting play of ideas, conventions, tone, sound, imagery, syntax, narrative viewpoint, compositional units, and much else."[4] Shimon Bar-Efrat describes the purpose of his inquiry with similar language. In his view, the goal of literary analysis is to "bring to light their artistic and rhetorical characteristics, their inner organization, and their stylistic and structural features."[5] Adele Berlin resorts to a metaphor noting that literary analysis involves examining the "cake" (the narrative) in an effort to determine how it was made.[6]

So to honor God as a storyteller means to ask questions that you might not be accustomed to asking about a Bible story. For example, the story of Jonah can be read in a matter of minutes. But it requires hours to analyze a story with questions such as these: Where do we find scene changes in the story? How does each of the scenes contribute to the plot? In which verses can we trace the rising and falling tension of the storyline? Where has the storyteller caused time to speed up, and where has the passage of time in the story been dramatically slowed? What methods of characterization has the inspired writer used? How do they shape my perception of Jonah? We note that the storyteller closes this story with a question. What kind of question is it? How does that impact the lingering influence of the story? These are the questions of narrative criticism that attend the Bible reader in pursuit of the story's meaning.

As a storyteller, God imbues the stories in the Bible with meaning. By carefully selecting content and managing the form of communication, the events of the past are turned into stories with an enduring meaning. In that light, consider the power of this comment by Robert Alter. Attention given to the "literary art is not merely an act of 'appreciation' but a discipline of understanding. The literary vehicle is so much the necessary medium through which the Hebrew writers realized their meanings that we will grasp the meanings at best imperfectly if we ignore their articulation as fine literature."[7]

Biblical Studies and Narrative Criticism

From the late nineteenth century through the middle of the twentieth century,[8] scholars devoted their attention to the history behind the text and the compositional development of the text itself. While a segment of the latter study was called "literary criticism," it had little to do with the topics found in this book. Perceiving Bible stories to be the product of various authors writing at different times and from different locations, this form of literary criticism sought to identify the boundaries between various sources, their authors, and the date of their composition.[9] However, by the middle of the 1980s, a true form of literary analysis began to challenge that historical paradigm. In fact, some scholars began calling such study the "new orthodoxy."[10] We will not provide a detailed history of that movement here, since it is adequately provided in other places.[11] But a check of the bibliography in this book will reveal the large number of scholars who have made their own unique contributions to this form of Bible study. While some of those studies are content with merely describing the narrative qualities of the text, many have pressed beyond mere definition and appreciation of the art in a bid to explain the rhetorical impact of a story on its readers.[12]

Objections to Reading the Bible with Narrative Criticism

The arrival of any new paradigm will typically face opposition and critical questions. A literary reading of Bible narratives is no exception to this rule. We begin with the question of relationship. How will this new form of analysis relate to more well-established forms of biblical inquiry? It would be imprudent to think that this form of analysis should be allowed to "excommunicate its predecessors."[13] Study of the Bible and its stories has profited considerably under the inspection of historical criticism, lower text criticism, source criticism, form criticism, redaction criticism, and canon criticism, to name just a few. Each of these methods asks and seeks to answer important questions that deserve the attention of every biblical scholar. Most of these methods of analysis focus on the origins and transmission of the text. Narrative criticism focuses on the text as it appears before us on the page. This is the text that reaches out into the lives of its readers, making a bid to impact their lives. Literary analysis of a Bible story does not deny that there may be a compositional history to the story, nor does it deny a transmission history to the text. Literary analysis, as a mode of inquiry, is not suited to make judgments on the historicity of the events portrayed. It sets those matters aside in favor of examining the story as it has come down to us. Thus it neither claims to supersede nor supplant other forms of investigation, but augments the various ways in which the Bible is already studied.[14] In the approach advocated in the pages ahead, we draw in an interdisciplinary way on other areas of study such as archaeology, history, anthropology, linguistics, and geography to obtain critical data needed to understand the language used within the story.

The advent of a new method of Bible study draws not only pointed questions but criticism as well. Within the evangelical Christian community, the validity of seeking the meaning of a Bible story using narrative criticism has drawn suspicious glances from those who contend that this method is not compatible with a strong commitment to the historical accuracy of the stories and the truth claims of historic Christianity. In 1987, as the narrative critical approach was finding its feet in biblical studies, Carl Henry expressed this concern: "The narrative approach seems not full befitting the historic Christian faith… One discerns here an enchantment with the affective, a flight from history to the perspectival that enjoins no universal truth claims."[15] Since many of the first articles linking narrative criticism to Bible study were written by scholars who questioned the historical reliability of the Bible, narrative criticism faced a tough audience in the evangelical community.[16] Because this form of analysis focuses more upon the text itself than the author and the author's context, some have linked a literary study of the Bible with historical minimalism.

But does a narrative critical approach necessarily demand historical minimalism and a full retreat from universal truth claims? The answer is no. First of all, the conventions used to compose a story are the same whether that story is purely fictional or whether it is historical.[17] In describing the way a historical event becomes a story, Long compares the work of the storyteller to the work of the representational artist. The artist must decide how the reality before him or her is going to be represented in the piece of art. This requires that many decisions be made with regards to matters such as: vantage point, boundaries, medium (oil, watercolor, etc.), the pallet of colors to be used, and the method with which to apply the colors to the palette. These choices in no way diminish the "reality" of the figure being painted, but they do guarantee that the portrait will be an edited representation of that reality.[18]

The storyteller is an artist who does the same thing. Instead of selecting colors and application techniques, the storyteller is making choices about whose voice is heard and whose voice is silenced in the story, what actions we see and which are hidden from sight, and where a metaphor or simile will be introduced. Thus the storyteller's use of narrative conventions and the analyst's use of narrative critical questions do not in themselves say anything about the historical reliability of the narrative or one's view of it.

Long further concluded that biblical narratives have three basic impulses, all of which invite our attention. The three impulses are historical, literary, and theological.[19] Consider the powerful implications of that observation. The same text can be studied by different scholars with different objectives. The historian may use the story in a bid to reconstruct the historical event behind the text. The narrative analyst may study the text to discern the literary art and rhetorical function of the text. The historian may seek the particular, and the literary scholar may pursue the universal.[20] But the study of one dimension of the text does not necessarily deny the existence of the other two. Both the literary scholar and the historian promise to make a meaningful connection to theology. Thus a narrative critical approach is very compatible with a high view of the historicity of the Bible and the claim to discover truth within it.

Yet another objection raised against this approach argues that modern, Western values are being imposed upon the text by using categories of analysis such as characterization, plot, and the strategic use of time. Certainly this is a potential concern given that the most recent book of the Bible was written centuries ago in a geographical and cultural context far removed from most Western readers. Leland Ryken responds to this concern in two ways. First of all, he notes that the "Bible has exerted a strong and formative influence on Western literature from the Middle Ages onward," so the forms we find in Western literature and the ways in which Western literature are studied are not necessarily foreign to our reading of biblical literature. Second, Ryken notes, "Literary forms tend to have certain inherent characteristics quite apart from the cultural situation in which they were written."[21] Given the influence of the Bible on Western culture and the inherent qualities found in stories across cultural boundaries, the risk of imposing Western cultural ideals on the interpretation process seems more remote. In the end, we must be aware of the possibility that someone writing thousands of years ago in the Middle East may have been employing a technique that is not current in Western literature. But there is good reason to expect that the methods of analysis developed to study Western stories will have validity in studying the stories within the Bible.

Finally, we respond to those who argue that narrative criticism lacks an objective set of criteria for analyzing a text and so results in a highly subjective reading of the text, one that validates all readings. This is really not a product of narrative criticism so much as it is a product of uniting narrative criticism with reader-response criticism. The latter, which seeks meaning in the reading experience rather than the text, will be discussed in detail below. But here we assert that the marriage of narrative criticism and reader-response criticism should not automatically be assumed. A careful reading of the text using the categories of narrative criticism can aid those who champion biblical inspiration and authority, for it honors the careful composition of those verses and seeks meaning that flows from the language and literary choices found there. Perhaps no finer example of this can be found than the scholarship of Tremper Longman III. He asserts, "Literary analysis of a historical book is not inconsistent with a high view of the historicity of the text, including the view that affirms the inerrancy and infallibility of Scripture."[22]

The Source of Meaning

While some scholars are content to analyze a Bible story using narrative criticism without taking the step of exploring its rhetorical intention or meaning (simply appreciating the art for art's sake, *ars gratia artis*), our intentions are to deploy narrative criticism in pursuit of a story's meaning. This brings us into the large and complex arena where well-thinking people are discussing the question of where the meaning of a text may be found. At the great risk of oversimplification, we have observed that three options stand before us: either the meaning will be sought in the intention of the author (*author*), or the language of the text (*text*), or within the experience of reading the text (*reader*). When articulating their own personal approach, Bible interpreters will typically emphasize one dimension of this triangle while assigning the other two dimensions a secondary role.[23]

In the first case, the author is seen as the one who has the authority to determine what a story means. Assuming this approach, the reader takes the responsibility to learn all one can about the author and the context of the writing experience to determine what may have motivated and excited the construction of a particular story in its own unique way. Of course, this approach works very well with living authors. But the problem of searching for the meaning imposed by the author becomes more complex when we are talking about a story whose author is either anonymous or dead, or both. Despite this challenge, many will still advocate the search for authorial intent in a story.

The problems associated with seeking meaning in the minds of anonymous or dead authors pressed the conversation about meaning away from the author and toward the text. In the mid-1940s two literary critics, W. K. Wimsatt and Monroe Beardsley, articulated an approach that seeks meaning in what the author has left behind, "the artifact"–their name for the text. The work of these scholars placed a high degree of confidence in our ability to decode the language and literary conventions deployed within a text. They argued that instead of looking *through* the text into the context and intentions of the writer, one ought to look *at* the text.[24] Thus New Criticism focused its attention on word choices, grammar choices, and literary choices in a bid to define the meaning of a text. Since the text was self-sufficient, they dismissed the notion of authorial meaning and the author's intentions (something they called the "intentional fallacy"). New Criticism was born, and the meaning of story would be sought *in* the text itself rather than *behind* the text in the author's intentions.[25] While most modern literary critics may view this absolute disconnection with the author as an extreme position, they would agree that meaning is not directly linked to the author's intentions.

In time, New Criticism, with its hopes set upon the capacity of the text to communicate meaning, met its own critics. The more people examined the connection between language and meaning, the more complex and slippery that relationship appeared to be. The very fact that we can and do misunderstand one another suggests that the relationship between language and meaning is less than perfect. In the 1960s and '70s Hans Georg Gadamer[26] and Paul Ricoeur[27] wondered aloud about how confident we should be in discovering meaning within texts, observing that people who were reading the same text came to different conclusions on what it meant. Is it possible that texts were merely silent shadows that carried no meaning in themselves until a listener or reader should come along?[28]

The questions about language and meaning erupted into an alternate theory that proposed that meaning was generated as the horizon of the reader and the horizon of the text merged. Meaning was created during the reading experience. Because each reader brought a different background, interests, and experiences to the text, one should expect that multiple meanings could and would flow from the interaction between text and reader. Thus, in application, reader-response criticism has produced a tapestry of interpretation associated with any one Bible story, a tapestry that reflects the diversity of the readers represented.[29]

Presuppositions of the Author

All of this brings us to the question of where *this* author and book will take their place in the current conversation about meaning and the method one might use to investigate it. First, the author of this book believes that the Bible is God's Word. I am persuaded that the Bible makes this claim for itself (2 Pet. 1:21; 2 Tim. 3:16 and Jn. 17:17). While some ontological proof can be summoned to support the truthfulness of this thesis, it is the power of the Holy Spirit, not logic alone, that has led me to this conviction.

Of course, that does not preclude legitimate questions from being raised about certain verses, stories, and statements in the Bible. Even for those who are able to penetrate past the veil of English translation to read the texts in Hebrew, Aramaic, and Greek, there remain questions about just how to understand the language being deployed in certain places. But I believe that the answers to those questions and challenges do not lie in impugning the Bible's authority or questioning its divine inspiration. Rather, I believe it best to see those challenges in light of our own shortcomings. The text may lack clarity because our language and literary competence falls short of what the author intended us to have. Or it may defy explanation because the original manuscript became contaminated during the transmission history of the text. Or we may struggle with a text simply because it exceeds the real frontier that will always be reached when mortals attempt to understand divine communication. The author and text may be absolutely clear, but fail to make sense for those of us who live with minds clouded by sin and so are incapable of attaining the full meaning placed there by a divine being who so exceeds us.

Second, although language does have the capacity for being misunderstood, I believe that language is very capable of housing meaning and motivating us to assume a perspective. As the inspired authors used language, selecting both the content and form of their stories, they left behind clues to how they wished a story to be read. Following in the footsteps of Meir Sternberg, we seek to meld an appreciation for the artful use of language with a search for the storyteller's agenda. We see the storyteller as a "persuader wielding discourse to shape response and manipulate attitude."[30] Thus the language of the text is the key to discovering the meaning of the story.

But how do we then account for the fact that multiple readers with a commitment to finding meaning in the text may come to different perspectives on what that text means? This may be the result of taking language out of its context, finding the meaning we wish to find in it. If an interpreter removes words, sentences, and even paragraphs from their larger literary context, that language can become very malleable. Such language can then be used to support an interpretation that flows against the general direction taken by a story and the intentions of its author. To guard against this risk, we propose that the meaning that most coheres with the narrative-critical crafting of the story be given the greatest credence. While it is true that different readers may read a text and come to different opinions about its meaning, not every proposed meaning has the same level of credibility when put in the same room with the textual evidence.

A second explanation for multiple interpretations rising from the same story is found in the work of E.D. Hirsch. He distinguishes between meaning and significance. Hirsch observes that meaning is that which the author places into the language signals within a text. Significance is that part of the meaning that the readers see due to the backgrounds and experiences they bring to the text. Thus the significance of a story may vary from one person to the next, but the meaning of the story remains the same.[31]

Finally, I am also persuaded that there is great value in investigating the historical, geographical, and social circumstances that surround the human authors, and that find their way into the language of our Bible stories. Of course, the power of those insights is conditioned by questions about the authorship and date of such stories. But we cannot dismiss the presence of these features within the language of the Bible. The reality of water and rainfall in the promised land, the rise of Assyria as an international superpower, the political parties of the first century, and dozens of other references like them all find their way into the stories of the Bible. In such cases, the storyteller often assumes we know much more than we might know. While we must be cautious about using background information, prudent use of geography, archaeology, and other historical sources can shed light upon the language choices that participate in delivering the meaning of the story.

Overview

The title and subtitle of this book can serve as a roadmap to what lies behind the cover, *God as Storyteller: Seeking Meaning in Biblical Narrative.* The first portion of this book will speak about the storyteller's craft, with a focus on how the divine storyteller takes the details of an event and moves them into story form. The latter part of the book will focus on the art of reading, with a view toward seeking meaning in the story.

Following this introduction, the first chapter in this book will discuss the way in which the storyteller leans on the literary context that surrounds the story and how the storyteller designs the structure within the story as part of the composition process. A Bible story never stands alone, but is always placed within a literary context where it interacts within a larger family of stories. That family of stories includes both the other stories within the book and the larger story being told across the various books of the Bible. In this way, Bible stories are designed to depend on one another. Internally, the details of the story are designed to participate in a plot and scenic structure. This plot is composed of various parts, including the presentation of a crisis, complication(s), climax, resolution, and conclusion. This plot line is carefully orchestrated to seize and sustain the reader's, or listener's, interest. Another way to divide the story internally is through recognizing the various scenes. Each may be marked by a change in place or time, or through a change in dialogue partners providing the focus of interest. We will explore the ways in which each scene makes its own unique contribution to the plot and delivery of the story's meaning.

Since Bible stories are filled with colorful and unique characters, the second chapter will focus on the storyteller's technique called characterization. Even though all the people we meet in a Bible story are real people with as much depth and complexity as any of us, the storyteller will not present every character in the story with the same amount of detail. We will investigate the different types of characters we meet in the story, both major and minor. In those instances where a character is presented in greater detail, we will look at the various ways in which the storyteller causes us to meet him or her. We will sensitize our reading to look for clues such as: what a character says, what a character does, what others say about that person, and how that character is named.

In the third chapter, our attention will turn to the "storyteller" within the story. That is the narrator. Whenever we find words in the story that are not assigned to one of the characters, the narrator is speaking to us. This storyteller within the story plays a critical role in shaping what we know as readers and when we know it. We will spend some time examining the credibility of the narrator and pay particular attention to the ways in which the narrator controls our point of view. As we noted above, the storyteller is interested in more than conveying the details of the story. The storyteller wants to influence our perspective as readers. The narrator plays a key role in accomplishing that end.

The fourth chapter will continue our exploration of the storyteller's craft by discussing the use of time and setting. In living life, we have very little control over the former. We live life twenty-four hours a day and sixty seconds every minute. We live life within the restricted flow that moves from past to present to future. That is not true in a story. A storyteller controls the amount of time we spend with an event, the speed with which time flows, and even the direction that time flows. We may experience the event in "real time," where the reading time and time of occurrence is nearly the same. But it is more often the case that the storyteller will change the speed of our experience, rushing us through certain segments of the story only to slow down our experience at other points of the story. Time may flow from past to future or we may find that the passage of time is reversed to help us revisit details from the past. In a similar way, every story will also have a physical and cultural setting that may be described in greater or lesser detail. The method of reading advocated in the pages of this book invites us to pay careful attention to the way in which the storyteller uses time and setting.

The fifth chapter will address the storyteller's artistic use of language. We noted that the language of the storyteller is not the language of ordinary speech but is composed more thoughtfully and more artistically. The word choices and word play the storyteller uses are woven into patterns that are both attractive and influential. In this chapter we will sample some of that artistry by exploring the use of repetition, irony, metaphor, personification, and the use of rhetorical questions.

The opening of the sixth chapter brings us to the second part of this book, which examines in greater detail the storyteller's use of geography. While other books on narrative criticism will typically include an introduction to the dimensions of storytelling discussed in the first five chapters, this chapter will deliver much more than is expected on this topic. The author's love for the outdoors and many trips to the Holy Land have filled him with an appreciation for the role that geography plays both in shaping biblical events and in the stories about those events. As we turn the pages of our Bible, we meet not just people, but people in various places, talking about places, and being influenced by the reality of place. Narrative geography inquires into the way a storyteller may use, reuse, and nuance geographical references to shape the reading experience. The relationship between story and geography has been noted in the analysis of secular novels. But even this exploration does not go as far as we will in reviewing the ways in which the storyteller uses geography. Since the amount of geographical detail varies from writer to writer and even from story to story, narrative geographical analysis will pay out differing dividends on different stories. But in those stories where the storyteller has elected to include more geographical detail, it can play a critical role in shaping the plot and characterization that are critical to our reading of the story. The sixth chapter of this book will take on the challenge of uniting the disciplines of geography and literature. This chapter on method will be quickly followed by chapter seven which seeks to illustrate in greater detail how attention to geography can impact the reading of a story. Here we will examine several stories from the Old and New Testament that are strongly influenced by the formal mention of geography.

The third part of the book will find a change in focus. While the first two parts have placed the spotlight on the storyteller, revealing the artful way in which the storyteller moves an event into story form, the third part of the book will focus on the reader and a method for seeking meaning in the craft of the storyteller. Chapter eight will get things started by offering a step-by-step procedure for reading a Bible story. This method will have us dissect the story into its various literary components. For example, we will identify the components of the plot. We will note how the main character is portrayed. We will observe the use of time in the story. And we will identify any examples of word play. Once we have disassembled the story and assessed the contribution of each literary component, we will reassemble the story to see how our new appreciation for the parts will influence our understanding of the whole. This chapter on method will be complemented by the next two chapters, which will illustrate this method of analysis using two stories, one from the Old Testament and one from the New Testament. Chapter nine will analyze the story of David and Goliath (1 Sam. 17), and chapter ten will analyze the story of Jesus in Samaria (John 4).

In the end, we hope that our readers are brought to a new place in their Bible reading. It is our prayer that this book will make you more sensitive to the fact that the God who is revealed to us in the Bible is a storyteller. By reviewing the tools that a storyteller may use to move the details of an event into story form, we hope that your eyes will meet the stories in the Bible in a new and fresh way, one that notices the structure of the plot, the careful design of characters, the strategic use of time, setting, and the pattering play of words. We also pray that you will be able to use this sensitivity to come to a deeper and fuller appreciation of the message God has placed into these stories for us.

Notes

[1]Leland Ryken, *How to Read the Bible as Literature* (Grand Rapids: Zondervan, 1984), 23.
[2]Robert Alter, *The World of Biblical Literature* (New York: Basic Books, 1992), 43.

[3]Moisés Silva, "But These Are Written That You May Believe," in *An Introduction to Biblical Hermeneutics: The Search for Meaning,* ed. Walter C. Kaiser and Moisés Silva (Grand Rapids: Zondervan, 1994), 109.

[4]Robert Alter, *The Art of Biblical Narrative* (New York: Basic Books, 1981), 12.

[5]Shimon Bar-Efrat, "Some Observations on the Analysis of Structure in Biblical Narrative," in *Beyond Form Criticism: Essays in Old Testament Literary Criticism,* ed. Paul R. House, Sources for Biblical and Theological Study (Winona Lake, Ind.: Eisenbrauns, 1992), 187.

[6]Adele Berlin, *Poetics and Interpretation of Biblical Narrative* (Winona Lake, Ind.: Eisenbrauns, 1994), 15.

[7]Alter, *World of Biblical Literature,* 63–64.

[8]For a survey of major works that have made a contribution to this movement, see R. Christopher Heard, "Narrative Criticism in the Hebrew Scriptures: A Review and Assessment," *Restoration Quarterly* 38 (1996): 29–43.

[9]Leland Ryken, "Literary Criticism of the Bible: Some Fallacies," in *Literary Interpretations of Biblical Narratives,* ed. R.R. Gros Louis (Nashville: Abingdon Press, 1974), 26.

[10]David M. Gunn, "New Direction in the Study of Biblical Hebrew Narrative," in *Beyond Form Criticism,* ed. Paul R. House, 412.

[11]For a more complete discussion of the new narrative critical emphasis in biblical studies see the following: Leland Ryken, "The Bible as Literature: A Brief History," in *A Complete Literary Guide to the Bible,* ed. Leland Ryken and Tremper Longman III (Grand Rapids: Zondervan, 1993), 49–68; David Rhoads and Kari Syreeni, *Characterization in the Gospels: Reconceiving Narrative Criticism* (Sheffield: Sheffield Academic Press, 1999), 17–23.

[12]James L. Resseguie, *Narrative Criticism of the New Testament: An Introduction* (Grand Rapids: Baker Academic, 2005), 30.

[13]John Barton, *Reading the Old Testament: Method in Biblical Study* (Philadelphia: The Westminster Press, 1984), 5.

[14]Adele Berlin speaks at some length about the important relationship between the diachronic forms of text analysis and narrative criticism. Berlin, *Poetics and Interpretation,* 111–34.

[15]Carl F.H. Henry, "Narrative Theology: An Evangelical Appraisal," *Trinity Journal* 8 (1987): 19.

[16]V. Philips Long, *The Art of Biblical History,* Foundations of Contemporary Interpretation 5 (Grand Rapids: Zondervan, 1994), 151.

[17]Meir Sternberg, *The Poetics of Biblical Narrative* (Bloomington, Ind.: Indiana University Press, 1987), 30.

[18]Long, *Art of Biblical History,* 70.

[19]Ibid., 167.

[20]Leland Ryken and Tremper Longman III, "Introduction," in *A Complete Literary Guide to the Bible,* ed. Ryken and Longman, 20.

[21]Ryken, "Literary Criticism of the Bible," 31–32.

[22]Tremper Longman III, *Literary Approaches to Biblical Interpretation,* Foundations of Contemporary Interpretation 3 (Grand Rapids: Zondervan, 1987), 58.

[23]Barton, *Reading the Old Testament,* 200.

[24]Ibid., 145.

[25]W.K. Wimsatt and Monroe Beardsley, "The Intentional Fallacy," *Sewanee Review* 54 (1946); reprinted in William K. Wimsatt Jr., *The Verbal Icon,* Studies in the Meaning of Poetry (New York, Farrar, Straus, 1958), 3–18.

[26]Hans-Georg Gadamer, *Truth and Method: Elements of Philosophical Hermeneutics* (New York: Seabury, 1975; reprint, Crossroad, 1982).

[27]Paul Ricoeur, *Interpretation Theory: Discourse and the Surplus of Meaning* (Fort Worth: Texas Christian University Press, 1976).

[28]Jan P. Fokkelman, *Reading Biblical Narrative: An Introductory Guide* (Louisville: Westminster John Knox Press, 1999), 20.

[29]Tremper Longman III, "Literary Approaches to Old Testament Study," in *The Face of Old Testament Studies: A Survey of Contemporary Approaches,* ed. David W. Baker and Bill T. Arnold (Grand Rapids: Baker Books, 1987), 108–9.

[30]Sternberg, *Poetics of Biblical Narrative,* 482.

[31]E.D. Hirsch Jr., *Validity in Interpretation* (New Haven: Yale University Press, 1967), 8.

PART ONE

The Storyteller's Craft:
The Event Becomes a Story

1

The Strategic Use of Context and Structure

While the historical event and the story are not the same thing, we believe an event lies behind each of the stories in the Bible. As the storyteller superintends the journey of that event into story form, the careful selection and shaping of those details gives the story its meaning. Part one of this book will examine the way in which an event becomes a story. In this chapter and those that follow closely after it, we will explore the various techniques that are part of that process. Together, those techniques combine to form the storyteller's craft. In the next pages in particular, we will focus on two dimensions of that craft, the use of literary context and literary structure.

While the individual stories in the Bible have varying degrees of autonomy, it is our perception that no story in the Bible was designed to function completely on its own. Every Bible story lies at the heart of a concentric circle of stories that surround it. Because we often hear Bible stories isolated from their larger context, this may call for some new thinking on our part. Sunday school classes and sermons often focus their attention on individual stories even if they form part of a Sunday morning series. There is nothing wrong with that focus as long as we do not lose sight of the larger literary context for a story and the impact that literary context has on meaning.

The first portion of this chapter will focus on the role of the story externally to the other stories around it. The second portion of the chapter will focus on the internal structures of the story. This will involve us in a discussion of plot and scene. A typical day in our lives is often filled with random encounters and chance conversations. That is not the case in a Bible story. Here the storyteller carefully arranges the order of events, meetings, and conversations into a plot line. We will label and define the various parts that comprise the plot in a typical Bible story and see how those components work together to keep our interest and to focus our attention on the enduring meaning of the story. This discussion of plot will lead naturally to a conversation about scenes, for we are carried along through the plot by the actions, encounters, and conversations that occur in one or more scenes. We will address both the division of the story in scenes and explore the unique contribution that such scenes make in moving the reader through the plot.

Reading in Context

Context is a necessary ingredient for effective communication. Only when we are able to link vocabulary and grammar to a context can effective communication occur. Consider the following short story in that regard. I know of a young girl who left home and ran for a short distance. She turned left three times, running as quickly as her feet would carry her past one person and then the next. Just after she made the last of her three turns, she was met by a masked man.

If you are puzzled by the story, it is unlikely that your confusion is caused by your inability to understand the vocabulary and grammar of those three sentences. What is missing is the appropriate context. If I told you that I saw this happening at my daughter's softball game, everything would make sense. Context plays a critical role in communication.

Of course, various forms of context impact the writing and telling of a story. These include the historical or temporal context, the social or cultural context, the geographical context, and on and on. To some degree, the storyteller will rely on the hearer's awareness of such context to understand what is being said. Alter points to the story of Moses in Exodus 2, in which both historical and literary allusion may play a role in the communication process.[1] In Exodus 2:3, the mother of Moses hides her child in an "ark" (NRSV translates "basket") since he is threatened by the Egyptian order that compels the death of every boy born to an Israelite family.

Within the larger ancient Near Eastern context, we are aware of another great leader who began his life in a basket. King Sargon of Akkad was nestled into a box made of reeds and placed into the Euphrates River. Is it possible that the storyteller includes this detail from Moses' young life to indicate that he, like King Sargon, would grow up to be a great leader? This allusion is certainly credible and may be one of the factors that influenced its inclusion. Another allusion seems even more likely, given the fact that it requires us to turn only a few pages in the Hebrew Bible. Alter proposes connection between the "ark" of Exodus 2 with the "ark" in Genesis 6. Before the reader hears a word about Moses and his "ark," the reader of the Torah meets Noah and his "ark." God instructs Noah to build an "ark" that will be the lifeboat for his family and the promise of the messiah. Noah rode in his ark and became the leader of all those who exited the ark. Does the storyteller select this detail from the life of Moses with an expectation that the reader will make this connection and see Moses as a rising star? Given the infrequency with which the word *ark* appears in the Bible, the connection seems likely. Thus reading the story of Moses within its larger literary context allows us to explore an allusion we would have missed had we treated this story in isolation from its larger literary context.

Literary Context

Every story in the Bible is part of a larger family of stories created by the divine storyteller. The storyteller will assume that the listener is using that literary context as a tool in decoding any individual story. For us as readers, that means we will treat each story as part of an interacting body of literature that reaches beyond the bounds of the story itself into the surrounding chapters, books, and testament. So while a story is a self-contained literary unit that can be studied in its own right, we will seek to understand how each participates within its larger literary context.[2]

A brief example may help clarify the point. The story about the tower of Babel is a story unit in itself (Gen 11:1–9). However, it lies within a larger matrix of stories told in Genesis 1–11 (the so-called "primeval history" of the world.) Thus we must define the tower of Babel's role in relationship to the story of creation, the story of Cain and Abel, and the story of Noah and the flood. What is more, the events related about the tower of Babel are part of an even larger story told in the book of Genesis, the book of beginnings. We must ask how the tower of Babel relates to the theme and message found in Genesis, with its patriarchal stories featuring divine promises. Since Genesis, too, is part of a larger sub-collection, the Torah, we must ask how the tower of Babel relates to the stories we read in the books of Exodus, Leviticus, Numbers, and Deuteronomy. Of course, the Torah is part of the Old Testament, and the Old Testament is part of the Bible that includes the New Testament, so we must inquire how the story of the tower of Babel fits within these larger frames as well. Whatever meaning we assign to this story will have to live in harmony with and contribute to the larger story being told in each of these circles of context.

The Bible's Literary Unity

All we have just said assumes that the entire Bible was authored and edited by a common mind. While some have argued that the Bible is a broken patchwork of disconnected literary contributions, a strong case can be made for the Bible's compositional unity. First of all, we note that the Bible itself contains a coherent story line, with a distinct beginning, middle, and ending that flows from the Old Testament to the New Testament.[3] The complication of a ruined creation pulls the reader forward toward a solution told in the gospels and an ultimate restoration pictured in Revelation. A second element that links the pages of our Bible is the ongoing awareness of God's presence and God's interaction in this world.[4] We see and hear his presence at Mount Sinai, at the baptism of Jesus, at the conversion of Saul (Paul), and on the streets of the New Jerusalem. People may come and people may go, but God persists as the eternal presence casting a shadow on every page and word of our Bible. The Bible stories we read are also linked by reoccurring themes that provide the Bible with a sense of continuity. These themes are all linked to the human condition as we watch real people navigate the challenges of real living. Among the recurring themes and topics that we find are: the meaning of physical suffering (Job 2:7–10; Jn. 9:1–12), the relationship of God to government (1 Sam. 8:1–22; Lk. 20:20–26), personal uncertainty (Gen. 15:1–3; Jn. 4:19), managing the temptations of Satan (2 Sam. 11; Mt. 4:1–11), giving personal possessions for divine service (1 Chr. 29:1–9; Mk. 12:41–44), and death (Gen. 23:1–20; Mk. 5:21–43). As the stories revolve around topics such as these, they grow upon and illuminate one another. Such signals of unity help us connect the books of the Bible and see them as part of an interacting unit.

We find similar signals within the books themselves. These formal linking devices may be more linear and obvious, such as the recurring formula that occurs in Genesis 2:4; 5:1; 10:1; 11:10; 11:27; 25:12; and 36:1. In each case, this segment of the story in Genesis is introduced by the same Hebrew expression that may be translated, "These are the generations of…," or, "This is the account of…"

The patterns used to link stories in a Bible book may also take the form of a repeating literary outline. Judges is an excellent example of that. The link between the individual stories becomes evident when we see that each is told with a similar outline. That outline is introduced to the reader in Judges 2:10–19. The Israelites begin to show devotion to the false gods of the people around them. God chastises his people for their lack of allegiance by allowing a foreign people to put military and economic pressure on them. The people cry out to the Lord for help. The Lord provides a judge who leads a successful campaign of liberation from the oppressing enemy. Then the land enjoys a time of peace as the people faithfully follow the Lord. In most stories within the book of Judges, all or a substantial part of the cycle is evident. It is that common outline that invites us to read each of the stories in Judges not only as an individual narrative but also as part of the larger story housed in the entire book.

At other times, the devices that link stories together may be more subtle. For example, the first and last chapters in the book of Matthew enclose all that lie between them with statements assuring the reader of God's abiding presence. In the very first chapter (Mt. 1:23), the divine author gives Jesus a special name, Emmanuel, "God is with us." Meanwhile, at the very end of the book, the last thing we hear Jesus say is, "I am with you always."

This is a subtle but powerful way of linking all the stories that lie between the first and last chapter of this book into a literary whole.[5]

So whether through more obvious or more subtle clues, the divine storyteller invites us to link the pages, chapters, and books of our Bible into a larger family of stories. It then becomes our job as readers to see each of the stories in the Bible not just as an isolated literary unit but as part of that larger family of stories that surround it.

Perhaps the best way to find those larger structures is to read larger segments of your Bible at one sitting. Instead of reading just the story of the tower of Babel, read the first eleven chapters of Genesis or, better yet, the entire book of Genesis over a couple of days. This will help you see connections and continuity of the message that can otherwise be lost. Others have read their Bibles in this way, and their observations are worthy of note. Consult the introduction to each book in your study Bible or within a Bible handbook. Those introductions will typically contain both an outline of the book and a discussion of themes within it. Both will help you place an individual Bible story within its larger unit of text.[6]

The Story of Cain and Abel in Its Literary Context

Let us consider how we might read the story of Cain and Abel with sensitivity to its literary setting. Many readers of Genesis see a natural division occurring in Genesis between chapters eleven and twelve.[7] The first eleven chapters talk about the history of the world and God's promise of a Savior since before the time of Abraham, while those that follow detail the history of the promise as it is linked to Abraham and his family. The story of Cain and Abel lies within the first eleven chapters, and immediately follows the story of the world's creation and the fall into sin.

Genesis 4 begins with the people we have already met in the first three chapters of Genesis, Adam and Eve. Those people and their experiences provide the setting for Genesis 4. We have witnessed their creation and the creation of the world in which they lived. But, most importantly, we have encountered the major problem that will inform our reading of the rest of the Bible. Sin was introduced into God's perfect world with all its consequences. Now there would be pain, discord in relationships, complexity in making a living, and death (Gen. 3:16–19). Humans were now destined to live their lives in this frustrating cycle perpetuated by their own sinfulness.

But alongside this discouraging message, the reader of Genesis 3 encounters a word of hope. For the same God who created the world in its perfect state is committed to restoring those separated from God by sin. The rescue plan takes shape as early as Genesis 3:15, when a descendant of Eve is introduced who will undo the power of Satan. The details of that rescue and rescuer are not painted in the detailed strokes provided throughout the rest of the Bible. But the fundamental problem and solution that occupy the rest of the pages in the Bible are already introduced to the reader by the close of Genesis 3.

Given the great significance of those early chapters, it is our assumption that the rest of Genesis 1–11 will have to grow and relate to what we find in them. Thus the reader of Cain and Abel's story does not enter this story without bringing along expectations that grow from the reading of the first three chapters in this book. Consider a few of those key expectations. After reading Genesis 3:18–19, we expect to be reading stories about people who are working hard to make a living. That is just what we find in Genesis 4. Abel was caring for flocks while Cain was farming. The reader of Genesis 3 was also warned about the potential for disharmony in relationships. Sure enough, chapter 4 provides another example of that as Cain is angry about the fact that the Lord looked favorably on his brother's sacrifice but did not look favorably on his own sacrifice. The reader of Genesis 3 also expects that death will occur. In chapter 4 we read not only about death but about a murder. Given these expectations, one way of fitting the story of Cain and Abel into its larger literary structure is to see it as a story told to illustrate the results of the fall into sin, in particular the complexity and horror that sin brought to the lives of families.

But we may also consider another role for this story, particularly as it relates to the promise of rescue. While the reader of Genesis 3 has heard the shadowy promise that a rescue was in the works, the persistence of God in keeping that promise has yet to be tested. The question lingers. Could human beings treat God and one another so badly that he would withdraw the promise of rescue? We would argue that this is one of the key ways in which all the stories of Genesis 4–11 function. Would God maintain his passion for rescue when most of the residents of his world had abandoned God (Gen. 6:1–3)? Following the flood, would God abandon his promises if the majority of people again thumbed their noses at him (Gen. 11:1–9)? Returning to Genesis 4, would God abandon his plan of rescue when one of his fallen creatures committed the act of murder? That act of murder seems to be the most extreme component and the most striking element in the story of Cain and Abel. One can hardly imagine a more heinous crime than the intentional taking away of a life God had given. Would God continue to show mercy, or would God now withdraw the promise of restoration in the face of the first murder blemishing human history?

The answer to that question comes in 4:25. The Bible would have been a very short book, only four chapters long, if the first murder would have terminated God's passion to bring rescue to the world. But the persistence of God to provide restoration, even in the face of this great sin, is signaled in 4:25. It explicitly says that God gives Adam and Eve a son, Seth, in place of Abel. This mention of a new son links again to the promise in Genesis 3:15 and the hope that a child of Eve will provide rescue from the predicament of sin. God provided a new son. Along with that child, God sent an important message. Not even the horrific sin of murder would terminate God's passion to save the world. Certainly the story of Cain and Abel can be used to teach an important lesson about the sanctity of human life and the horror of murder. It clearly illustrates the outcome of the fall in a vivid way. But to stop there is to miss the critical connection between this story and the promise of restoration. The story of Cain and Abel teaches us something extraordinary about God's passion to fulfill the promise of a Savior.

Whether or not we have correctly placed our finger on the meaning of the story of Cain and Abel is for you to decide. More importantly, we hope that it illustrates the way in which reading the larger story can influence the reading of a smaller narrative unit. This is not necessarily a linear process, but rather a process of experimentation as one considers the necessary and circular relationships between larger and smaller units of text.[8] It is very easy to allow preconceptions about the story or the need for theological dogma to guide our reading of a story. One way to get the storyteller back in the lead is to carefully consider how the story might best be interpreted within its larger literary context.

Literary Structure

Those with a passion to listen to the divine storyteller with more discerning ears will not only pay careful attention to the literary context of the story but will also examine its literary structure. The Bible consists of shorter stories contained within larger story units. For example, the story of Joseph and Potiphar's wife (Gen. 39) is housed within the larger story of Joseph that begins in chapter 37 and extends to chapter 50. While we could define a plot structure in that larger narrative unit extending over many chapters, our focus here will be on identifying the boundaries of smaller narrative units. That will be the first topic for discussion in what follows. From there our attention will turn to the plot of the story. We will identify and define the various parts of the plot, noting their respective contributions to the listening experience. Finally, the chapter will come to a close with a look at the participation of scenes in that plot structure.

Boundaries of a Narrative

One way to establish the boundaries of a smaller story unit is to use the chapter divisions and the headings found on the pages of your Bible. But while helpful, they were not placed there by the author. They reflect editorial decisions made by later Bible readers, so we would encourage you to test those decisions and even edit the drawing of those boundary lines by reading carefully for clues the storyteller left behind. A variety of devices can be used to mark the beginning and ending of a story unit. These include the imposing of a task, birth and death, explicit introductions, patterns in content, time indicators, and location changes.[9]

A few illustrations of those boundary markers at work will help get us off to a good start. The inspired writer may be organizing the stories in a book according to a pattern, as we have seen in the book of Judges. When we read the closing verse of chapter 5 and the opening verse of chapter 6 in Judges, we sense the entrance into a new story. As the story of Deborah and Barak comes to a close, we read, "And the land had rest forty years" (Judg. 5:31b). This is followed immediately with the sentence, "The Israelites did what was evil in the sight of the LORD, and the LORD gave them into the hand of Midian seven years" (Judg. 6:1). If we are reading the book of Judges with an awareness of the way its stories are written, then this language will signal to us that one story is closing while another is opening.

This marking of a sub-story can also be done with an *inclusio*. An *inclusio* or envelope structure is a literary device that uses a similar theme or phrase to mark the beginning and ending of a literary unit. Genesis 4 provides us with an example. This chapter begins and ends with the announcement of a birth. The birth of Cain begins the chapter (4:1), and the birth of Seth (4:25) closes the chapter. These two births function as a front and back door to the story, an envelope that marks the beginning and close of this story unit.

The transition between sub-stories may also be marked by a change in location. In reading between Matthew 8:1 and 9:1, we see six changes in location. Following the Sermon on the Mount, Jesus comes down from the mountain (8:1). He enters Capernaum (8:5). He enters Peter's house (8:14). He gets into a boat (8:23). He arrives on the far side of the lake (8:28). And he returns to "his own town" (9:1). Physical exits, entrances, and returns to places of previous residence can all indicate that a new sub-story has begun.

Time indicators can also point to such a transition. The storyteller may commence a new sub-story by announcing that a specific time has come. The narrative describing the first celebration of the Lord's supper begins like this, "On the first day of Unleavened Bread, when the Passover lamb is sacrificed…" (Mk. 14:12). Also watch for language like "at that time" (Gen. 21:22), "after these things" (Gen 22:1), "when evening came" (Mk. 11:19), and "in the morning" (Mk. 11:20). These explicit time indicators may also signal to the listener that a new sub-story has begun.

Chapter divisions and headings in your study Bible will be helpful to you in marking the boundaries of story units. But remember that these are editorial suggestions provided long after the storyteller's work had come to a close. Do not hesitate to edit those suggested boundary lines as you observe the various patterns noted above that the storyteller will use to indicate the presence of a sub-story within a Bible book.

Plot Structure

Once we have formally noted the boundaries of the story, we may explore the structure within it. The way in which we experience life on a day-to-day basis is very different from the way we encounter life in the stories of the Bible. If we were to write down every experience we are having this day and then read about them tonight, we would find that our day is full of random, mundane, and unconnected events and experiences. By contrast, the stories we read in the Bible are purged of all extraneous details and focus on interconnected and meaning-filled chains of events.[10] If this chain of events has a clearly defined beginning, middle, and end, then we have the ingredients needed for a story, according to Aristotle.[11] In the most basic of terms, the beginning, middle, and end form the plot. This is the organizing force[12] that gives the story a sense of flow and movement that captures our interest, sustains our interest, and finally lets us go.

The Purposes of the Plot

Storytellers organize their narratives along such patterns for two important reasons. On the one hand, the plot arouses our emotions and our interest as readers. Once the storyteller has begun to speak, he or she does not want our attention to waiver until the story has come to a close. This happens again and again on the pages of the Bible. We want to know what Jesus is going to do when faced with five thousand hungry people and no apparent way of feeding them (Jn. 6:1–15). We must know what is going to happen to Peter and his passion to share the gospel when the murdering King Herod arrests him (Acts 12).

To keep our attention, a well-designed plot quickly summarizes the necessary background we need to enter the story and then plunges quickly into a problem or crisis that demands resolution. The complications that attend and grow from that crisis draw us even more deeply into the story. We want solutions. We want resolution. We cannot put the story down until it comes to a point of greater peace or resolution.

Since the goal of the divine storyteller always includes delivering a meaning, the plot structure becomes another tool in directing the listener to the appropriate details. Random conversations, actions, and encounters make it very difficult for an audience to find the purpose of the story, so they disappear from the story. Organizing the events into a plot devoid of unnecessary details imbues the story with meaning[13] and pushes the eyes of the reader forward in a bid to make sense of it all.[14]

The Components of the Plot

In most cases, the stories in the Bible have a classic organizational pattern that includes an exposition, crisis, complication, climax, unraveling (resolution), and conclusion.[15] We will spend a few moments discussing this typical plot sequence before illustrating it in the story of Abraham and Isaac (Gen. 22).

The exposition of the story provides the reader with the necessary background with which to enter into the rest of the plot. Typically the key characters are introduced together with their current circumstances.

The number of words dedicated to the exposition will vary significantly depending on how well we know the characters and the circumstances from our previous experience with them. The length of the exposition may be housed within a single verse or travel the length of several verses. For example, the story in Genesis 16 begins with a very brief exposition. "Now Sarai, Abram's wife, bore him no children. She had an Egyptian slave-girl whose name was Hagar." With just two sentences of exposition, the storyteller launches us into the crisis.

On the other hand, note the length of the exposition in the story of Hannah:

> There was a certain man of Ramathaim, a Zuphite from the hill country of Ephraim, whose name was Elkanah the son of Jeroham son of Elihu son of Tohu son of Zuph an Ephraimite. He had two wives; the name of the one was Hannah, and the name of the other Peninnah. And Peninnah had children, but Hannah had no children. Now this man used to go up year by year from his city to worship and to sacrifice to the LORD of hosts at Shiloh, where the two sons of Eli, Hophni and Phinehas, were priests of the LORD. On the day when Elkanah sacrificed, he would give portions to his wife Peninnah and to all her sons and daughters; but to Hannah he gave a double portion, because he loved her, though the LORD has closed her womb. Her rival used to provoke her severely, to irritate her, because the LORD had closed her womb. So it went on year by year; as often as she went up to the house of the LORD, she used to provoke her. Therefore Hannah wept and would not eat. (1 Sam. 1:1–7)

No matter if the exposition is long or short, the crisis will quickly follow. The crisis is an unmistakable problem or tension that has risen in the life of key person(s) in the story. This may be an unfulfilled passion, a failure to understand, a lack of ability, an invalid perception, complication in a relationship, or a moral crisis.[16] For example, the tempter comes to Jesus in the wilderness bent on destroying the ministry and mission of Jesus at its very inception (Mt. 4). Will Satan succeed? While Moses is receiving the instructions of God on Mount Sinai, the Israelites indulge themselves in pagan revelry (Ex. 32). How will the Lord respond to this blatant act of sin? Information is withheld, or gaps are intentionally built into the story and left in place as long as necessary to hold our attention and interest.[17] If the way out of the crisis were direct and easy, it would not be much of a story, so additional complications are often included that will deepen the sense of crisis and leave the outcome more deeply in doubt.

The tension of the story often builds throughout the early verses of the story until a climactic moment is met. This may lie along a direct path with exposition leading to crisis leading to climax, or the climactic moment may be delayed. In the latter case, expect a series of intermediate or incomplete semi-climactic moments (so-called false climaxes). But once the story has reached the ultimate turning point, the tension truly begins to subside during the resolution phase (also called the unraveling or the *dénouement*). The reader breathes a sigh of relief as an insight is gained, a power is discovered, a passion is fulfilled, or the correct moral path is pursued. If the crisis focuses and holds our attention on the critical events or circumstances from which the lesson of the story will come, it is often in the resolution that we find the meaning of the story conveyed.

Finally, the story arrives at a concluding paragraph or sentence that restores a sense of calm. The listener must know that the story has come to its close. But the storyteller does not return us to the same world as before. It is a different place, a place that has given the reader an insight to apply to his or her own life.

The Plot Structure of Genesis 22

The story of Abraham and Isaac in Genesis 22 reveals the outline discussed above very clearly. The exposition of the story is handled in half a verse and relies heavily on the reader's previous experience with the principle characters in the story. We are told that God is going to test Abraham. Before our minds can wander for a moment into the realm of what that might mean, we hear it for ourselves. The crisis drops on us in the second verse, shocking us as it must have shocked Abraham by its horror and terseness. "Take your son, your only son Isaac, whom you love, and go to the land of Moriah, and offer him there as a burnt offering on one of the mountains that I will show you" (Gen. 22:2). From this moment on, the storyteller has us. We do not know what else Abraham may have planned to do that day. We are not told what he was wearing or what he may have said to his wife at this time. All extraneous details of the event are shed. The crafting of the plot has begun. Our focus goes to the crisis, raising questions that demand answers. How can a God who abhors human sacrifice make such a request? How could a father think of doing this to his son? What does this mean for the promise of rescue, since Isaac was to provide the family from which the messiah would be born? Will Abraham really do this? The tension of the crisis drives our reading forward in a bid to answer questions just like these.

But the trip to resolution will not be short or easy. Once the crisis is introduced, we meet additional details that tug at the heart of the listener and complicate the outcome. The journey to the place of sacrifice will take several days. Servants are accompanying Abraham and Isaac. Then comes Isaac's probing question, "The fire and the wood are here, but where is the lamb for a burnt offering?" and his father's mysterious reply, "God himself will provide the lamb for a burnt offering, my son" (Gen. 22:7–8). At just the place the reader wishes that the story would move quickly, the narrative slows to carefully detail the preparation of the altar for the sacrifice. All of these complications delay our necessary arrival at the climax of the story, either clouding the outcome or tricking us into thinking that the resolution lies down some other path.

The climatic moment comes in verses eleven and twelve as Abraham reaches out and picks up the knife to kill his son, ready to splash his blood over the wood and stones of the altar. At just this moment, the test comes to its conclusion. Abraham has demonstrated that his faith in the Lord is uncompromised–even by the relationship to his son. Once again a voice from heaven booms directions: "Do not lay your hand on the boy or do anything to him; for now I know that you fear God, since you have not withheld your son, your only son, from me" (Gen. 22:12).

We take our first breath since reading the second verse and listen as the story winds down to its conclusion. During the resolution a substitute sacrifice is offered, and Abraham gives voice to the conviction that we may carry with us from the story: "The LORD will provide" (Gen. 22:14). No matter how difficult or impossible our circumstances may seen at the time, it is possible to negotiate them if we believe, as Abraham did, that the Lord will provide.

This magnificent demonstration of faith results in a reaffirmation of God's promises given to Abraham. Abraham's family would grow, and the family of Isaac would bring the messiah into the fallen world that so desperately needed him. As Abraham returns to Beer-sheba (22:19), we know that the story has come to its close and we may return to our lives. But we do not return the same. We have witnessed a remarkable act of faith. The divine storyteller challenges us to emulate that faith by trusting that the Lord will provide answers to us when we face seemingly impossible challenges. The crisis in Abraham's life provides the teachable moment, presented in the resolution.

Scenes

Yet another way to look at the organization of the story is to examine the way in which the storyteller uses scenes to advance the plot line. This form of analysis can be very helpful, particularly when you are dealing with a longer story that has a more complex plot. The scene within a Bible story is typically defined by the interaction of two characters at a given place and time. A change in scene becomes apparent when we observe a change in principle characters who are occupying the center of our attention, a change in the character's location, or a formal announcement that there has been a change in time.[18]

While the changing scenes give the story a sense of movement, each individual scene plays an important role in advancing a component of the plot line. After reading through a story once and identifying its plot line, we can return to the story and mark off individual scenes. Again, watch for changes in characters, place, or time as a way of segmenting the plot into scenes. Then each individual scene can be analyzed and its contribution to the plot assessed.

Scenes in Genesis 22

We will now return to the story of Abraham and Isaac to break out the scenes and consider the ways in which they function within the plot structure we discussed above. Within the nineteen verses that comprise this story, we find six different scenes represented. Following the brief exposition that occupies the first half of verse one, we enter the first scene (22:1–2). As we discussed above, this scene immediately introduces the crisis. There are two participants in the scene, God and Abraham. God calls to Abraham. Abraham indicates his attentiveness, and then God drops the "bombshell." Abraham is to take his one and only son, the one that he loves dearly, and sacrifice him on a mountain God will show him. Without a word of protest from Abraham, that scene ends, but not before setting the crisis in place.

The second scene is entirely contained within verse three. The change in scene is indicated by the announcement of time and shift in characters on the stage. The voice of God is now absent, leaving the spotlight on Abraham as the sun rises early the next morning. He saddles a donkey, assigns two servants to go along, and cuts the wood for the offering. Then the travel toward the somber destination begins. This scene further complicates the crisis because the actions of Abraham all seem so mundane. It is as if Abraham is packing up to go on an ordinary trip, not one that will result in the death of his son. We wonder what role the two servants will play. Is Abraham hoping that they will intervene and prevent him from acting? Will they be used to hold down Isaac so that Abraham can take his life? There are no answers to these questions here. What is more, we are confused by the silence of Abraham. We have seen this man argue with God to save the lives of people in Sodom, most of whom he did not know (Gen. 18:16–33). Why, when it involves the life of his own son, is Abraham not arguing his case? Thus scene two is brief, but it raises further questions and concerns in our minds that complicate our path toward resolution of the crisis.

Scene three jumps ahead to "the third day, when the mountain is in view (22:4–6). The scene begins with Abraham's instructions for the servants who had accompanied them to this point. They are instructed to remain behind. We are not sure why they were asked to come this far, but no matter. They will no longer be playing a key role in the story. We also note that the donkey is also going to be left behind. That creates a concern for the wood that Abraham had split. Who is going to carry the wood now that this pack animal will be left behind? The answer comes quickly as Abraham places the wood on Isaac. Now this young man is carrying the very wood on which his body is to be burned. If we could stop reading we would, but we cannot.

While this act of putting the wood on Isaac startles us, it is Abraham's language that further complicates our travels. When Abraham finally speaks, he addresses the two servants left behind. "Stay here with the donkey; the boy and I will go over there; we will worship, and then we will come back to you" (Gen. 22:5). The last phrase contributes even more uncertainty to the story. The assertion of return is offered in a strong volitional form that communicates both Abraham's passion and confidence in this statement. Abraham is boldly asserting that he and Isaac will return. The reader of this story in this setting does not have the insight offered by Hebrews 11:17–19, so we are pulled even more deeply into the mysterious language of Abraham. What does he mean when he asserts that they will return?

Scene three comes to a close as Abraham and Isaac continue their journey. On the way, scene four takes place (22:6–8). This scene presents the dialogue between Abraham and Isaac that is particularly painful to hear. In his own naiveté, Isaac ironically asks about the absence of a sacrificial animal. He sees wood for a sacrifice, fire, and a knife; but where is the sacrificial animal? Once again this scene complicates the crisis as Abraham offers an enigmatic answer, "God himself will provide the lamb for a burnt offering, my son" (Gen. 22:8). The positioning of the words "offering" and "my son" in such close proximity shakes the reader to the core. But once again Abraham's statement puzzles us. What does he mean God will provide? Is he attempting to fool Isaac? Is he deluding himself? Or is this going to be the answer to the crisis? We have but one choice, to read on.

Scene five brings us to the climax and resolution of the story. This scene brings us to the setting where the long-expected sacrifice will take place. The storyteller is about to answer our questions. Will Abraham really take the life of his own son? Will God really accept a human sacrifice? What about the promise of the messiah that is linked to the children of Isaac? This scene (verses 9–18) is the longest in the story. It begins with Abraham's slow preparation of the altar and binding of Isaac, building to the climatic moment when the sacrifice is interrupted. The faith of Abraham is celebrated, a substitute sacrifice is provided, and the promises given to Abraham in the early verses of Genesis 12 are confirmed.

With the close of this crucial scene, the emotional roller coaster comes to an end, but we still are awaiting a signal that says the story has come to a close. That signal comes in the final scene housed in verse nineteen. Abraham returns to pick up the servants. All those who began the journey return together to Beer-sheba, where all this had begun. Thus the story of Abraham and Isaac in Genesis 22 is composed of six scenes, each carefully designed to make its own contribution to the plot.

Conclusion

As the storyteller moves the historical events from Bible times into the Bible itself, we see that part of the storyteller's craft relates to context and structure. First of all, the Bible presumes itself to be a large ongoing story from beginning to end in which each individual story must find its place and role. We must always inquire how a particular sub-story advances the cause of the book, the testament, and the Bible itself. As we make that inquiry, we can also identify the sub-stories in the larger story so that we may more closely examine the way they have been organized to make them meaningful to the listener. This involves us in identifying the structure of the plot and the ways in which the individual scenes within the plot function. We now have our start at examining the storyteller's craft as the storyteller moves the historical event into Bible story form. In the next chapter, we will turn our attention to the careful shaping of the characters who participate in the plot.

Notes

[1]Robert Alter, *The World of Biblical Literature* (New York: Basic Books, 1992), 110.

[2]Shimon Bar-Efrat, "Some Observations on the Analysis of Structure in Biblical Narrative," in *Beyond Form Criticism: Essays in Old Testament Literary Criticism,* ed. Paul R. House (Winona Lake, Ind.: Eisenbrauns, 1992), 188.

[3]Leland Ryken and Tremper Longman III, "Introduction," in *A Complete Literary Guide to the Bible,* ed. Leland Ryken and Tremper Longman III (Grand Rapids: Zondervan, 1993), 35.

[4]Ibid., 34.

[5]James L. Resseguie, *Narrative Criticism of the New Testament: An Introduction* (Grand Rapids: Baker Academic, 2005), 58.

[6]If you are reading in the Old Testament and wish to see a more sophisticated effort to bring all the pages of that testament together, see David A. Dorsey, *The Literary Structure of the Old Testament: A Commentary on Genesis-Malachi* (Grand Rapids: Baker Books, 1999).

[7]Gleason L. Archer Jr., *A Survey of Old Testament Introduction* (Chicago: Moody Press, 1964), 180. David A. Dorsey, *Literary Structure of the Old Testament,* 48.

[8]John H. Sailhamer, *The Pentateuch as Narrative: A Biblical-Theological Commentary,* The Library of Biblical Interpretation (Grand Rapids: Zondervan, 1992), 26.

[9]Shimon Bar-Efrat, *Narrative Art in the Bible,* JSOT Bible and Literature Series 17 (Sheffield: Almond Press, 1984), 94; Yairah Amit, *Reading Biblical Narratives: Literary Criticism and the Hebrew Bible* (Minneapolis: Fortress Press, 2001), 19–21.

[10]Bar-Efrat, *Narrative Art in the Bible,* 93.

[11]K.A. Telford, *Aristotle's Poetics: Translation and Analysis* (South Bend, Ind.: Gateway Editions, 1961), 15.

[12]David M. Gunn and Danna Nolan Fewell, *Narrative in the Hebrew Bible,* The Oxford Bible Series (Oxford: Oxford University Press, 1993), 101.

[13]Bar-Efrat, *Narrative Art in the Bible,* 93.

[14]Gunn and Fewell, *Narrative in the Hebrew Bible,* 105.

[15]Bar-Efrat, *Narrative Art in the Bible,* 121.

[16]Leland Ryken, *How to Read the Bible as Literature* (Grand Rapids: Zondervan, 1984), 40–41.

[17]Meir Sternberg, *The Poetics of Biblical Narrative: Ideological Literature and the Drama of Reading,* Indiana Studies in Biblical Literature (Bloomington: Indiana University Press, 1987), 235–36.

[18]Adele Berlin, *Poetics and Interpretation of Biblical Narrative* (Winona Lake, Ind.: Eisenbrauns, 1994), 46.

2

The Critical Role of
Characterization

Perhaps the most striking quality of the stories we read in our Bible is the colorfulness of the characters we meet there. People such as King David, Ruth, Peter, and Paul have been fleshed out with such vivid language and such intimate detail that we feel a personal connection to them. They are not just paper cutouts or cartoon characters, but real people who are working through life's issues much as we do on a daily basis. Such people lie at the very heart of Bible stories. Of course, plenty of other books tell stories from the lives of real people. But what makes the Bible different from those other books is God's presence on its pages. Through interaction with people in these stories, God is at work defining himself and telling us what we might well expect from God. In turn, we are also learning what it means to have a relationship with God by observing the men and women in these Bible stories work out their relationship with God. Thus the message for us in any given Bible story will have an intimate connection to the people who are in it.

If we had met the people who appear on the pages of our Bible personally in ordinary time and place, we would have formed our own impressions of them. Had we taken a chair next to Naomi in church, or next to Goliath at a neighborhood picnic, we would have introduced ourselves and begun the slow and natural process of becoming acquainted. But our impressions of Bible characters are not formed in this ordinary way. Rather, our acquaintance is mediated by the storyteller. What we know about the men, women, and children in our Bible, what remains hidden about them, and how we react to them is part of the careful crafting of the story. As the storyteller transfers an event into story form, the process of characterization becomes a task of critical importance.

This chapter will explore the critical role of characterization in Bible stories. First of all, we will consider the different types of characters introduced to us on the pages of these stories. Some are fully developed, well-round characters who get the bulk of our attention, while others are merely agents or types who support the story that surrounds the main character(s). We will then investigate the various ways by which the storyteller shapes our knowledge about and impressions of these characters. By controlling what we hear them say and what others say about them, by giving and changing their names, and by describing appearance and actions, the storyteller shapes our first and subsequent impressions of the characters.

Varieties of Characters

While every book in the Bible is blessed with a retinue of interesting characters, not every character is blessed with the same level of prominence and attention. This is analogous to my experience in daily living. Some of the people I meet and work with today will be very important to me. I know them very well. They have the power to change my life in deep and dramatic ways. By contrast, other people I encounter today will play a very minor role. I may not even know the name of the person who cuts my hair or of the clerk who tells me where to find the baked beans in the grocery store. Their small roles in shaping this day stand in dramatic contrast with the roles that my wife or my children will play.

Round Characters

In the same way, some of the characters within a Bible story will play a more prominent role than others. We get to know them well. They become the focus of our interest and attention. These characters are called "round" characters since our knowledge and connection to them is more complex and fully developed.[1] It is not unusual for such characters to be introduced and developed over many pages or over an entire book. Consider the intimate knowledge we have of people like Joshua, Ruth, Jesus, or Peter who are introduced to us through many pages, chapters, and even multiple books of the Bible.[2]

Flat Characters

By contrast to such round characters, the storyteller will also employ "flat" characters. The term flat is not a reference to their personal girth, but a reference to the thin amount of information shared with us about them. These flat characters can either function as agents or types.[3] The agent, while often given a name, is destined to play little more than a supporting role in the story. That role is limited to assisting the main character live out the details of the plot.

Several examples will illustrate the nature of that supporting role. In 1 Kings 1:1–4, we meet a woman named Abishag who is quickly introduced to us and who just as quickly leaves the pages of this chapter. She functions only as an agent who illustrates the diminished capacity of the once virile King David. Another example of such a minor character is Orpah, whom we meet in the book of Ruth. Orpah and Ruth are both Moabite women married to the sons of Naomi. When the husband and the two sons of Naomi die, her daughters-in-law join her in her widowhood. At this time, Naomi encourages both Ruth and Orpah to return to their families of origin rather than committing themselves to the uncertain life that lay ahead for her. Orpah accepts Naomi's invitation to return to her family of origin, causing the selfless act of Ruth, who remains with Naomi, to stand out (Ruth 1:14).

The nameless armor-bearer stands with King Saul on Mount Gilboa. After he was mortally wounded, Saul asked this agent to draw his sword and kill him (1 Sam. 31:4–6). By refusing to strike down the King of Israel, this young man sets the stage for Saul to take his own life. The armor-bearer, Abishag, and Orpah are examples of flat characters who function as agents. Their primary role is to set up the speech and actions of the main character in the story.

Another form of "flat" character is the type. The type is the character who either represents a group or who namelessly participates with a group. Like the agent, the person who functions as a type is only there to advance the movement of the plot in association with the main character(s) in the story. The type may be illustrated by the people who confront Aaron at the base of Mount Sinai when Moses' return from the summit is delayed. As a group, they express their misgivings on the leadership of the now vanished leader and demand that Aaron provide a deity for them to worship (Ex. 32:1). No one individual's voice or actions stand out. These individuals function as types. The disciples who were sent for a colt that Jesus might ride into Jerusalem (Mk. 11:1–7) and the soldiers who stood at the foot of the cross (Jn. 19:16–18) may also be classified as types. Such characters have even less definition than agents and have a much more reserved role to play in the story.

So in a typical Bible story, we may encounter a number of different individuals, some of greater prominence and some of lesser prominence. While there is room for discussion on just how a character should be classified in a particular story, these categories of round and flat characters, main and supporting characters can help us parse out the difference in importance between characters. This is an important step in seeking meaning within a Bible story. Rather than focusing on a minor character, we will want to read with our attention on the main character, since the meaning of the story will be most closely associated with that person.

Methods of Characterization

We now turn our attention to the various methods that a storyteller may use when characterizing the individuals we meet in the plot. We come to know the people in a Bible story in much the same way we get to know others we meet in our day-to-day living. We get to know others through what they say, what they do, and how others respond to them, assembling and assimilating the insights we gain.[4] Although we are meeting people in Bible stories indirectly, the storyteller uses the same kinds of clues to introduce the participants to us. We will explore and illustrate a sample of the methods used in the characterization process: direct quotations, statements about a character, actions, contrasting actions and quotations, appearance, and naming. During this overview, we will see that main characters in the story are often presented with complex and even contradictory traits. This is no surprise since we are talking about real people who are as complex in their personalities and nature as we are. But the complex and, at times, contradictory traits we see in a Bible story call for us to press even more deeply into what we have been told to eliminate the ambiguity.

Direct Speech of a Character

As we go through our day, we are bombarded by the speech of those around us. Because it would be most undesirable, if not impossible, to attend to every word, we disregard a great deal of what we hear people saying. That is a listening strategy that will not transfer well when analyzing the storyteller's craft within a narrative, since the storyteller has already edited out the words that are inconsequential for the story, preserving only that language that is critical. Since those quotations have an important role to play in the way we perceive the persons within the story, we will pay particular attention when we see quotation marks appearing on the pages of our Bible.

The words we see within quotation marks may either reflect the actual words or the unspoken thoughts of the person being quoted.[5] Everyone who was in the room with Jesus would have heard the words he spoke to the disabled man in Capernaum. The majority of those words exchanged with this man are unreported by the storyteller. However, Mark does preserve what he perceives to be the powerful core of what Jesus had to say to the man: "Son, your sins are forgiven" (Mk. 2:5). These words tell us something extraordinary about Jesus. The crowd and even those who brought the man to Jesus thought they understood this disabled man's deepest need. But Jesus saw past the obvious challenge this man faced and directly addressed what was truly his greatest need.

At other times, the storyteller uses quotation marks to house the inner thoughts rather than the externalized speech of an individual. When it became clear to David that he could no longer remain in the court of King Saul without risking his life, the storyteller allows us access to David's thoughts. "David said in his heart, 'I shall now perish one day by the hand of Saul; there is nothing better for me than to escape to the land of the Philistines; then Saul will despair of seeking me any longer within the borders of Israel, and I shall escape out of his hand'" (1 Sam. 27:1). So whether through direct speech or inner speech, we have the opportunity to meet and to know the characters in the story through the content of their own thoughts and words, as presented by the storyteller.

Careful analysis can take us beyond the content of the speech to note other qualities of that speech that will shade its impact on us. Communication is much more than just the arranging of vocabulary according to the grammatical rules. For example, I can say, "It is raining outside." That simple sentence can be shaded to express celebration, surprise, or anger. Consequently, I need to pay attention not only to what is said but also to how it is being said. The decoding of how something is being said may be as fundamental as noting the introduction to the quotation offered by the narrator. When Jesus was anointed in Bethany, Mark introduces and then quotes some of the people: "But some were there who said to one another in anger, 'Why was the ointment wasted in this way?'" (Mk. 14:4).

In the absence of this formal identification, the grammatical structure of a sentence can also betray inner conflict and struggle. Shimon Bar-Efrat challenges us to watch for just this kind of language pattern that reflects a more emotionally disturbed state.[6] When we are upset about something, the way we organize our sentences often reflects our emotion. The same is true of the speech patterns reflected in the direct quotes of the Bible. Unfortunately, some English translations smooth those quotations, making them flow more naturally than the Greek or Hebrew that lies behind them. For example, when Ahimaaz comes to David with news about the campaign to put down the rebellion of his son, Absalom, David asks Ahimaaz if Absalom is well. Ahimaaz stumbles at this point, not wanting to report the death of the king's son, and his language reflects his distress. "I saw the great disturbance at the sending of the servant of the king, Joab and your servant, I do not know what" (2 Sam. 18:29, author's translation). Both the roughness of the grammar and disjointedness of the content betray the inner conflict within Ahimaaz.

Another dimension of direct quotation that invites our attention is the quantity of speech allocated to the participants in the story. If a character is given a great deal of time to speak, it typically signals that he or she is important to the story and has something powerful to contribute to the meaning of the story. The story of David and Goliath provides a helpful illustration. In a chapter in which most participants are allowed little more than a sentence of direct communication at any one time, David gives a speech that extends over the course of three verses (1 Sam. 17:45–47). Since direct speech is one of the ways we get to know a character well, the storyteller invites us to listen to David for a longer time as he articulates the faith that makes him fit to lead the people of God. By contrast, consider the message that is sent to the reader about Judas in the gospel of John. When we investigate the amount of speaking time allotted to him, we find that Judas remains silent for nearly the entire book. He is permitted only one sentence of direct speech. When he does speak that sole sentence, it plays a powerful role in his characterization, particularly as it is explained by the narrator. As Jesus was being anointed at Bethany by Mary, Judas objected, "Why was this perfume not sold for three hundred denarii and the money given to the poor?" (Jn. 12:5). Then the narrator comments: "(He said this not because he cared about the poor, but because he was a thief; he kept the common purse and used to steal what was put into it)" (Jn. 12:6).

Together with the length of speech, the careful reader will also consider the position of the speech within the story. First speeches are often designed to be the first impression, so they deserve greater attention.[7] At the start of Daniel, we read that he and his colleagues have been pressed into training for service in the Babylonian royal court. We do not hear Daniel speak a word until the twelfth verse of the book that bears his name. But that first speech reveals both the faith and intelligence of this young man. When Daniel and his colleagues were told by their captors to eat food that God had forbidden them to eat, Daniel suggested a way out of the seeming conflict of interests: "Please test your servants for ten days. Let us be given vegetables to eat and water to drink. You can then compare our appearance with the appearance of the young men who eat the royal rations, and deal with your servants according to what you observe" (Dan. 1:12–13). Because these are the very first words from Daniel's lips, they play an even greater role in the characterization process than if they had been buried more deeply in the story.

Prominence in the story is also given to direct speech that falls during or shortly after the climax in the plot. During the climactic moment or during the resolution phase, a clue about the intended meaning of the story is often placed on the lips of the main character.[8] In the previous chapter, we observed this very phenomenon in the story of Abraham and Isaac. Immediately after the climax of the story, Abraham gives voice to this conviction, "The LORD will provide" (Gen. 22:14). We had wondered throughout the story how to make sense of Abraham's words and actions. His commitment to this premise is what helps us make sense of it all. The one short sentence establishes the meaning of the story for us.

The absence of direct speech when it is expected also can also be used in the process of characterization.[9] When one of David's sons criminally rapes one of David's daughters in the royal palace, we expect this great man, capable of profound speech, to speak. How could a father remain silent when a son and daughter within his own family were involved? While his rage is recorded for us, we do not hear a word from him on the matter (2 Sam. 13:21). The storyteller uses the absence of expected speech to shape our impressions.

Thus speech plays a major role in the process of characterization. While we do not hear everything that everyone would have said when the event took place, the storyteller does select direct quotes for us to hear.

By paying careful attention to the content, the style, the length, and the position of that direct speech, we can come to know the person speaking in a more intimate way.

Statements about a Character

Another way in which a storyteller introduces a character to the reader is through what others have to say about him or her. This can come either via another character's statement or through a statement from the narrator.[10] In the first case, one participant in the story makes a statement about another person. When Jesus was discussing his true identify with his followers near Caesarea, Peter gives this profound description of who Jesus is: "You are the Messiah, the Son of the living God" (Mt. 16:16). The storyteller provides the listeners with Peter's words since they clearly illuminate the true nature of his teacher.

Less often, the narrator directly characterizes a participant, providing us with a very clear and unmistakable impression.[11] In some cases, we find that the narrator provides a very positive report: "Noah was a righteous man, blameless in his generation; Noah walked with God" (Gen. 6:9b). This declaration leaves no doubt about the characterization of Noah. In the same way, we cannot mistake Cornelius' true nature. The narrator succinctly describes him: "In Caesarea there was a man named Cornelius, a centurion of the Italian Cohort, as it was called. He was a devout man who feared God with all his household; he gave alms generously to the people and prayed constantly to God" (Acts 10:1–2).

By contrast, the narrator's assessment may be much less than positive. The narrator would not have won a favored position in Ahab's court when he told the real story of Ahab: "Ahab son of Omri did evil in the sight of the LORD more than all who were before him" (1 Kings 16:30). Commenting on Judas' objection that the perfume used to anoint Jesus could have been sold to the poor, the narrator reports, "(He said this not because he cared about the poor, but because he was a thief; he kept the common purse and used to steal what was put into it)" (Jn. 12:6). So it is not just what characters say but what others say about them that leaves a lasting impression with us.

Actions

A third way in which the storyteller introduces characters to us is through what they do. Not everything that we do or that we observe others doing is filled with meaning. But when a storyteller brings a character's actions before our eyes, we will want to pay attention, because such actions often speak louder than their words when it comes to their true nature and traits.[12] We find this very early in the book of Genesis with Adam and Eve. Here the storyteller tells us that Adam and Eve hid from the Lord among the trees of the garden. That act signaled a critical shift in their relationship with God that came upon the heels of eating from the forbidden tree (Gen.

3:8). These are no longer the same people whom we had met just a few verses earlier who talked easily and fearlessly with their God. Their act of hiding bespeaks a profound change in who they have become and what their relationship with God has come to be.

While the actions of Adam and Eve propel us toward a more negative assessment of them, a widow's simple action in Jerusalem casts her in a very positive light. As Jesus sat in Jerusalem within sight of the place where people came to place their offerings, he observed many rich people placing large amounts of money into the treasury. A widow gets our attention and his when she puts in two very small copper coins (Mk. 12:41–42). This gift flowed from her great poverty rather than her great wealth, and so the story of her gift leads us to celebrate the quality of this giving, as Jesus does. Similarly, often Jesus' acts in the gospels give us the clearest sense of who he is. From the moment he turns water into wine, through his many acts of healing, down to the very way he entered Jerusalem, riding on a colt, Jesus' actions more often than his direct claims lead us to see him as the promised Messiah.

Two unique forms of action also merit special attention: repeated action and clusters of action. Actions that are repeated become closely linked to the characterization process.[13] When we read that David's son, Absalom, was in the habit of cutting his hair and having it weighed, we are led to see him as one filled with self-absorbed pride–the royal, rich kid who is going to be nothing but trouble (2 Sam. 14:26). By contrast, when we read that Job's regular custom was to offer a burnt offering every day on behalf of his children just in case they had committed a serious sin, we are left with the impression that Job is both a concerned father and a faithful follower of the Lord (Job 1:5).

We will also want to watch for clusters of actions reported by the narrator. When God told Abraham to take his son Isaac to the region of Moriah and sacrifice him there, Abraham did not respond with words but with a cluster of actions that indicate his obedience to God's command. Abraham gets up early the next morning, puts a saddle on the donkey, arranges for servants to go along, cuts fire wood, and sets out on the journey (Gen. 22:3).

Clusters of actions can also reinforce a sense of futility and failure. When Elijah is engaged in a contest with the prophets of Baal on Mount Carmel, we find the Baal prophets involved in just such a cluster of meaningless acts. They prepare a sacrifice, call on the name of Baal all morning, dance around the altar, shout more loudly, slash themselves with swords and spears, and increase the intensity of their pleading throughout the afternoon (1 Kings 18:26–29). We get quite a different impression through the cluster of actions reported in the first chapter of Jonah. These actions are all associated with the pagan mariners caught on the storm-tossed ship that was carrying Jonah. We come to appreciate their level of fear and desperation as we watch them crying out to their gods, throwing cargo overboard, casting lots, interrogating Jonah, and vigorously digging in to bring the ship closer to land (Jonah 1). As the storyteller works to shape our impressions of the people we meet in such stories, actions can play a key role in the characterization process. Since the stories have been purged of unnecessary details, we can be certain that reported actions, inaction when action is expected, repeated action, and clusters of action deserve our careful attention.

Contrasted Speech and Actions

Not just what a character says and does in a narrative shapes our perceptions. The way in which a main character's words and actions contrast with the speech and actions of others we meet in the narrative also molds our understanding.[14] This contrast in character qualities plays a critical role in the reading of David and Goliath (1 Sam. 17). The storyteller invites us to compare the leadership of the sitting king, Saul, and the anointed king, David. Both are confronted with the same national crisis as the Philistine army has invaded the Elah Valley. Both are faced with the daily challenge Goliath makes to provide a warrior to fight him. Both hear the giant Philistine warrior their nation and their God. As the story unfolds, the storyteller invites us to compare and contrast the speech and actions of David in response to all this to determine who has the qualities to lead God's people effectively. The verbal misgivings of Saul are contrasted with David's words of confidence. David says, "Let no one's heart fail because of him; your servant will go and fight with this Philistine" (1 Sam. 17:32). In the very next verse Saul attempts to negate that confidence. "You are not able to go against this Philistine to fight with him; for you are just a boy, and he has been a warrior from his youth" (1 Sam. 17:33). In the subsequent speech and actions of David, he clearly shows that he is taking into account a divine presence and strength that Saul has long forgotten. In the end, when we compare all that David says and does to what Saul says and does, David clearly comes out the more appropriate leader.

While David is clearly the winner in this comparison, he does not fair so well in 2 Samuel 11. After impregnating the wife of Uriah, a faithful solider in his army, David summons Uriah back from the front in a bid to cover up his sinful act. But at every turn, Uriah's speech and actions cast David in an increasingly negative light. While David is more than ready to sleep with Bathsheba while her husband and the soldiers of Israel are engaged in the field, Uriah sleeps at the entrance of the palace, not in his own bed or with his own wife. Note how the words of Uriah sting with irony as he explains his actions, "The ark and Israel and Judah remain in booths; and my lord Joab and the servants of my lord are camping in the open field; shall I then go to my house, to eat and to drink, and to lie with my wife? As you live, and as your soul lives, I would not do such a thing" (2 Sam. 11:11). Uriah would not, but David did. Here the contrast of speech and actions places David in a very negative light.

Jesus uses this technique of contrasting speech and action when he tells a story about a Pharisee and a tax collector who had come to the temple for worship. The speech and actions of the Pharisee betray a self-righteous pride in and of themselves. "The Pharisee, standing by himself, was praying thus, 'God, I thank you that I am not like other people: thieves, rogues, adulterers, or even like this tax collector. I fast twice a week; I give a tenth of all my income'" (Lk. 18:11–12). But notice what happens when we take the speech and actions of the Pharisee and place them next to the speech and actions of the tax collector. They become even more powerful by contrast. "But the tax collector, standing far off, would not even look up to heaven, but was beating his breast and saying, 'God, be merciful to me, a sinner!'" (Lk. 18:13).

Appearance

Yet another technique available to the storyteller with which to shape our response to the participants in the narrative is the description of their appearance. Typically, the inspired writers give us very little information on the appearance of the people we meet. It is virtually impossible for us, using the language of Scripture, to draw an accurate representation of even one of the Bible's characters. But the descriptions of appearance are not meant to be used by an artist to draw a picture. Rather, readers are to use information about physical appearance or dress to form impressions about these individuals.[15] When we meet Rachel and Leah, marriage prospects for Jacob, we are provided with information on the physical appearance of the two. "Leah's eyes were lovely, and Rachel was graceful and beautiful" (Gen. 29:17). The attractive appearance of Joseph will also play a role in his story, so the storyteller reports that he is "handsome and good-looking" (Gen. 39:6). As we enter the story of Ehud, the careful reader will note that while he is left-handed (Judg. 3:15), his Moabite adversary is a fat man (Judg. 3:17). Those seemingly small details will play an important role in the way the story unfolds and concludes. Saul is both handsome and taller than average (1 Sam. 9:2). The reader finds great detail in the story of David and Goliath with regards to the appearance and dress of the giant. Here the storyteller dedicates four verses to the description of Goliath's height and armor (1 Sam. 17:4–7). Even in this case, we may not be able to draw an accurate picture of Goliath with the details given to us about his appearance, but we may use descriptions like this to better understand the people we meet and their role in the story.

Naming

Finally, we come to the matter of naming. As the story unfolds, the inspired authors will give some of the participants proper names while others are merely given appellations or designations, for example "the woman," "a servant," or "the rich man." Here we will discuss the function of naming, the importance of noticing the changes in name or appellation during the course of a story, and the matter of meaning that may or may not be directly associated with the etymology of a person's personal name.

The assigning of a name or designation to a person in the story can have several functions. At the lowest level, the name or function allows us to differentiate between participants in the story, distinguishing one character from another. But beyond that, the name or designation can play a role in differentiating between the importance of various characters and even indicate something about their personalities or traits.[16]

As a general rule, the storyteller will give proper names to key players in the narrative, while withholding the personal names of minor participants. When we encounter personal names like Moses, David, Esther, Mary, or John, our inclination as readers is to pay greater attention to such people, assuming that they will play more critical roles in the narrative and in communicating the meaning of that narrative. In reading the gospel of John, one encounters many healing miracles. But in all of those miracles, the personal name of only one individual being healed is provided. Because the names of the sick are withheld, our reading more naturally focuses on Jesus in those stories. However, when Lazarus is given a name, we recognize that this man is to share the stage with Jesus in a more important way.[17] The reason for his naming in John 11 becomes clear within just a few verses. This miracle animates the anger of the religious leaders in Israel to the point that they begin more aggressive action against Jesus (Jn. 11:45–53). While there are exceptions to the rule, those who are not given a proper name usually play a supporting role.[18] Such nameless characters are often not less critical to the plot but, in most cases, we will know less about them and focus less upon them. Thus it is important to note who is given a personal name in the story and from whom such naming is withheld.

A storyteller may well change the naming of a character as that character goes through changes throughout the course of the story. For example, it is interesting to track the development of David's naming through the early part of his story that begins in 1 Samuel 16. Here the Lord sends Samuel to the family of Jesse with direction to anoint the next king of Israel from among Jesse's sons. David is not identified at first with a personal name. Rather he is identified as one of Jesse's sons (16:1), "the one" (16:3), "the youngest" (16:11), and again as "the one" (16:12). Only at verse thirteen do we find his personal name. Sternberg sees this progress in naming as part of the strategy in the chapter that withholds the use of David's personal name until his status changes at the time of his anointing.[19]

Another interesting study is the naming of Bathsheba in 2 Samuel 11–12. At first she is just "the woman" whose public bathing caught the eye of King David. He sent for this "woman," and this "woman" became pregnant (11:2, 3, 5). Her personal name is provided in 11:3. But the use of her personal name gives way to the designation "wife of Uriah," that becomes the most persistent appellation used for her in these two chapters (11:3, 11:11, 11:26,

12:9, 12:10, and 12:15). It is the designation Nathan used for her even after she has become the wife of David. This designation calls attention again and again to the indiscretion of David. Her personal name is finally restored after the death of her child as David is consoling her (12:24).

This sort of development in naming is also evident in the gospels. For example, consider the naming of Mary Magdalene in John 20. On Easter Sunday morning, Mary remained outside the tomb of Jesus crying. When she looks into the tomb, she sees two angels who address her as "woman" (20:13). She turns around and stands before Jesus but does not recognize him. Jesus inquires about her grief again calling her "woman" (20:15). Then Jesus says her name, "Mary" (20:16). As the "woman" becomes "Mary," she is reunited with her Lord and becomes a key witness to Jesus' resurrection. Thus it is not just the naming of a character but also the change in name or appellation during the course of the story that invites our attention, for this, too, is part of the art of storytelling that helps us sort the primary participants in the plot and allows us to track their development within the story.

There remains the question of using the etymology of proper names as a tool in assigning traits to biblical characters. Many of the personal names in the Bible have an interesting etymology that lies behind them. For example, "Saul" is the "the one requested" and "Jonah" is "a dove." The question is whether or not the divine storyteller wishes us to use the etymology of such names in the characterization process. It seems the safest interpretive strategy in this regard is to avoid making something of those etymologies unless the storyteller has formally signaled that we ought to do so.[20]

And that does happen. In the book of Ruth, Naomi certainly faced more than her share of personal tragedy. Her family was displaced by a famine. Her husband and both of her sons died during their time in Moab. When Naomi returns to Bethlehem, she brings up the etymology of her name. In Hebrew, the etymology of "Naomi" suggests something "pleasant." Given all she has been through, she suggests her name be changed to "Mara," the Hebrew equivalent of "bitterness" (Ruth 1:20–21).

A descendant of Naomi, King David, draws attention to the etymology of Solomon's name as having significance for his role in Israel. Although King David had longed to build the Lord a temple in Jerusalem, the Lord had told David that he was not the one to do it since he was a man of war (1 Chr. 22:8). Rather it would be his son, King Solomon, who would build that temple. The personal name, Solomon, is built from the Hebrew word that means "peace." Note how the storyteller makes use of that etymology in what God says to David. "See, a son shall be born to you; he shall be a man of peace. I will give him peace from all his enemies on every side; for his name shall be Solomon, and I will give peace and quiet to Israel in his days" (1 Chr. 22:9).

Something similar happens in the New Testament near Caesarea Philippi. When Jesus asks his disciples who they believe him to be, Peter gives the stellar answer: "You are the Messiah, the Son of the living God" (Mt. 16:16). This is a dramatic moment in naming in and of itself. In what follows, Jesus does something with Simon's name. In verse seventeen, he refers to Peter as "Simon son of Jonah." In the very next verse he says, "And I tell you, you are Peter, and on this rock I will build my church..." This new name Peter is derived from the Greek word for "rock," again creating an important connection between this man and his rocklike confession. So while many of the personal names used in the Bible have etymologies that offer insights into the people they name, it seems the best interpretive strategy to reserve the use of those insights to times when the divine storyteller signals approval.

Clarifying the Characterization

The process of characterization is rarely based on one instance of naming or one speech by a character. It is the weight of the combined evidence that leads readers to view Bible characters as they do. When the various pieces of evidence are considered together, we often find information that stands in apparent contradiction. That is because characters in our Bible stories are presented as the very real and complex people that they were. So, in the very same chapter (Gen. 12), we meet Abraham as the man ready to step out in remarkable faith traveling to a new country at the Lord's request, *and* as a man willing to share his wife sexually with an Egyptian leader to avoid being harmed by that leader. Who is the real Abraham? Of course, the answer is that he is both the man of faith and the man of weakness, for he is a real person just as we are.

As we read a Bible story, it often becomes necessary to navigate between conflicting impressions about a person to better understand him or her. Just as in real life, we must often compare words and actions, first and last impressions, public and private moments to feel we really know someone.[21] That is certainly the case with Jonah. In the very first chapter of his book, we are met with conflicting information. On the one hand we have Jonah inexplicably thumbing his nose at the Lord's directive that he preach in Nineveh while just verses later we find him announcing, "I am a Hebrew...I worship the LORD, the God of heaven, who made the sea and the dry land" (Jon. 1:9).

In the face of such conflicting evidence, Robert Alter offers a plan for clarifying the characterization. He places the credibility of the evidence on the following scale.[22] At the lowest level, he places a character's actions and appearance. Since actions and appearance require the most inference in creating an impression, he gives them the least amount of credibility in evaluating a character. Just beyond actions and appearance comes direct speech and speech about a character. Here we are weighing verbal claims that require less inference but still may be clouded by personal prejudice. The highest level of certainty may be attached to the inner speech of a character and the words of the narrator, which offer the most certain insights. And of that data, the narrator offers the most believable reports since the credibility of the narrator is on par with the credibility of God within Bible stories.[23]

While Alter's matrix is helpful, we should be cautious never to reduce the interpretation of a story to a scientific formula. Since direct comments from the narrator are generally rare, we are largely left with the evidence of speech and actions. While speech may offer us more direct access to characterization, we need to honor the fact that people in the Bible stories are in fact real people who may either misunderstand what they are talking about or who may speak in ways that edit reality to foster their own self-interests.

So when we look at the speech of characters on the pages of our Bible, we need to ask if, in fact, they are getting it right. Clearly Satan has it wrong when he says to Jesus, "All these I will give you, if you will fall down and worship me" (Mt. 4:9). But Jesus has it right when he says, "Worship the Lord your God, / and serve only him" (Mt. 4:10). Clearly the crowd is right when they say, "Never has anything like this been seen in Israel" (Mt. 9:33), after witnessing Jesus perform an exorcism. But the Pharisees are equally wrong when they say, "By the ruler of the demons he casts out the demons" (Mt. 9:34).

Self-interested inaccuracies are more easily picked out in these narratives, but that is not always the case. The characterization of Jonah in chapter 1 of his book presents us with a perplexing dilemma. Should we accept his proclamation at face value when he says, "I am a Hebrew...I worship the Lord, the God of heaven, who made the sea and the dry land" (Jon. 1:9)? If we apply Alter's matrix rigidly, then we would have to believe what Jonah said more than what he did. But a look at all the evidence that characterizes Jonah in the first chapter of his book clearly leads to the conclusion that Jonah's quotation is an ironic misstatement of his convictions. This is not the confession born of deep spiritual conviction, but one born of a spiritual delusion. Thus in the face of conflicting evidence we must do what we always do in life when we meet someone we are attempting to understand. We will look at all the evidence and come to a conclusion on who they are, realizing that this is particularly important when we examine Bible stories, since the meaning of the story is often closely connected to the characters we meet in those stories.

A Method for Character Analysis

As we read or listen to the stories in the Bible, our views of the various characters are naturally being shaped by the storyteller. We suspect that you were not very attracted to Goliath and Judas long before you read the treatment of them in this chapter. But to more accurately discern the meaning of a story, we can explore the way we meet the characters by using the method outlined here.

The first step in that process is to identify and distinguish the different characters in the story. Who are the main characters who are the focus of the story? Who are the supporting characters (agents and types)? The main characters are typically given proper names and introduced in the exposition of the story. In reading the story, we will find that the structure of the plot is intimately connected to them while others are playing supporting roles. For example, the story of Abraham and Isaac (Gen. 22) is clearly a story that defines a challenge in the life of Abraham. Even though Isaac is given a proper name here, his is in a supporting role rather than a lead role in the story.

Once we have distinguished the roles of the characters, it is time to formally mark or identify the specific method(s) used to introduce us to those participants in the plot. This can be done by highlighting the text using different colors for different characterization techniques or using different colors to mark the characterization of various characters. If you would prefer not to mark a text, you can accomplish the same thing by generating a list of characters and then noting the various techniques used within the story to shape our perception of them. What does the character say? What is directly said about that character by another person in the story or by the narrator? What does the individual do? What is said about the appearance of the character? How is the character named? In what ways do the actions and words of the other characters influence our view by comparison? Your analysis will likely demonstrate that the storyteller does not use all these techniques, but it will lay bare the distinctive way in which our meeting with the characters in the story has been designed. We can then ask ourselves the critical questions. What is the cumulative impact of all the characterization techniques on my perception of that person? What changes or developments, if any, do we see during the course of the story?

Jonah 1

We can illustrate such analysis by using characterization we find in the first chapter of Jonah. This is a wonderful story for illustrating the ways in which the divine storyteller carefully manipulates our meeting with Jonah and guides our response to him. Of course, the story of Jonah is much larger than the first chapter. But in the first chapter, the storyteller sets up the crisis closely associated with the character of Jonah. It is necessary for the reader to meet him in this very unfavorable light so that the ultimate purpose of the story can be achieved: to show that the power of God's Word does not lie in the messenger but in the message itself.

In Jonah 1, two main characters are introduced to us in the exposition, both given proper names—the Lord and Jonah. While the first chapter of the story focuses our attention on the discordant relationship between these two, it also dedicates a considerable amount of space to the supporting characters in the story, the mariners and the captain. For the sake of simplicity, we will treat the mariners and captain together. In what follows, we will examine the techniques used to characterize three participants in the plot: the Lord, Jonah, and the mariners.

In characterizing the Lord, the writer of this story relies heavily on the reader's larger understanding of God's revelation in Scripture. Thus the storyteller can get by with dedicating very few verses to the characterization of God even though the Lord's mission to Nineveh lies at the heart of this story. The storyteller articulates that passion in God's only direct quote addressed to Jonah in the first chapter. "Go at once to Nineveh, that great city, and cry out against it; for their wickedness has come up before me" (1:2). The Lord is also presented to us through two distinctive actions. In verse 4, God "hurls a great wind upon the sea"; and in verse 17, God provides a large fish that swallows up Jonah. From his own words, we learn that the Lord has a message for Nineveh and a mission for Jonah. From God's actions, we realize that God is serious about it.

While we know a great deal about the Lord from the other pages in the Bible, we get to know Jonah well only within the pages of this book. The characterization of Jonah in the first chapter is accomplished by a mixed bag of quotations and actions that, on their own, leave us somewhat puzzled. Since Jonah has been identified as a spokesperson for the Lord, we want to listen carefully to what he says. In fact, we may assume that an insight on the meaning of this story will come from his mouth. But he is silent through the first eight verses of the story. He first speaks in verse nine with what appears to be a very orthodox confession. "I am a Hebrew…I worship the LORD, the God of heaven, who made the sea and the dry land" (1:9). We nod our approval. But this confession in the greatness and power of God is followed by another speech that appears to be made in resignation rather than faith: "Pick me up and throw me into the sea; then the sea will quiet down for you; for I know it is because of me that this great storm has come upon you" (1:12). So who is Jonah? Is he the orthodox willing to surrender his life to save the crew? Or is Jonah the man of little faith who hopes to escape the mission assignment by ending his own life?

If that speech of Jonah leaves us a bit uncertain about him, the actions leave little doubt. Following God's command to Jonah, calling for him to go to Nineveh, Jonah initiates a cluster of activities that are designed to avoid this call. Jonah sets out for Tarshish through a series of steps described in 1:3. He goes to the harbor at Joppa, finds a ship, pays the fare, gets on board, and sets out for Tarshish, a direction that takes him away from Nineveh rather than toward it. These actions of Jonah weigh more powerfully than his first speech. This leads us to read his confession of faith as an empty formula and to see his invitation to the sailors as a bid at the ultimate escape from the mission rather than an honorable offer to save the crew. From what we hear Jonah say and what we see Jonah do, the close of the first chapter leaves us certain that this man is poorly suited for his mission as a prophet of God.

While it is clearly the Lord and Jonah who are the focus of this book and of the first chapter in this book, it is the supporting characters, the mariners and the captain, who actually receive more attention than the Lord and Jonah. Almost half the words in this story are used to describe them, their actions, and their words. This does not elevate their status in the story. They remain the supporting cast who have no personal names assigned to them. But our understanding of them plays a critical role in further increasing our distaste for Jonah. For through the positive characterization of these pagan mariners, Jonah's character is further diminished in our eyes.

While the Lord speaks once and Jonah twice in this chapter, the direct speech of the mariners is recorded on five different occasions. With a storm raging outside, the captain comes to Jonah with the very question the reader has been asking. "What are you doing sound asleep? Get up, call on your god! Perhaps the god will spare us a thought so that we do not perish" (1:6). We can hear the exasperation in his voice. This nameless captain knows nothing of the Lord's true identity and full power. Jonah has much to teach him, but it is this pagan mariner who calls Jonah's attention to the power of God and to prayer. The confusion of the mariners is again highlighted in a conversation they have among themselves. "Come, let us cast lots, so that we may know on whose account this calamity has come upon us" (1:7). Once Jonah has been identified as a person of interest, we hear the anxious questions they ask: "Tell us why this calamity has come upon us. What is your occupation? Where do you come from? What is your country? And of what people are you?...What shall we do to you that the sea may quiet down for us?" (1:8, 11a). Finally, as they prepare to cast Jonah to the sea, they plead with the Lord they have come to know, though imperfectly. "Please, O LORD, we pray, do not let us perish on account of this man's life. Do not make us guilty of innocent blood; for you, O LORD, have done as it pleased you" (1:14). The desperation in their voices comes through loud and clear. We do not know the names of these men, yet our hearts do go out to them. They have been caught in a storm meant for another.

The storyteller also dedicates considerable space to the description of the mariners' actions. In response to the storm, they cry out to their gods and throw cargo off the ship (1:5). Even when Jonah tells them that the solution to the problem is for them to throw him into the sea, they instead dig in to turn the ship closer to land (1:13). After the storm suddenly ceases, they offer sacrifices to the Lord and make vows (1:16). Again, the desperate actions of the mariners stand in stark contrast to Jonah's sleep, and their acts of worship stand in sharp relief to the faithless actions of Jonah. We hear the fear in their voices and see the desperation in their actions. They, like the people of Nineveh, need to hear from a prophet of the Lord. So the silence of Jonah and his inaction stand out even more powerfully against this background.

In the end, the listener's impressions of Jonah are largely directed by contrasting the response of Jonah and the mariners to the crisis before them. While Jonah responds with callous and hollow language, the mariners respond with clusters of action, pleading language, and the beginnings of humble faith. At the close of chapter 1, we are left with an unfulfilled mission to Nineveh and some deep concerns about Jonah. Will he even survive the experience in the belly of the fish? If he does, could God possibly use someone like this to preach effectively in Nineveh? Since Jonah looks much like me in so many respects, could God use someone like me as an effective messenger even in the face of all the shortcomings that I bring to the task? Of course, the reader must read on for the answers to those questions and for the revelation of the meaning of the story. But en route, chapter 1 and its characterization of Jonah play a key role in setting the stage for that revelation.

Conclusion

The colorful people we meet in the Bible, such as Jonah, become just that through the careful planning of the storyteller. We have not met the people in our Bible stories personally, but we have been introduced through the careful process of characterization. We can identify the prominence of the main characters and the roles of the supporting characters. We can examine the strategic reporting of language, actions, appearance, and naming to see how we have been introduced. By carefully examining that process, we not only can come to appreciate the storyteller's craft but ultimately find a clearer insight into the meaning of the story itself.

Notes

[1] Adele Berlin, *Poetics and Interpretation of Biblical Narrative* (Winona Lake, Ind.: Eisenbrauns, 1994), 23; James L. Resseguie, *Narrative Criticism of the New Testament: An Introduction* (Grand Rapids: Baker Academic, 2005), 123.

[2] David Rhoads and Donald Michie, *Mark As Story: An Introduction to the Narrative of a Gospel* (Philadelphia: Fortress Press, 1982), 103; Kari Syreeni, "Peter as Character and Symbol in the Gospel of Matthew," in *Characterization in the Gospels: Reconceiving Narrative Criticism,* ed. David Rhoads and Kari Syreeni (Sheffield: Sheffield Academic Press, 1999), 234.

[3] Berlin, *Poetics and Interpretation of Biblical Narrative,* 23–24.

[4] David M. Gunn and Danna Nolan Fewell, *Narrative in the Hebrew Bible,* The Oxford Bible Series (Oxford: Oxford University Press, 1993), 47.

[5] Robert Alter, *The Art of Biblical Narrative* (New York: Basic Books, 1981), 68.

[6] Shimon Bar-Efrat, *Narrative Art in the Bible,* JSOT Bible and Literature Series 17 (Sheffield: The Almond Press, 1989), 65.

[7] Alter, *Art of Biblical Narrative,* 74.

[8] Walter C. Kaiser Jr., "I Will Remember the Deeds of the Lord: The Meaning of Narrative," in *An Introduction to Biblical Hermeneutics: The Search for Meaning,* ed. Walter C. Kaiser Jr. and Moisés Silva (Grand Rapids: Zondervan, 1994), 72.

[9]Alter, *Art of Biblical Narrative,* 79.

[10]Bar-Efrat, *Narrative Art in the Bible,* 53.

[11]Gunn and Fewell, *Narrative in the Hebrew Bible,* 60.

[12]Bar-Efrat, *Narrative Art in the Bible,* 80.

[13]Ibid., 81.

[14]Alter, *Art of Biblical Narrative,* 72–73; Berlin, *Poetics and Interpretation of Biblical Narrative,* 40.

[15]Berlin, *Poetics and Interpretation of Biblical Narrative,* 34; Yairah Amit, *Reading Biblical Narratives: Literary Criticism and the Hebrew Bible* (Minneapolis: Fortress Press, 2001), 47.

[16]Adele Reinhartz, *"Why Ask My Name?" Anonymity and Identity in Biblical Narrative* (Oxford: Oxford University Press, 1998), 6.

[17]Raimo Hakola, "A Character Resurrected: Lazarus in the Fourth Gospel and Afterward," in *Characterization in the Gospels,* ed. Rhoads and Syreeni, 234.

[18]Ibid., 12.

[19]Meir Sternberg, *The Poetics of Biblical Narrative: Ideological Literature and the Drama of Reading,* Indiana Studies in Biblical Literature (Bloomington, Ind.: Indiana University Press, 1985), 330.

[20]Ibid., 330.

[21]Jan P. Fokkelman, *Reading Biblical Narrative: An Introductory Guide* (Louisville: Westminster John Knox Press, 1999), 66.

[22]Alter, *Art of Biblical Narrative,* 116–17.

[23]Bar-Efrat, *Narrative Art in the Bible,* 54.

3

The Nuances of the Narrator

By contrast to the vivid and memorable characters we meet on the pages of our Bible, the narrator assumes a more quiet and reserved presence in the story. Just as quiet waters can run deep, we dare not underestimate the power and influence of the narrator. The narrator is the storyteller within the story, empowered to nuance the details of the story that shape our reading experience. Every shift in speaker, every action undertaken by a character, every detail of the event that is revealed or hidden is done so at the direction of the narrator. As the event becomes the story, it is God the storyteller that employs the narrator within the story to shape that transition, all the while imbuing the story with meaning.

In this chapter, we will explore the nuances of the narrator. Since it is so easy to read past the unassuming voice of the narrator, we will begin by addressing how we may formally mark the narrator's voice within the story. We will explore the knowledge and credibility of the narrator. Then, after surveying the variety of roles the narrator may play within the story, we will focus on the role of the narrator in establishing the ideological point of view that both shapes the presentation of the story and that, in turn, seeks to shape the reader of the story. "For the narrator is always at the reader's elbow, shaping response to the story even, and especially when, the reader is least aware of it."[1]

Identifying the Narrator's Voice

To examine the role of the narrator, we must first remove the literary camouflage. Unlike the painter, composer, or even the author, the narrator is present within the art form, hiding among the words of the story.[2] Within the words used to tell the story, we will be able to identify and trace the quiet tracks of the narrator. Although the author will generally use caution to call as little attention to the narrator's voice as possible, we can discover the narrator's voice by observing one simple maxim. The narrator's voice becomes audible whenever the voices of characters are silent. The narrator's voice is right there before us in the printed edition of the story. Any word in the story that does not reside within a set of quotations marks is a word spoken by the unassuming narrator.

When we mark and look more closely at those words that lie outside the quotation marks in our Bible, we will find that the narrator tends to speak in the more distant third person.[3] This means that the narrator tells the story from the outside, referring to the characters either by proper name, designation, or third person personal pronouns. Here is an example drawn from the early verses of Matthew 2. To make the language of the narrator stand out, we have italicized those words.

> *In the time of King Herod, after Jesus was born in Bethlehem of Judea, wise men from the East came to Jerusalem, asking,* "Where is the child who has been born king of the Jews? For we observed his star at its rising, and have come to pay him homage." *When King Herod heard this, he was frightened, and all Jerusalem with him; and calling together all the chief priests and scribes of the people, he inquired of them where the Messiah was to be born.* (Mt. 2:1–4)

First, note how easy it was for us to identify the voice of the narrator. The narrator is speaking when the other characters in the story are silent. And when we read those words, we note that the narrator is always referring to people in the story by proper name (King Herod, Jesus, wise men, etc.) or through the third-personal personal pronoun (he and them). This is classic third-person narration, a form of narration that relates the story from a position outside the story's scenes.

Almost all biblical narratives are written from the perspective of the third-person narrator. One significant exception to this general rule occurs in the "we" passages of Acts (Acts 16:10–17; 20:5–15; 21:1–18; and 27:1–28:16). In these verses, the narrator is not telling the story from a remote location that lies outside the story. He is actually living the story himself, telling the story as a reflection of his own personal experience. This is called first-person narration. In the example from Acts 16, the words of the narrator have again been italicized.

> *A certain woman named Lydia, a worshiper of God, was listening to us; she was from the city of Thyatira and a dealer in purple cloth. The Lord opened her heart to listen eagerly to what was said by Paul. When she and her household were baptized, she urged us, saying,* "If you have judged me to be faithful to the Lord, come and stay at my home." *And she prevailed upon us.* (Acts 16:14–15)

The narrator does use personal pronouns and third-person personal pronouns when referring to others in the story (a woman, she, the Lord, etc.). But because the narrator is also a participant in the plot (at least, some of the time), we also find first-person pronouns deployed in the storytelling. In this particular case, Lydia was listening to "us." And she urged "us" to stay longer with her. Like all stories in the Bible, whether related in first-person or third-person, the voice of the narrator can always be identified by marking the words of the text that are not the direct speech of one of the characters.

Knowledge and Credibility

Having identified the narrator's voice, we may further inquire about the knowledge and credibility of the narrator. How much does this guide in the story actually know? Can I trust the narrator when he or she speaks to me in the story? The answer to both questions flows from the fact that the voice of the narrator and the voice of God are intimately linked to one another in the stories of our Bible. When the narrator is speaking, God is speaking.

This intimate link between the voice of God and the voice of the narrator becomes evident in a variety of ways. First, the narrator is aware of events and conversations that transpired when no mortal was present to know about them. At the time of creation, the narrator reports.

> In the day that the LORD God made the earth and the heavens, when no plant of the field was yet in the earth and no herb of the field had yet sprung up—for the LORD God had not caused it to rain upon the earth, and there was no one to till the ground; but a stream would rise from the earth, and water the whole face of the ground—then the LORD God formed a man from the dust of the ground, and breathed into his nostrils the breath of life; and the man became a living being. (Gen. 2:4b–7)

Even though no mortal was present to observe these events, the narrator has intimate knowledge of all that happened that day. Consider also the opening verses of Job. Here the narrator makes us aware of a conversation that occurs behind the veil that separates the realm of mortals from the realm of heavenly beings:

> One day the heavenly beings came to present themselves before the LORD, and Satan also came among them. The LORD said to Satan, "Where have you come from?" Satan answered the LORD, "From going to and fro on the earth, and from walking up and down on it." The LORD said to Satan, "Have you considered my servant Job? There is no one like him on the earth, a blameless and upright man who fears God and turns away from evil." (Job 1:6–8)

The close relationship between God and the narrator is further demonstrated by his access to the private thoughts and emotions of God and of mortals. Just before the flood, the narrator discloses the following information drawn from the private reflections of the Lord. "And the LORD was sorry that he had made humankind on the earth, and it grieved him in his heart" (Gen. 6:6). The narrator knows what God thinks and feels, and also has access to the private thoughts, dreams, and secrets of mortals. The narrator knows about the personal correspondence David sent to his general Joab directing him to mismanage the assault on Rabbah so that Uriah, the husband of Bathsheba, would be killed (2 Sam. 11:14–15). The narrator knows that King Herod has no intention of paying homage to the new king born in Bethlehem, and so tells us about a dream that redirected the steps of the Magi away from Herod (Mt. 2:8–15). The narrator knows about a private note that Pilate received from his wife informing him about a troubling dream: "Have nothing to do with that innocent man, for today I have suffered a great deal because of a dream about him" (Mt. 27:19b).

This close connection between God and the narrator in these stories influences the answer to the two questions we raised earlier. How much does this guide in the story actually know? Can I trust the narrator when she (or he) speaks to me in the story? The answers are "everything," and "absolutely." The narrator is omniscient and truthful. First, the narrator is omniscient—that is, all-knowing. While the amount of information communicated to the reader may reflect only a part of that deep knowledge, the guide who leads us within the story really does know it all.[4] As the narrator shares that knowledge with the reader, the reader can be certain that the narrator is not going to mislead, for the narrator is trustworthy and credible. When the narrator offers an insight or makes a qualitative judgment, we can rest assured that the information and perspective being offered is accurate.[5]

For those seeking meaning in a Bible story, this is very crucial information. When characters speak, we must always pause before accepting their perspective as valid. When the narrator speaks, we do not have to pause and evaluate the credibility of the statement, for, when the narrator speaks, we are hearing the infallible perspective of God. We can be assured that we are being pointed in the right direction.

Roles of the Narrator in the Narrative

With the voice of the narrator disclosed and armed with an understanding of the narrator's knowledge and credibility, we can explore the various ways in which the narrator functions in the stories we hear. We will see that the narrator is the one who provides the exposition for the story, reports on the actions and appearance of the characters, defines changes in time or location, and offers value judgments that direct our reading. While this list of the narrator's functions is not complete, it reflects the more significant ways in which the narrator works.[6] We will briefly explore and illustrate each of these roles that the narrator can play.

First of all, the narrator often opens the story with an exposition. As we noted earlier, this exposition provides an introduction to the characters, time, location, and circumstances that will participate in shaping the plot. As the story of Jesus and the Samaritan woman begins in John 4, it is the narrator who tells us that Jesus' journey through Samaria had brought him to Sychar, near a piece of land that had a history with Jacob. We learn that Jesus was tired out by his travels and that he was sitting alone near Jacob's well when a Samaritan woman approached the well (Jn. 4:4–8). This detailed exposition allows us to enter the heart of the story.

With the exposition out of the way, it becomes the narrator's responsibility to disclose the images and sounds that will be part of the story. This means identifying changes in speaker, describing actions the characters undertake, and the appearance or dress of a character that might be pertinent to the plot. Many times when the narrator informs us of a change in speaker, that notification is bland and mundane. "Jesus said to her…," followed by, "The woman said to him…" At other times these direct-speech introductions call greater attention to themselves because they indicate a sense of urgency, emotion, or the volume with which something is said. When David gives Joab instructions on how to handle his rebellious son Absalom, the quotation is introduced by the phrase, "The king ordered" (2 Sam. 18:5). As Stephen was being stoned because of his testimony about Jesus, his final words call for the forgiveness of his attackers. They are introduced by the expression, "[Stephen] cried out in a loud voice" (Acts 7:60). These less than ordinary speech introductions may be used to draw our attention to critical quotations that invite deeper attention from the reader.

Because we as listeners do not have the ability to observe what the characters are doing, it is up to the narrator to hide or to report on such actions. For example, before David met Goliath in combat, the narrator tells us, "He took his staff in his hand, and chose five smooth stones from the wadi, and put them in his shepherd's bag, in the pouch; his sling was in his hand, and he drew near to the Philistine" (1 Sam. 17:40).

A special technique, called mirroring of language and actions,[7] deserves special mention in this regard. This technique permits a character to describe what he or she wishes to happen or desires to do. The narrator then reports on the actual happening, but in doing so mirrors the language the character used. A wonderful example occurs in Genesis 24, where Abraham has sent his trusted servant to find a wife for his son Isaac. The servant is passionate about finding just the right person for Isaac and makes a very specific prayer request, "I am standing here by the spring of water, and the daughters of the townspeople are coming out to draw water. Let the girl to whom I shall say, 'Please offer your jar that I may drink,' and who shall say, 'Drink, and I will water your camels'—let her be the one whom you have appointed for your servant Isaac (Gen. 24:13–14). In the verses that follow, the narrator reports on the actions of Rebekah and discloses a dialogue between Abraham's servant and Rebekah that perfectly mirrors the individual requests the servant made in his prayer. This mirroring technique is no accident but part of the narrator's strategy used to affirm that Rebekah is the Lord's choice for Isaac.

A third role for the narrator is found in the way he (or she) keeps the listener abreast of the key time and location details that change the conditions reported on in the exposition. For example, as Abraham and Isaac set out on their fateful journey toward Mount Moriah, the narrator puts the story on fast forward, moving breathlessly through three days and dozens of miles. "On the third day Abraham looked up and saw the place far away" (Gen. 22:4).

Finally, the narrator presents overt value judgments that define characters, motives, actions, and events. Typically, the divine storyteller will allow the words and actions of the characters in the story to lead the listener to the appropriate conclusions. At times, however, the narrator's voice steps to the stage to interpret the meaning of the story. This becomes clear when we contrast the two editions of Saul's death recorded in 1 Samuel 31 and in 1 Chronicles 10. The details provided by the storyteller are nearly the same in both accounts. The Israelites under the leadership of Saul had lost the battle and were in full flight before the Philistines. As the Philistines continued to wage war on the retreating Israelites, each of Saul's sons was killed and Saul himself mortally wounded. Saul asks his armor-bearer to finish him off with a sword. When this young man demurs from the gruesome task, Saul takes his own life. The Philistines use the body of Saul in a public relations campaign that celebrates their victory before the body is rescued by the residents of Jabesh-gilead, who bury Saul and his sons at Jabesh. The story in 1 Samuel ends here, allowing the reader to draw his or her own conclusions about the meaningfulness of Saul's death. However, the narrator of 1 Chronicles steps to the stage and offers the following commentary on Saul's death:

> So Saul died for his unfaithfulness; he was unfaithful to the LORD in that he did not keep the command of the LORD; moreover, he had consulted a medium, seeking guidance, and did not seek guidance from the LORD. Therefore the LORD put him to death and turned the kingdom over to David son of Jesse. (1 Chr. 10:13–14)

Such overt value judgments about a story obviously play a critical role in leading us to the meaning of the story when they are present.

Given all the tasks and the power that lies in the hands of the narrator, scholars have used various metaphors to describe the narrator's role. Perhaps the most helpful is the metaphor of the "movie director." Like the movie director, the narrator is the one who determines what images are brought into view and for how long, whose voice is heard and who is silenced.[8] The narrator controls what we see, what we hear, what we know, and when we know it. Characters are introduced and dismissed, details are revealed and hidden, our eyes are turned one direction then another. So either by editing our experience with the event or by directly offering an evaluation of the event, the narrator is always controlling our experiences in a bid to shape our perceptions. Ultimately, this storyteller within the story controls our point of view.

Point of View

Every historical narrative is composed of two basic dimensions: details of the event and a viewpoint from which those details are delivered.[9] In the case of a Bible story, our right to survey the details of the event, to listen to whom we wish to listen, to see what we wish to see has been usurped. The storyteller acting through the narrator in the story makes those decisions for us. Those decisions are not made thoughtlessly but strategically in a bid to influence our adoption of a specific, ideological point of view.[10] If we follow the leading of the narrator, we do not get to cheer for Goliath, even though we may have been able to find some things in his real life to celebrate. Ultimately, we are not permitted to side with King Saul. Rather we are cajoled into celebrating the rise of David at the expense of both Goliath and Saul. The narrator is leading us to adopt this point of view.

In contrast to what some may call "fair and honest reporting," the narrator typically directs the camera and the microphone so that the reader meets only those actions and words that ultimately reinforce the intended perspective of the narrator. Thus the goal of the divine storyteller is not merely to inform about the past but to transform the future by impacting the reader's values and attitudes.[11] It is the "re-presentation of past events for the purpose of instruction."[12]

This manipulation of our point of view can take a very overt form, such as we just saw in the story of Saul's death; or it can be done with great subtlety, even allowing the participants in the story to express multiple and contradicting points of view before ultimately landing the reader on the side of the narrator.[13] A story drawn from the life of Jesus illustrates this storytelling technique in action. Traveling in the region of Tyre and Sidon, Jesus exchanges words with a Canaanite woman desperately in need of help. This woman, who is an outsider in the estimation of most Jews at the time, came to Jesus with this plea: "Have mercy on me, Lord, Son of David; my daughter is tormented by a demon" (Mt. 15:22b). She expresses the point of view that Jesus' ministry should extend beyond the descendants of Abraham, particularly in the case where a child's well-being is at stake. While this perspective is ultimately confirmed in the story, it is not immediately affirmed until the alternative perspective is explored in a way that may make the reader cringe a bit. At first Jesus ignores her; and then the disciples urge Jesus to send her away (15:23). Jesus' silence and the words of his students seem to undermine the woman's perspective. But nothing has prepared us to hear Jesus slam the door shut with the words that follow. Jesus turns to the pleading mother and says, "I was sent only to the lost sheep of the house of Israel…It is not fair to take the children's food and throw it to the dogs" (15:24–26). Now both views have been forcefully expressed, leaving the reader in tension between the two. Is Jesus the loving presence of God whose work extends to people of all nationalities, or is he the more narrowly focused messenger sent exclusively to those of Jewish descent?

This deadlock is broken when the afflicted woman speaks again. She directs her response as much to the reader as to Jesus. "Yes, Lord, yet even the dogs eat the crumbs that fall from the master's table" (15:27). Here is a new and highly persuasive way of presenting her point of view. In playing off of Jesus' comment and lowering herself and those outside the Jewish family to the role of scavenging dogs, she again reasserts her perspective. Only now in this brief story does Jesus align himself with her point of view, affirming the quality of her faith and healing her daughter as a sign of that affirmation. Although Jesus was Jewish and the history of his cause was steeped within Judaism, Jesus' ministry was intended for those who were not part of Abraham's family. So while the narrator does at times allow more than one perspective to surface within the dialogue and details of the story, there is no indication that the narrator is impartial.[14] The tension is finally broken as the narrator leads the listener to the intended point of view.

In contrast to using this more subtle form of manipulation in the storytelling process, the storyteller can also direct the narrator to be more direct in expressing the point of view that the storyteller wishes the reader to adopt. During the ministry of Jesus, his identity and his claim to be the Messiah were often contested. But the narrator in Mark leaves no doubt as to where the reader is being led in this gospel, since this narrator himself calls Jesus "the anointed one" and "the Son of God."[15] A similar directness is evident in the book of Judges. As one spiritual catastrophe follows another, the narrator steps in to offer commentary on the situation, "In those days there was no king in Israel; all the people did what was right in their own eyes" (Judg. 17:6; 21:25) There is nothing subtle about that, as there is nothing subtle about the narrator's evaluation of the rulers in 2 Kings: "[Ahaz] did not do what was right in the sight of the Lord his God, as his ancestor David had done, but he walked in the way of the kings of Israel. He even made his son pass through fire, according to the abominable practices of the nations whom the Lord drove out before the people of Israel" (2 Kings 16:2b–3). No matter what else we might read about the legacy of Ahaz, this evaluation delivered through the words of the infallible narrator will taint his record. By contrast, note the way in which the narrator shapes our perspective on Hezekiah:

> He did what was right in the eyes of the LORD just as his ancestor David had done. He removed the high places, broke down the pillars, and cut down the sacred pole. He broke in pieces the bronze serpent that Moses had made, for until those days the people of Israel had made offerings to it; it was called Nehushtan. He trusted in the LORD the God of Israel; so there was no one like him among all the kings of Judah after him, or among those who were before him. (2 Kings 18:3–5).

Thus through both subtle nudging and forceful nuancing, the narrator proposes a point of view and seeks to convict the reader's adoption of it.

Seeking Meaning in the Nuancing of the Narrator

The narrator is used by the author as the participant within the narrative controlling the structure of the plot and the characterization within in the story. By understanding the role and function of the narrator, we learn to seek meaning in the narrative itself. Here we will begin with a brief word about the risk of "psychologizing," speak about reading with an awareness that we are being manipulated, and then illustrate the role of the narrator by using the Bible passage Judges 3:12–30.

By design, the narrator will leave gaps in the story. These gaps are designed to influence our reading. Often gaps left in the narrative are related to a character. As listeners, we may be inclined to rush in at such moments and attempt to fill in the storyteller's gaps through a process called psychologizing. The story of Jonah will illustrate what we mean. At the start of this story, Jonah is instructed to travel to Nineveh and cry out against it because of the city's and nation's wicked behavior (Jon. 1:2). Jonah responds to the Lord's command with a series of actions that take Jonah farther away from Nineveh, making it impossible for him to carry out his mission. Jonah does explain his actions. The storyteller has left a gap in the narrative. Why did Jonah refuse to fulfill his assignment in Nineveh? Here is where the risk of psychologizing comes into play. If we attempt to answer this question about Jonah, we may begin to lead this story down a path of our own choosing rather than pausing to ask how it is that this important gap impacts our experience as readers. That is the difference between psychologizing and the path we recommend here.

When a narrator places a gap in the story, our goal is to explain the impact the gap has on the reading experience rather than attempting to fill the gap with our own reflections. In the case of Jonah, the storyteller knew why Jonah fled his mission to Nineveh, but has strategically elected to remove that information from our sight. The lack of information on Jonah's motives for running puts his actions in an even more austere and unsympathetic light. Rather than learning that Jonah was afraid of this mission or disinclined due to his fear of failure or unwilling to aid the nation's enemies, all we have is the cold, hard facts of his flight. Instead of filling the gap in the story, we observe that this technique places the character of Jonah in a more negative and unsympathetic light.

This reading of narrative gaps with an awareness of their impact on us as readers really can be broadened to the entire story. We can read each detail of the story with an awareness that it is designed to manipulate us. If we are seeking meaning in the careful crafting of the story, we will be better served by a more aware and active reading that from time to time asks the question, How is the narrator attempting to manipulate our knowledge, feelings, and attitude through the way in which the story is being told? This active reading will help direct our attention to the meaning that the storyteller is building into the narrative.

Since the narrator's role in shaping a story is often so very subtle, we will need to identify the language within the story that specifically belongs to the narrator. Once again, the formal marking of the narrative can be helpful in surfacing this language for review and observation. This can be done by highlighting or marking those segments of the text that belong to the narrator. We will do just that in the story of Ehud (Judg. 3:12–30). Below, the text of that story is presented with the words of the narrator italicized. This will help you identify specifically the words of the narrator and allow you to ask how it is that this narrator is seeking to manipulate you as the reader.

> *The Israelites again did what was evil in the sight of the* Lord*; and the* Lord *strengthened King Eglon of Moab against Israel, because they had done what was evil in the sight of the* Lord*. In alliance with the Ammonites and the Amalekites, he went and defeated Israel; and they took possession of the city of palms. So the Israelites served King Eglon of Moab eighteen years.*
>
> *But when the Israelites cried out to the* Lord*, the* Lord *raised up for them a deliverer, Ehud son of Gera, the Benjaminite, a left-handed man. The Israelites sent tribute by him to King Eglon of Moab. Ehud made for himself a sword with two edges, a cubit in length; and he fastened it on his right thigh under his clothes. Then he presented the tribute to King Eglon of Moab. Now Eglon was a very fat man.*
>
> *When Ehud had finished presenting the tribute, he sent the people who carried the tribute on their way. But he himself turned back at the sculptured stones near Gilgal, and said,* "I have a secret message for you, O king." *So the king said,* "Silence!" *and all his attendants went out from his presence. Ehud came to him while he was still sitting alone in his cool roof chamber, and said,* "I have a message from God for you." *So he rose from his seat. Then Ehud reached with his left hand,*

took the sword from his right thigh, and thrust it into Eglon's belly; the hilt also went in after the blade, and the fat closed over the blade, for he did not draw the sword out of his belly; and the dirt came out. Then Ehud went out into the vestibule, and closed the doors of the roof chamber on him, and locked them.

After he had gone, the servants came. When they saw that the doors of the roof chamber were locked, they thought, "He must be relieving himself in the cool chamber." *So they waited until they were embarrassed. When he still did not open the doors of the roof chamber, they took the key and opened them. There was their lord lying dead on the floor.*

Ehud escaped while they delayed, and passed beyond the sculptured stones, and escaped to Seirah. When he arrived, he sounded the trumpet in the hill country of Ephraim; and the Israelites went down with him from the hill country, having him at their head. He said to them, "Follow after me; for the LORD has given your enemies, the Moabites into your hand." *So they went down after him, and seized the fords of the Jordan against the Moabites, and allowed no one to cross over. At that time they killed about ten thousand of the Moabites, all strong, able-bodied men; no on escaped. So Moab was subdued that day under the hand of Israel. And the land had rest eighty years.* (Judg. 3: 12–30)

When viewing the language of the narrator in this more visual way, it becomes clear that we have no story without the narrator's voice. Apart from the narrator, we hear Ehud speak three times, twice with a message for the king and once with a message for the Israelites. In an ironic twist, we hear only one word from the quiet king, and that word is "Silence!" Finally, the servants get one sentence that adds a bit of comic relief. They interpret the locked door as suggesting the king's modesty while relieving himself.

Given the significant role that the narrator plays in this narrative, we will consider that role in greater detail. First, note how deep and pervasive the knowledge of the narrator is. This narrator knows God's perspective on Israel's actions, knows about a special sword that was made, knows about the architecture of Eglon's palace, and knows what Ehud said privately to the king. This is clearly the omniscient narrator at work.

Given the close link between the narrator and God, there is no mistaking the point of view from which the story is being told. Court recorders in the palace of Moab would have told the story very differently, but the Moabite point of view is not important here. This is God's story, so the divine point of view will direct its narration. Every act and every word is marshaled to support God's perspective on the events as they transpire.

Given the infrequency with which characters speak in this story, the descriptions of the people, their actions, and the organization of the plot really illustrate the narrator's hand. The exposition of the story (verses

12–17) provides us with all the background needed to read the story in the way the narrator would like it to be read. The series of events that repeats again and again in the book of Judges is felt here. God's people have again entered into perversion that has resulted in their oppression. This time Eglon, in an alliance with Ammonites and Amalekites, is the oppressor. Things have gotten so bad that the enemy has taken the key city of Jericho ("city of palms"). In their distress, the Israelites cry out to the Lord, who provides a deliverer, Ehud. The exposition also provides us with a few details that pique our interest. Ehud is left-handed. He has made a special sword and strapped it to his right thigh. In a very unusual moment of physical description, the narrator has told us that Eglon is fat.

Those details all have a role to play in the plot that begins to take shape. It begins with the complication found in the quotation of Ehud. After he had given Eglon the protection money Israel had sent, he says, "I have a secret message for you, O king" (Judg. 3:19). A secret—now the storyteller has our attention as well as that of the king. As Ehud is about to deliver the message to the king in private, he notes that this particular message is "from God for you" (3:20). The climax comes quickly as the message is delivered, not one that the king expected. Suddenly, all the details come together—the left-handed judge, the sword on the right thigh, and even the king's fat belly play a role.

Following this climax, the resolution follows. Ehud escapes, aided by the delay of the servants who think their leader is relieving himself in the locked room. Once he has returned to Israel, Ehud gathers fighters from Ephraim, speaking the words that provide the meaning for this story. While the narrator does not give voice to the significance of the events, the lead character, who had a "message" for the king of Moab, is permitted to deliver a "message" to us that pulls it all together. "Follow after me; for the LORD has given you enemies the Moabites into your hand" (Judg. 3:28). Ehud is inviting those around him to not only follow him physically, but to follow his lead in trusting the Lord. A failure to trust the Lord had brought Israel into conflict with their God and into submission to Moab. By contrast, trust in the Lord and full dedication to God and God's cause will bring freedom from this oppression. To confirm the truth of this message, the narrator tells the story of the defeat of Moab that restores peace in Israel. Ehud not only said it, the narrator affirmed it in providing the details of the victory.

Conclusion

If God is the storyteller outside the narrative, God's representative within the story is clearly the narrator. While the voice of the narrator is designed to remain subtly in the background, that voice plays the critical role in shaping the meaning of the story. Clearly, when we as readers take the time to expose the narrator in a more direct way, the roles of the narrator in designing the plot, shaping characters, and sculpting the ideological point of view become clearer. That clarity not only exposes the craft of the storyteller but also directs our attention to the meaning within the story.

Notes

[1]David Rhoads and Donald Michie, *Mark as Story: An Introduction to the Narrative of a Gospel* (Philadelphia: Fortress Press, 1982), 39.

[2]Shimon Bar-Efrat, *Narrative Art in the Bible,* JSOT Bible and Literature 17 (Sheffield: The Almond Press, 1989), 13–14.

[3]Walter C. Kaiser, "Preaching from Historical Narrative Texts of the Old Testament," in *Giving the Sense: Understanding and Using Old Testament Historical Texts,* ed. David M. Howard Jr. and Michael A. Grisanti (Grand Rapids: Kregel, 2003), 444.

[4]Robert Alter, *The Art of Biblical Narrative* (New York: Basic Books, 1981), 157; Bar-Efrat, *Narrative Art in the Bible,* 17; Adele Berlin, *Poetics and Interpretation of Biblical Narrative* (Winona Lake, Ind.: Eisenbrauns, 1994), 44; Meir Sternberg, *The Poetics of Biblical Narrative: Ideological Literature and the Drama of Reading,* Indiana Studies in Biblical Literature (Bloomington, Ind.: Indiana University Press, 1987), 84–85.

[5]Yairah Amit, *Reading Biblical Narratives: Literary Criticism and the Hebrew Bible* (Minneapolis: Fortress Press, 2001), 95; David M. Gunn and Danna Nolan Fewell, *Narrative in the Hebrew Bible,* Oxford Bible Series (Oxford: Oxford University Press, 1993), 52.

[6]Sternberg, *Poetics of Biblical Narrative,* 120.

[7]Alter, *Art of Biblical Narrative,* 77.

[8]Amit, *Reading Biblical Narratives,* 94.

[9]John H. Sailhamer, *The Pentateuch as Narrative: A Biblical-Theological Commentary* (Grand Rapids: Zondervan, 1992), 25.

[10]The term, "point of view," is employed to describe a number of different perspectives associated with the narrator including: ideological point of view, spatial point of view, temporal point of view, and psychological point of view. For a more full treatment of the topic, see Berlin, *Poetics and Interpretation of Biblical Narrative,* 55–56; James L. Resseguie, *Narrative Criticism of the New Testament: An Introduction* (Grand Rapids: Baker Academic, 2005), 170–73.

[11]Bar-Efrat, *Narrative Art in the Bible,* 16.

[12]Sailhamer, *Pentateuch as Narrative,* 25.

[13]Berlin, *Poetics and Interpretation of Biblical Narrative,* 82.

[14]Bar-Efrat, *Narrative Art in the Bible,* 33.

[15]Rhoads and Michie, *Mark as Story,* 36.

4

Tinkering with Time and Setting

We live each day of our lives bound by the constraints of time and place. While it often escapes us, this reality attends every moment of our day. We are continuously occupying, and traveling through, space. The kids need to be dropped off at school by 7:30 a.m. We have a thirty-minute lunch meeting with our colleague at a local restaurant. We need to be home for dinner by 5:30 p.m. so that we can make it to the 7:00 p.m. church meeting that will last one hour.

Because the people of the Bible were real people, they, too, lived their lives under the constraint of time and place. While the places in which they lived and the ways in which they marked the passage of time looked different than our own, Moses, Ruth, Mary, and others in the Bible occupied space and responded to the passage of time just as we do in our daily living. As the divine storyteller brings their stories to our day, some of this information about time and place makes the transition between event and story. As we will now see, this becomes another dimension of the storyteller's craft, tinkering with time and place.

As we often pass unconsciously through the time and place markers in our own lives, so our eyes may not always catch the time and place markers within a Bible story. The goal of this chapter is to raise our attentiveness to the passage of time within the story and the formal mention of specific time and place. Once we have raised our attentiveness to their presence in the story, we will explore how the storyteller's use of time and place may impact the listener and assist with the development of the story's meaning.

The last page of this chapter will not be the last word of this book on the topic of setting, particularly the topic of geographical setting. While this chapter will introduce the possibility of a storyteller using geography in telling a story, chapters 7 and 8 will push back the frontier on this discussion to explore at even greater depth the various ways in which the storyteller may employ geography as part of the storytelling process.

Time

Time is like an ever-rolling stream whose rate of flow and direction we cannot change or control. Our weeks march forward in predictable fashion, moving relentlessly from past to present to future. At times, we may wish that our birth certificate had come with a remote control, with pause, rewind, and fast-forward features. Such a remote control would allow us to fast-forward through those days or weeks in our lives that are filled with distress and discomfort. It would allow us to rewind and review an event that confused us. It could pause our lives at those precious times when we announce, "Life does not get better than this."

We do not have this kind of remote control, but in one sense the storyteller does. While the events that lie behind the biblical story flowed under the same constraints of time we experience, the divine storyteller who recasts those events in story form can edit the flow, direction, and mention of time. Experiences that lasted but seconds under the governance of real time may, in fact, be recast so that they occupy several minutes of our listening or reading time. Events that lasted for days and even years may be compressed and retold so that our experience with them lasts just a few seconds. The storyteller may sequence the details of a story so that they occur in the same order as the events did in history, or the storyteller may reorder those details so that we meet them in a sequence that better serves the artful and rhetorical intentions of the author. The storyteller may choose to make us aware of the specific time of day, year, or season. Alternatively, those details may be removed from our view. Like all other facets of the storytelling craft, this tinkering with time is not serendipitous but intentional, strategic, and functional.[1] We will now take time to discuss each of these storytelling options and the way in which they can impact us as listeners.

Duration of Time

The first matter we consider is the duration of time. As the storyteller brings the story to our eyes and ears, the objective time needed for the event to occur in real time may be reflected exactly, may be compressed, or may be expanded in the recasting of that event in story form.[2] In other words, we can distinguish between the amount of time an event took to occur in real time contrasted with the amount of time it takes to read the report of the event. When the biblical author presents the story in scenic fashion, reflecting a great deal of the dialogue that occurs between participants in the story, then the reader's experience with duration of time would come very close to the passage of real time during the event.[3] Consider the following scenic account from the life of Abraham. The Lord had indicated to Abraham the Lord's preparations to annihilate the cities of Sodom and Gomorrah. At this point, Abraham immediately engages the Lord in a dialogue, the purpose of which is to allay that judgment:

> Then Abraham came near and said, "Will you indeed sweep away the righteous and the wicked? Suppose there are fifty righteous within the city; will you then sweep away the place and not forgive it for the fifty righteous who are in it? Far be it from you to do such a thing, to slay the righteous with the wicked, so that the righteous fare as the wicked! Far be that from you! Shall not the Judge of all the earth do what is just?" And the LORD said, "If I find at Sodom fifty righteous in the city, I will forgive the whole place for their sake." Abraham answered, "Let me take it upon myself to speak to the Lord, I who am but dust and ashes. Suppose five of the fifty righteous are lacking? Will you destroy the whole city for lack of five?" And he said, "I will not destroy it if I find forty-five there." Again he spoke to him, "Suppose forty are found there." He answered, "For the sake of the forty I will not do it." Then he said, "Oh do not let the Lord be angry if I speak. Suppose thirty are found there." He answered, "I will not do it, if I find thirty there." He said, "Let me take it upon myself to speak to the Lord. Suppose twenty are found there." He answered, "For the sake of twenty I will not destroy it." Then he said, "Oh do not let the Lord be angry if I speak just once more. Suppose ten are found there?" He answered, "For the sake of ten I will not destroy it." And the LORD went his way, when he had finished speaking to Abraham; and Abraham returned to his place. (Gen. 18:23–33)

In the very few minutes that it took you to read this dialogic exchange between the Lord and Abraham, you were experiencing the passage of time much as you would have experienced it had you been there. This is the outcome when the storyteller presents the account in scenic fashion, retelling the story through the dialogue of the participants in that story.

In contrast to scenic reporting, the storyteller may also present the events in summary fashion, which limits or eliminates the use of dialogue completely. The net result of this form of storytelling is to compress the passage of time significantly. Events that may have taken months or even decades are experienced in seconds of reading.[4] Consider the following examples. As Elijah vied with the prophets of Baal on Mount Carmel, we are told that the Baal prophets were first to prepare their sacrifice and call on Baal to prove himself with fire from heaven. They spent several hours that morning preparing the sacrifice and calling out to their god. But those hours are compressed into the seconds it takes to read one verse. "So they took the bull that was given them, prepared it, and called on the name of Baal from morning until noon, crying 'O Baal, answer us!' But there was no voice, and no answer. They limped about the altar that they had made" (1 Kings 18:26).

The passage of days can likewise be compressed into seconds. Consider again the story of Abraham and Isaac. After Abraham completes the preparation for their journey to Mount Moriah, he, his son, and his servants begin a trip that will take at least three days. Without providing any details on what transpired during those three days, the narrator whisks through them in less than three seconds. "On the third day Abraham looked up and saw the place far away" (Gen. 22:4).

Months and years can be compressed in a similar way for the reader. When the Lord opened the womb of Leah, the months that passed during her pregnancy are reported with just six words. "Leah conceived and bore a son, and she named him Reuben" (Gen 29:32). Years of Jesus' early life on this earth are also presented in compressed fashion. Jesus' first visit to the temple in Jerusalem would have occurred when he was just a little over a month old. After this story is told, we leap past eleven plus years of Jesus' young life. The only comment on these years comes from the narrator, "The child grew and became strong, filled with wisdom; and the favor of God was upon him" (Lk. 2:40). Just two verses later, the storyteller informs us that the infant Jesus is now twelve years old. Thus our experience with time changes at the whim of the storyteller. The divine storyteller can either approximate the passage of real time, accelerate time, or slow the passage of time.

The remote control in the hand of the storyteller also has a pause button. In certain instances, the listener can note that the passage of time comes to a complete stop. This happens when a writer wishes to offer an interpretation or explanation of what the reader has experienced, evaluate a character, or offer a description that allows the reader to better visualize what is occurring.[5] In John 4, as Jesus approaches the well in the village of Sychar, the biblical author pauses time twice to explain circumstances that attend the events about to unfold. As Jesus requests a drink of water, the narrator stops time to explain that Jesus and the woman were alone at the well, since "His disciples had gone into town to buy food" (4:8). Then, after the woman wonders aloud about the appropriateness of their exchange, Jesus being a Jew and she being a Samaritan, the narrator again pauses the story's action for commentary. "Jews do not share things in common with Samaritans" (4:9).

In a similar way, time is stopped when the narrator feels a need to formally express views on a character. As listeners, we have already assembled a very negative opinion of Ahab and Jezebel by the time we reach the twenty-first chapter of 1 Kings. However, just in case the reader missed it, the storyteller pauses time to reinforce the point with the following observation. "Indeed, there was no one like Ahab, who sold himself to do what was evil in the sight of the LORD, urged on by his wife Jezebel. He acted most abominably in going after idols, as the Amorites had done, whom the LORD drove out before the Israelites" (1 Kings 21:25–26).

Finally, the passage of time can be halted briefly to describe what the reader is unable to see on his own. This can be a lengthy description, such as the report on the appearance of Goliath, a description that goes on for four verses (1 Sam. 17:4–7); or it can be done within the span of one verse. As Jesus prepared to provide a miraculous meal for five thousand people, the storyteller pauses time to tell us what we cannot see. "Now there was a great deal of grass in the place; so they sat down, about five thousand in all" (Jn. 6:10).

From all that precedes, it is clear the storyteller is controlling our experience with the duration of time. The story can be told in a way that mirrors the passage of real time, that compresses real time into mere seconds of reading time, or that stops time entirely.

But what does this have to do with the meaning of the story? Since the storyteller can vary the speed of time we experience in listening to the story, we can benefit as interpreters of the story from paying attention to this storytelling technique. Compression of the story into a realistic amount of time for telling the story requires that certain matters be passed through more quickly. Without such compression, it could take years to listen to just one story in the Bible. Those quiet moments are best left as quiet moments. When the storyteller causes time to flow very quickly, leaving gaps in our awareness of what transpired, we can move more quickly past this information gap, knowing that the meaning of the story will not be found in what is untold.

It may be tempting to conjecture about what was occurring in a bid to fill the gap. For example, we may wish to speculate on the nature of the conversations and reflect on the thoughts crossing Abraham's mind during the three days when he traveled with Isaac toward the site of the sacrifice, the region of Moriah. Since the divine storyteller has remained silent on this topic, rushing to fill that gap seems to be an imprudent approach. As noted in chapter 3, the better approach is to observe the impact such a gap in reporting has on the reading experience. Once we have observed that impact, it is best to move along to those places in the narrative where the storyteller has provided greater details for us to digest.

A markedly different strategy is called for as actions and conversations come at us in greater detail. At places where time slows, the storyteller is creating emphasis and focus.[6] This means that I will spend very little time with the three days that pass quickly in Abraham's story (Gen. 22:4). But it also means that I will pay very close attention to that part of the narrative where the passage of time slows dramatically, for often the slowing pace of the story corresponds to the climax of the story, as it does in Genesis 22. As this story reaches its culminating moment, every act of Abraham seems to be put into slow motion. He constructs an altar, he arranges the wood, he binds the hands and feet of Isaac, he lifts him, he places him on the wood, and then reaches his fingers toward the knife (Gen. 22:9–10). The slowing movement of time sharpens the apex of the plot and focuses the mind of the listener to the key moment of the narrative.

The gospel of Mark provides a similar experience for its readers. David Rhoads and Donald Michie note that the inspired storyteller moves quickly in the early narratives within the book, changing the setting frequently. But at the close of the story, we focus on Jesus in Jerusalem moving day-by-day, and then hour-by-hour, toward the moment of climax, the time of Jesus' crucifixion.[7] Thus, by noticing the rate at which time is passing in our experience with the story, we may detect something about our proximity to the climactic moment of the plot.

Sequence of Time

Along with the duration of time, the storyteller also controls the sequence in which we experience events. While we have all read stories filled with flashbacks that reverse the course of time regularly, the divine storyteller typically allows the historical events recounted in the story to flow in the same sequence as they have occurred in real time. This gives the stories we read within the Bible a natural, incessant, and even dynamic flow.[8] At the same time, it allows the storyteller to take advantage of two outcomes that naturally attend a story told in this way. On the one hand, the listener's understanding grows naturally as one event precipitates the next. Action leads to further action. One speech leads naturally to the next. On the other hand, the storyteller exploits the suspense that naturally comes from not knowing exactly how things will play out in the future.[9]

Still, at times the interest of the divine storyteller will lead to reordering the events, either in a bid to help the listener better understand what she or he is hearing or in a bid to focus attention on the event(s) placed out of order. In the first instance, the storyteller may use a flashback to help the listener get a better sense of what is currently happening in the story. For example, as the author of 1 Kings is summarizing the various activities of the wise and wealthy King Solomon, this author mentions a number of key cities that Solomon fortified to protect his kingdom. Gezer is listed among those cities, a city that could provide heightened security for the city of Jerusalem since Gezer guarded the key attack route most frequently used against Jerusalem. But what the reader may not know (since it is unmentioned in 1 Kings) is how this city, with its crucial location, had come into Solomon's possession. So here the storyteller uses a flashback to fill that gap: "Pharoah king of Egypt had gone up and captured Gezer and burned it down, had killed the Canaanites who lived in the city, and had given it as a dowry to his daughter, Solomon's wife; so Solomon rebuilt Gezer" (1 Kings 9:16–17a). In similar fashion, Jonah 1 includes a flashback. As the mariners interrogated Jonah with questions in a bid to understand the storm that was pummeling their ship, the narrator provides a flashback that offers the reader fresh insights on their fear. "For the men knew that [Jonah] was fleeing from the presence of the LORD, because he had told them so" (Jon. 1:10b). Such flashbacks occur rather infrequently in Bible stories and are used to simply clarify a part of the story.

The storyteller may also reorder the events in ways that are subtler than the flashback. It takes a more sophisticated eye and ear to observe them. Genesis 22 again provides an example for us. After the Lord gave Abraham the horrifying instructions that required the sacrifice of his son, the narrator records a series of actions: "So Abraham rose early in the morning saddled his donkey, and took two of his young men with him, and his son Isaac; he cut the wood for the burnt offering, and set out and went to the place in the distance that God had shown him" (Gen. 22:3). If we are reading quickly and less attentively, the shifting order of events may elude us. But if we listen more carefully for the sequence of events, one of Abraham's actions reported in this list is out of order: the cutting of the wood. Our expectation is that the wood would have been cut before the donkey was loaded, since the pack animal would have been used to carry such supplies for the trip. This subtle reordering of the events serves to delay that component of the preparation that had the closest connection to the anticipated sacrifice of Isaac, sparing for emphasis a detail that that evokes a powerful, emotional response from us. The father is actually taking time to split the wood on which his son's body will be burned. The storyteller reports this event out of sequence to draw our attention to the act and so increase the drama and tension in the plot.[10]

The early chapters of John's gospel account may also contain a reordering of events designed to make a larger rhetorical splash. The gospels contain a story that details Jesus' cleansing of the temple in Jerusalem. For Matthew, Mark, and Luke, this cleansing is reported among the last acts of Jesus' earthly ministry. But John reports the temple cleansing in 2:12–25. If Jesus cleansed the temple only once, and if that cleansing occurred during Jesus' final days on earth, then John radically changes its position. By taking this event from Jesus' life and rushing it forward, John puts emphasis on it and its significance in ways that the other gospel writers do not. Thus, in the story of Abraham and the story of Jesus recounted in John, the careful listener will benefit not only from attending to the duration of time but also to the sequencing of events within the passage of time for keys to the storyteller's emphasis.

Specific Time

The third dimension of time use that resides at the discretion of the storyteller is the reporting of specific time. While some stories are told without any reference to specific time, others do note either the time of day, day of the week, or time of the year when the events of the plot are occurring.

Specific time notation can set the story within a certain time during the day. For example, as Abraham sent his servant in search of a wife for his son, the storyteller does not tell us what time of day the servant initially received the assignment or what time of day the servant left. But as the servant arrives outside the city of Nahor, we learn, "It was toward evening, the time when women go out to draw water" (Gen. 24:11b). The specific time is key, since it provided the Lord the opportunity to direct the servant to Rebekah. At another time of day, the women would not have been there. Another striking example of denoting the specific time of day occurs in John 13 as Jesus is celebrating the Passover during his last week on earth. Just as the meal began in the upper room, Jesus directed Judas to go and do his deed quickly. Following Judas' exit, the time of day is reported succinctly but powerfully: "And it was night" (13:30b).

At times, it is not the time of day that is critical to the story but the day of the week. This happens again and again in Jesus' ministry as his acts of love come up against the misperceived restrictions of the Sabbath. Luke 6 opens very casually, "One sabbath while Jesus was going through the grainfields…" (6:1). At first, we may not even notice this inconspicuous reference to the day of the week. But in short order it becomes the focus of the story. When Jesus' disciples pick grain from the field, some of the Pharisees accuse them of breaking the Sabbath laws that prohibited God's people from doing farm work on the Sabbath. This event that occurs on the Sabbath gives Jesus the opportunity to explain that he is, in fact, the Lord of the Sabbath.

Apart from the time of the day or time of the week, the time of the year can also be critical for the setting of the story. As the storyteller records the Israelites miraculous entry into the promised land during the time of Joshua, the Israelites are faced with a very risky river crossing.[11] That drama and associated message of that crossing is definitely enhanced as the storyteller reports on the time of the year. "Now the Jordan overflows all its banks throughout the time of harvest" (Josh. 3:15a). The time of the year is also reported when a new chapter in the book of 2 Samuel also opens a new chapter in the life of King David, a darker chapter that sees him wrestle with the sins of adultery and murder. "In the spring of the year, the time when kings go out to battle, David sent Joab with his officers and all Israel with him; they ravaged the Ammonites, and besieged Rabbah. But David remained at Jerusalem" (2 Sam. 11:1). The spring season brought an expectation that went unfulfilled in the life of David, a signal to the listener that things were about to change for the worse.

Perhaps one of the most striking uses of specific time is found in John 7. The exposition of the story tells us that the Jewish festival of Booths was at hand (7:2). Lest the reader lose sight of this critical time reference, the word for "festival" is mentioned five more times in the next verses (7:8 [twice], 10, 11, and 14). By the time we reach 7:37, we have reached the "last day of the festival." Now all this festival talk is about to make sense. During the festival of Booths, texts from Zechariah 9–14 were read, fueling messianic expectation. These words from Zechariah speak about a coming king and about water that would flow from Jerusalem, making even the Dead Sea come to life. As this harvest festival comes to a close, water is brought from the Gihon spring through the Water Gate. After the celebrants have walked around the altar singing verses from Psalm 118, the water is poured out near the altar.[12] At this moment of highly charged messianic expectation that employs water as a symbol of a new era, Jesus says, "Let anyone who is thirsty come to me, and let the one who believes in me drink. As the scripture has said, 'Out of the believer's heart shall flow rivers of living water'" (7:37b–38). That language is powerful in and of itself, but just look at what happens when the storyteller places that declaration on the last day of the feast.

While we do not have the ability to control time, the storyteller speaking to us from the pages of our Bible does just that. We have seen that the storyteller may expand, compress, or stop the passage of time we experience in a given story, that the storyteller may either preserve or alter the sequence of events within a story, and may either withhold or mention the specific time at which the events of a story are unfolding. In each case, careful reading of the text will reveal the storyteller's craft and point to verses and concepts that deserve the special attention of the listener.

Setting

This use of time stands in concert with the storyteller's use of setting. The setting is the physical location or social setting that serves as the backdrop for the actions recorded in the story.[13] Every event that finds its way onto the pages of our Bibles enjoyed a certain physical and social setting. But like the other details that are placed into the narrative by the storyteller, the details of an event's setting are only reported when their presence makes a contribution to the story being told. This means that the formal reporting of setting is never random, but rather strategic and intentional.[14] We will now explore this dimension of the storytelling craft, illustrating the way in which geographical setting, architectural setting, and social setting may be employed.

Geographical Setting

When it serves the larger purposes of the storyteller, specific mention is made of geographical setting. This includes reference to places such as cities, rivers, mountains, and plains. This will not be so surprising to us if we honor the important connection between geography and the promise of rescue that lies at the heart of the Old Testament. When God came to Abraham and spoke directly with him about this rescue plan and the role of his family in it, geography was right there. Abraham was promised that his family would grow to become a great nation (Gen. 12:1–3). He was promised that this great nation would have its own land (the future land of Israel). And he was promised that all people on earth would be blessed through him, a blessing that would be realized when the Messiah came into this land (Acts 3:13, 25–26; Gal. 3:8). The rest of Genesis, the rest of the Torah, and in fact the rest of the Hebrew Bible demonstrates a great deal of attentiveness to land, given its close relationship with the promise of the Messiah.

Consequently, the land becomes an important player in many Bible stories in the Old Testament. It fills Abraham's purchase of property in the promised land with new significance (Gen. 23). It creates a tension as his grandson, Jacob, leaves that land (Gen. 29), and a sense of relief when he returns and Esau welcomes him (Gen. 33). It explains the great hesitation that both the reader and Jacob feel as a famine drives his family from the promised land into Egypt, a tension that is only abated when the Lord speaks to Jacob in a vision at Beer-sheba assuring him that this family will return to the promised land (Gen. 46:1–5). So it is from page to page and place to place that the stories of the Bible become intimately linked to location.

But the formal mention of geography does not always get the attention it merits either in our personal study of God's Word or in the scholarly world of biblical studies. Our absence of geographical experience with the promised land and our lack of intimacy with its geography may cause us to read very quickly past such geographical references, missing their mention as well as the critical role that they can play within the story. For that very reason, we will be spending two full chapters later in this book discussing and illustrating the use of geography.

Architectural Setting

At times, the storyteller's purposes are achieved through the formal mention of the architectural setting for speeches and actions of the characters. Take, for example, the story of Rahab. As the Israelites were poised to reenter the promised land following the long stay of Jacob's family in Egypt, Joshua sent spies ahead to investigate the status and capabilities of the fortress city of Jericho, which controlled a critical access point into the land of Canaan. When the spies entered Jericho, they came to the house of a prostitute named Rahab who provided critical information about the city and also protection for the two Israelite spies. In the process of telling this story, the storyteller provides details about her home. When the king demanded her assistance in finding the Israelite spies, she deflected his inquiry, telling the king that they had left her home earlier. But the storyteller shows us her true allegiance, using the setting of her actions to demonstrate her passions: "She had, however, brought them up to the roof and hidden them with the stalks of flax that she had laid out on the roof" (Josh. 2:6). Following an exchange during which she declares her commitment to the

Israelite cause, she again exploits the architecture of her home to facilitate the safe return of the spies to Joshua. "Then she let them down by a rope through the window, for her house was on the outer side of the city wall and she resided within the wall itself" (Josh. 2:15).

Architecture also plays an important role in demonstrating the persistence of men who were determined to bring their paralyzed friend to Jesus. Jesus was speaking in the small room of a home in Capernaum that allowed for a very limited audience. The entire courtyard outside this home was crammed with people who strained to hear Jesus' words. Getting near Jesus was problematic even for a healthy, young person, so the four men carrying their paralyzed friend must have been discouraged at the sight. Their passion for this man to be in the presence of Jesus led to creative thinking and innovation. They carried him to the roof. After removing the organic materials and mud that separated their friend from hope, they carefully lowered him into the presence of Jesus. The storyteller informs us, "And when they could not bring him to Jesus because of the crowd, they removed the roof above him; and after having dug through it, they let down the mat on which the paralytic lay" (Mk. 2:4).

Social Setting

Finally, the concept of setting has also been extended to include the social realm, since our relationships and the quality of conversations can be impacted by our social context as much as by our physical context. Meals frequently provided the setting for clashes between social groups in the New Testament stories. Consider the meal that followed Jesus' calling of Matthew. The divine storyteller reports that Jesus was having dinner with tax collectors and sinners (Mt. 9:10). Playing by the social rules of Jesus' day, the sharing of a meal meant that you were declaring approval of and connection to the other dinner guests. Thus Jesus' sharing of a meal with tax collectors and sinners deeply troubled the Pharisees. You can hear the venom and horror in the question they direct to the disciples: "Why does your teacher eat with tax collectors and sinners?" (Mt. 9:11) Certainly, they felt, any rabbi whose words were worth a shekel would avoid such a compromised social setting. Their sense of social propriety gives Jesus the opportunity to demonstrate that their social boundaries are not boundaries he recognized, nor would he allow their boundaries to limit the reach of the gospel message.

Social boundaries that inhibited the spread of the gospel surface again in the early chapters of Acts. As Peter continued his work as an apostle in the very Jewish seaport city of Joppa, the Lord called him to witness to the gospel in the Gentile seaport of Caesarea (Acts 10). At first, Peter objected to what he saw as the crossing of an inappropriate social boundary. But a vision, provided *three times* by the Lord, brought him to a different understanding of society under the charter of the gospel. This vision caused

Peter to leave the Jewish city of Joppa for the Gentile city of Caesarea. When he arrived, he formally addressed the topic of social setting. "You yourselves know that it is unlawful for a Jew to associate with or to visit a Gentile; but God has shown me that I should not call anyone profane or unclean" (Acts 10:28).

To more fully appreciate the storyteller's craft, it is again necessary for us to elevate the subtle and inconspicuous references to setting. In doing so, we will see that the storyteller is at work shaping our experience with these settings. First of all, recall that a shift in time or setting is one of the key ways in which we identify the breaks between scenes in a narrative. Shimon Bar-Efrat points to Genesis 24 as a classic example of this technique at work. As Abraham seeks a wife for Isaac, the setting of the story shifts back and forth between Canaan and Mesopotamia, creating both scene breaks and an envelope structure (or *chiasm*) within the larger narrative.[15]

Canaan (vv. 1–10)
Mesopotamia (well) (vv. 11–31)
Mesopotamia (house) (vv. 32–61)
Canaan (vv. 62–67)

As we observed in the story of the paralytic and his four friends, the architectural setting for Jesus' teaching provided an obstacle that the friends of the paralyzed man needed to overcome. Their persistence in overcoming this obstacle betrays their deep passion for bringing their friend to Jesus. The social setting that caused Peter to hesitate at the Lord's invitation to speak to Gentiles in Caesarea becomes intimately linked to the message that story delivers. The gospel message was meant for people from every social setting. In these stories and others like them, the formal mention of setting may play a variety of roles: structuring the plot, enhancing the conflict within the plot, shaping the characters we meet within that plot—all the while influencing the meaning that the storyteller wishes to deliver.[16]

Conclusion

We live each day of our lives bound by the constraints of time and place. Although we are not always be aware of it, we are always responding to the flow of time and moving through various physical and social settings during our day. If we carry the same lack of awareness into our reading of a Bible story, we may miss a part of the storyteller's craft designed to influence our reaction to the narrative. In this chapter, we have seen that the storyteller controls our experience with time: the speed with which time moves, the direction in which time moves, and our awareness of specific time within the day, week, or year. In a similar fashion, the specific location of a story—whether that be geographical, architectural, or social—can also be elevated to a position of importance in the recasting of the event. By increasing our attentiveness to the way in which a storyteller may tinker with time and setting, we will obtain new insights into familiar stories.

Notes

[1]Shimon Bar-Efrat, *Narrative Art in the Bible,* JSOT Bible and Literature Series 17 (Sheffield: Almond Press, 1989), 142.

[2]Yairah Amit, *Reading Biblical Narratives: Literary Criticism and the Hebrew Bible* (Minneapolis: Fortress Press, 2001), 104; Bar-Efrat, *Narrative Art in the Bible,* 143.

[3]Mark Allan Powell, *What Is Narrative Criticism?* Guides to Biblical Scholarship (Minneapolis: Fortress Press, 1990), 38.

[4]Bar-Efrat, *Narrative Art in the Bible,* 150.

[5]Ibid., 146.

[6]Amit, *Reading Biblical Narratives,* 143; Bar-Efrat, *Narrative Art in the Bible,* 151.

[7]David Rhoads and Donald Michie, *Mark as Story: An Introduction to the Narrative of a Gospel* (Philadelphia: Fortress Press, 1982), 45.

[8]Ibid., 147.

[9]Meir Sternberg, *The Poetics of Biblical Narrative: Ideological Literature and the Drama of Reading,* Indiana Studies in Biblical Literature (Bloomington: Indiana University Press, 1985), 284.

[10]Yair Mazor, "Genesis 22: The Ideological, Rhetorical and the Psychological Composition," *Biblica* 67 (1986): 85.

[11]John A. Beck, "Why Do Joshua's Readers Keep Crossing the River? The Narrative-Geographical Shaping of Joshua 3–4," *JETS* 48 (2005): 694–96.

[12]James L. Resseguie, *Narrative Criticism of the New Testament: An Introduction* (Grand Rapids: Baker Academic, 2005), 114.

[13]Tremper Longman III, *Literary Approaches to Biblical Interpretation,* Foundations of Contemporary Interpretation 3 (Grand Rapids: Zondervan, 1987.

[14]Amit, *Reading Biblical Narratives,* 124.

[15]Shimon Bar-Efrat, "Some Observations on the Analysis of Structure in Biblical Narrative," in *Beyond Form Criticism: Essays in Old Testament Literary Criticism,* Sources for Biblical and Theological Study 2, ed. Paul R. House (Winona Lake, Ind.: Eisenbrauns, 1992), 199.

[16]Tremper Longman III, "Biblical Narrative," in *A Complete Literary Guide to the Bible,* ed. Leland Ryken and Tremper Longman III (Grand Rapids: Zondervan, 1993), 74; Rhoads and Michie, *Mark as Story,* 63; Resseguie, *Narrative Criticism of the New Testament,* 87.

5

The Patterning Play of Words

Language is the medium via which the divine storyteller transforms an event into a story. Yet that language is far from ordinary. While the Bible speaks about everyday affairs in human life, it does not use everyday language to do so. During our day-to-day conversations, we use language in a very common, even mundane way. The verbal exchanges we have with our family or coworkers display very few figures of speech and are in general less artistic and dramatic in their composition. That is not the case with the language we find in a Bible story. Here the divine storyteller presses language into a much more refined service far from the language of everyday conversation. Robert Alter calls the language of the Bible, "language straining against the decorum of ordinary usage."[1] The storyteller has upgraded from ordinary language to a style of communication that employs many more figures of speech and intricate verbal patterns. David Gunn and Danna Nolan Fewell draw all the various figures of speech together under the heading of the "patterning play of words."[2] That will be the title and subject of this chapter.

Bullinger's treatment of the topic in his *Figures of Speech Used in the Bible, Explained and Illustrated*[3] encompasses well over a thousand pages! The goal of this chapter will be much more modest. We seek to sample the figures of speech used in Bible stories and to sharpen our awareness of them. Our sample of the patterning play of words will include: the use of repetition, the use of metaphor and simile, personification, verbal irony, and rhetorical questions. We will see that each of these is part of the storyteller's craft that participates in delivering the meaning of the story.

The Function of the Patterning Play of Words

When the divine storyteller deploys figures of speech within the process of telling a story, our reading of the story is impacted in at least two important ways. On one hand, the patterning play of words provides the stories with a literary elegance that is befitting divine communication. It is a signal that we are no longer listening to the idle chatter of the public market or mundane drivel flowing from our television sets. This special language suggests that we are in the presence of something greater.

Beyond that, the intrusion of this higher level of language arrests the reader or listener's attention. If our attention has dared lapse or has drifted to other details of our day, the figure of speech summons us to return and reengage the story with renewed attentiveness.[4] Such word play is designed into the structure of the story "to add force to the truth being conveyed, to add emphasis to its statement, and to add depth to its meaning."[5] Given this reality, readers seeking meaning in Bible stories will have particular interest in this elevated form of language, for figures of speech are designed to get our attention and to participate in the process of shaping our response to the story.[6]

Examples of the Patterning Play of Words

Similar to so many other dimensions of the storyteller's craft, the ability to evaluate the use of wordplay begins by sensitizing our reading or listening to its presence. Toward that end, the next pages will introduce and illustrate a variety of those forms of speech—from various forms of repetition to the use of rhetorical questions. In each case, we observe that the word play is not associated with a minor component of the story but always is associated with a topic closely connected to the story's message.

Repetition

It is characteristic for Hebrew thinkers and for those influenced strongly by this background to develop a persuasive argument or to drive home a key concept through repetition, revisiting the same point again and again.[7] This repetition can sound somewhat foreign, even primitive to the ears of a modern Western reader.[8] Alter points Bible readers to Numbers 7 as an extreme example that tests the patience of contemporary readers.

In Numbers 7, the leaders of the twelve Israelite tribes are each bringing an offering on successive days as the tabernacle is being dedicated. Nahshon from the tribe of Judah is the first to bring his offering. After introducing him, the storyteller uses five verses to detail the offering that this leader of Judah brings:

> His offering was one silver plate weighing one hundred thirty shekels, one silver basin weighing seventy shekels, according to the shekel of the sanctuary, both of them full of choice flour mixed with oil for a grain offering; one golden dish weighing ten shekels, full of incense; one young bull, one ram, one male lamb a year old, for a burnt offering; one male goat for a sin offering; and for

the sacrifice of well-being, two oxen, five rams, five male goats, and five male lambs a year old. This was the offering of Nahshon son of Amminadab. (7:13–17)

At this point the storyteller could simply have made the statement that during the next eleven days, eleven other leaders brought and presented the same offering as Nashon from Judah. But such abbreviation is not what follows. Instead, the story continues by introducing the second leader, Nethanel of Issachar, who brings his offering on the second day. Once again, five verses are used to detail the offering.

> He presented for his offering one silver plate weighing one hundred thirty shekels, one silver basin weighing seventy shekels, according to the shekel of the sanctuary, both of them full of choice flour mixed with oil for a grain offering; one golden dish weighing ten shekels, full of incense; one young bull, one ram, one male lamb a year old, for a burnt offering; one male goat as a sin offering; and for the sacrifice of well-being, two oxen, five rams, five male goats, and five male lambs a year old. This was the offering of Nethanel son of Zuar. (7:19–23)

By this time, the contemporary reader, who has little stomach for such repetition, may already be paging ahead in the Bible for something that sounds more natural to the modern ear. But the storyteller presses on with the same technique, recounting what happens the third, fourth, and subsequent days. Each day a new tribal leader is introduced, and the description of the offering is given in exactly the same language again and again and again and again. The net result is that we have twelve paragraphs in this chapter (7:12–89) that are virtually identical. A modern editor would recoil from this kind of writing. Within its original culture and context, this use of repetition helped communicate an obedience and tribal unity that resonated with the literary expectations and tolerances of the early audience.

Not all repetition we find in our Bible stories is so obnoxiously obvious. Yet because of its importance as a literary device within the repertoire of the divine storyteller, we will explore it more fully than the other figures of speech in this chapter. This summary of repetition will include a brief visit in each of the following categories: sound, word, phrase, motif, and series of threes and fours. Some of these forms of repetition may be difficult to trace in our English translations due to the difficulty in recreating the literary experience during the translation process from the parent languages of Hebrew and Greek. But we will present even those forms of repetition for those who have access to the original languages of the Bible or for those who are willing to investigate Bible commentaries that address the use of such figures.

SOUND

The biblical authors may employ figures of speech that repeat either the sounds of the consonants (alliteration) or the sounds of vowels (assonance).[9] The blood that stained the hands of David, the warrior, made it inappropriate for him to build the temple as a house of peace. But God had promised David that he would have a son who would build the temple. His name would be Solomon (*šĕlōmō*) because God would provide him with *šālōm*, the Hebrew word for peace (1 Chr. 22:9). The repetition of the consonant and vowel sounds that link Solomon's name with the word for peace calls attention to this naming and reinforces the point. The Lord's temple could not be built by a man of war but must be built by a man of peace.

In the New Testament, Jesus used sound to emphasize the destruction of wicked tenant farmers in the parable of the tenants (Mt. 21:33–41). The landowner sent representatives to the farmers to see how work in the vineyard was progressing, but the tenant farmers severely mistreated these representatives. When the landowner sent his own son on the same mission, they murdered him. Jesus asked his listeners what they thought would happen to those tenant farmers. The response of the people employs the repetition of sound, which the NIV attempts to simulate with the following translation: "He will bring those wretches (*kakous*) to a wretched (*kakōs*) end ..." (21:41, NIV). This repetition of sound catches the ear of the listener and draws attention to the fate of those who dared to treat the son of the landowner in this way.

WORD

The storyteller may also use the repetition of a single word. This vocabulary repetition or use of a "leading word" (*Leitwort*) sounds more than a little strange to us who live in a culture in which the use of synonyms is championed in more refined forms of writing.[10] Thus for stylistic reasons some Bible translations will avoid reproducing this kind of word repetition. But even Bible translators who wish to reproduce this phenomenon can be undone by language limitations. Often the repetition of a Hebrew or Greek word will play upon its various meanings. This can cause problems for translators since the difference in the semantic range of a word (that is, the breadth of meanings assigned to a particular word) is rarely equivalent between a word in English and a similar word in Greek or Hebrew. For example, the Hebrew word for "house" has a much wider semantic range than the word *house* in English. For English speakers, the word *house* conjures the picture of a residential dwelling. However, in Hebrew the word may signify a personal residence, a temple, a family, or a royal dynasty. When the inspired author elects to repeat a word like this, language limitations may prevent the English translator from passing that phenomenon along to the English reader. Despite these stylistic and language limitations, tracing key-word repetition in our Bible translations can yield wonderful insight into the storyteller's craft. Two examples will illustrate that point.

The book of Jonah contains a wonderful example of *Leitwort* in the very first chapter. After the Lord directs Jonah to deliver a message to the residents of Nineveh, Jonah falls silent. What follows is not Jonah's speech but a series of actions, all described with the same Hebrew verb form that is the direct antonym of the verb the Lord used. The command from the Lord is clear. "Arise, go to Nineveh" (Jon. 2:1, NIV) Note the imperative; Jonah was to "arise." But this command to "arise" precipitates a series of "descents," all reported with the same Hebrew word. Jonah *went down* to Joppa (1:3). After identifying a ship for passage and paying his way, he *went down* (boarded) into it (1:3). As the divine storm raged around the ship, Jonah *went down* into the inner most part of the ship (1:5). In his poetic analysis of what had happened, Jonah reports that he had *gone down* to the foundations of the mountains (2:6; Hebrew 2:7). The repetition of this word highlights Jonah's failure to "arise and go" and characterizes Jonah's actions as a series of linked "descents," profiling not only his physical actions but his spiritual descent as well.

While the word repetition in Jonah serves to demonstrate the negative qualities in Jonah, this figure of speech can also be deployed to deliver good news as it does in the first two chapters of Luke. When the angel of the Lord appeared to Zechariah to announce the birth of his son, John the Baptist, the angel directed him to "stop being afraid" (Lk. 1:13). Just a few verses later, as the angel Gabriel informed Mary that she would be the mother of Jesus, the same language was used, "Stop being afraid" (1:30). As the shepherds in the fields outside Bethlehem trembled in the presence of the angel of the Lord, those fearful shepherds were addressed with the same word, "Stop being afraid" (2:10). This repetition sends a message about the new era that has dawned in this sinful world. In the old era, people feared the Lord because of the shadow the sin of Adam and Eve cast on humanity. The very first reaction of Adam and Eve to God's presence, after the fall into sin, was fear. Throughout the Old Testament, whenever mortals are confronted by the power and presence of the holy God, their first reaction is fear. But Christmas morning saw the dawn of a new era. Through the use of repetition, the gospel writer has emphasized that this is now a time for fear to cease since the Savior of the world had been born.

PHRASE

Sometimes the repetition takes the form of a unique and distinctive phrase. The account of Jesus' resurrection in John provides us with an example of such phrase repetition. The deep love of Mary Magdalene for Jesus brought her to the tomb early on Easter morning. Her only wish at the moment was to be near the physical remains of the Lord she loved so deeply. Finding that the stone had been removed from the tomb entrance, she felt robbed again. Her living Lord had been taken from her, and now she had lost his body, too. Mary dashed to Peter and John and breathlessly declared, "They have taken the Lord out of the tomb, and we do not know where they have laid him" (Jn. 20:2). All three returned to the tomb. After Peter and John examined the tomb and found the discarded funeral attire, Mary looked into the tomb. She saw the two angels sitting where Jesus' body had been. She still could not make sense of it all. She says to them, "They have taken away my Lord, and I do now know where they have laid him" (20:13). The repetition of this phrase helps us see both the desperation and confusion that gripped Mary. Emphasizing the problem sets up the celebration as Jesus reveals himself as her risen friend.

Motif

Apart from repeating sounds, words, and phrases, the biblical storyteller may also repeat a motif. A motif is a concrete image that reoccurs in more than one story and that helps to connect and to inform the reading of the stories linked by that motif.[11] Consider the use of clothing in the story of Joseph. Jacob loved Joseph more deeply than his other sons. He made this fact evident to the rest of the family when he provided Joseph with a distinctive robe (Gen. 37:3). This special treatment of their younger brother caused his older siblings' jealousy to pulse with increasing passion. When Joseph was alone with them in a remote location, the feeling of jealousy erupted into a murderous plan. As Joseph arrives on the scene, the first thing they do is strip that distinctive robe from his shoulders (Gen. 37:23). The robe is set aside briefly but reappears again in this story as a piece of evidence that would dissuade their father from ever looking for Joseph:

> Then they took Joseph's robe, slaughtered a goat, and dipped the robe in the blood. They had the long robe with sleeves taken to their father, and they said, "This we have found; see now whether it is your son's robe or not." He recognized it, and said, "It is my son's robe! A wild animal has devoured him; Joseph is without doubt torn to pieces." (Gen. 37:31–33)

The mention of clothing that occurs eight times in connection with Joseph in chapter 37 resurfaces again in chapter 39, where Joseph's clothing is mentioned six times. While Joseph was working in the home of Potiphar, Potiphar's wife made sexual advances in Joseph's direction. At one point, she became so aggressive that she grabbed Joseph's garment as he fled from her (39:12). Potiphar's wife would use this garment that she kept by her side as a tool with which to punish her desired lover. She presented it to her husband as evidence that Joseph had attempted to molest her (39:13–16).

Following this miscarriage of justice, Joseph was placed in an Egyptian prison where his ability to interpret dreams found expression as he interpreted the dreams of his fellow inmates. Subsequently, when Pharaoh was disturbed by his dreams, Joseph was summoned to court to interpret them. Before he was brought into Pharaoh's presence, his clothing was changed (41:14). Following the successful interpretation of those dreams, this capable man was put in charge of a massive public works project. Once again his clothing changes as Joseph is given a fine linen garment to wear in his capacity as overseer (41:42).

As a man of wealth and influence, Joseph meets the brothers who had sold him into slavery and faked his death. A famine that swept the region brought the sons of Jacob to Egypt. When Joseph finally revealed himself to these brothers who had taken his robe, the circle was completed as Joseph then gave these brothers new clothing (45:22).

A motif is a concrete image, such as clothing, that recurs in a set of stories. As we have seen above, that repetition not only links those stories. It can also be used as a literary signal. We have seen that the story of Joseph is very closely attended by the taking, exchange, and giving of garments. By carefully reading the text, we find that Joseph and clothing are mentioned eighteen times in this story cycle. Those changes in clothing are always associated in some way with the changing fortunes of Joseph.

REPETITION IN THREES AND FOURS

The final form of repetition that we will illustrate is the repetition of three or four events that have a great deal of similarity to one another. The reader senses movement each time the event occurs, with the culminating event being the last in the series.[12] The parable of the good Samaritan clearly shows this pattern. Jesus tells the story of a man who was robbed, stripped, and beaten by thieves. A priest traveling the road comes upon the injured man and passes by on the other side. Next, a Levite comes along the road, happens upon the injured man, and also passes by on the other side. The reader familiar with this pattern of three will expect that the third rendition of the pattern will result in a change. In this case, the third man to come down the road is a Samaritan who stops to aid and care for the injured traveler (Lk. 10:25–37).

This threefold pattern is also evident as the Lord deals with the apostasy of King Ahaziah of Israel (2 Kings 1). When this king was injured in a serious fall, he sent messengers to Baal-zebub, the god of Ekron, to learn if he would recover from his injuries. Elijah intercepted the messengers and sent them back to Ahaziah with a message from the Lord. This king would die in his bed. The message so angered Ahaziah that he sent a portion of his army to seize Elijah. Note how the story is told:

> Then the king sent to him a captain of fifty with his fifty men. He
> went up to Elijah, who was sitting on the top of a hill, and said
> to him, "O man of God, the king says, 'Come down.'" But Elijah

answered the captain of fifty, "If I am a man of God, let fire come down from heaven and consume you and your fifty." Then fire came down from heaven, and consumed him and his fifty. (2 Kings 1:9–10)

In the second act of the story, King Ahab responds to this by sending yet another fifty-one soldiers to Elijah and repetition is put into play:

Again the king sent to him another captain of fifty with his fifty. He went up and said to him, "O man of God, this is the king's order: Come down quickly!" But Elijah answered them, "If I am a man of God, let fire come down from heaven and consume you and your fifty." Then the fire of God came down from heaven and consumed him and his fifty. (2 Kings 1:11–12)

The recounting of these two events with nearly the same language rouses an expectation in the reader that a third set of soldiers will be sent and that the story will move forward in a new way in the third repetition. This is the rule of three. That is exactly what happens:

Again the king sent the captain of a third fifty with his fifty. So the third captain of fifty went up, and came and fell on his knees before Elijah, and entreated him, "O man of God, please let my life, and the life of these fifty servants of yours, be precious in your sight. Look, fire came down from heaven and consumed the two former captains of fifty men with their fifties; but now let my life be precious in your sight." Then the angel of the LORD said to Elijah, "Go down with him; do not be afraid of him." So he set out and went down with him to the king. (2 Kings 1:13–15)

Although less frequent, the more typical threefold repetition leading to a climax or change may be replaced by a fourfold repetition that leads to the change or climax in the fourth rendition. Chapter 1 of Job provides us with an example of this storytelling technique. As Satan was permitted to press the faith of Job to the breaking point, the storyteller has us join Job on a most dreadful day. First a messenger comes with the news that Job's oxen and donkeys were carried off by the Sabeans. This messenger was the only one of the servants tending those animals that was able to escape death (1:14–15). While he was still speaking, a second servant arrives. Fire had fallen from the sky and burned up the sheep in the pastures. Again the servant who was reporting the matter was the only worker to have survived this catastrophe (1:16). While he was speaking, a third messenger arrives. Chaldean raiding parties had carried off the camels, killing all the servants who were tending them. This witness was the sole survivor of the attack (1:17). At this point, the listener may assume that he or she has heard the worst of it. But now a fourth messenger arrives with the worst news of all.

Job's children were all celebrating at a party held at the oldest brother's house when a wind collapsed the entire structure, killing everyone inside but this one witness (1:18–19). Thus the tension flows past the third repetition, reaching its climax only with the horrible news of the fourth messenger.

This survey makes it clear that the storyteller employed repetition as an important tool. These examples that have shown the repetition of sound, of words, of phrases, of motifs, and of events in patterns of three and four form just a small sample of the many places that repetition makes itself evident in biblical storytelling. While this device is less familiar to Western ears, we have seen that it does play an important role in the recasting of events into story form, directing the reader to key people and events that shape the meaning of the narrative.

Metaphor and Simile

From repetition in its various forms, we now turn to the use of metaphor and simile. These two forms of speech are similar to one another and therefore easily confused. A metaphor uses a form of the linking verb (is, are, was, were, etc.) in its formulation. For example, "The Lord is my rock." In the metaphor, the language artist is not saying that "A" literally equals "B," but rather is saying that "A" represents or resembles "B," similar to the way a photograph represents a family member.[13] I may say to a colleague, "This is my son," while pointing to a photograph that resides on my desk. Of course, I am not saying that the paper image is literally "my son." But the colleague will correctly assume that I am saying that this photograph is representative of his appearance. In the same way, the Lord is not a literal rock. But the Lord has certain qualities that are similar to those of a rock.

A simile does something very similar to this but is formulated with the words "as" or "like." After being served a particularly bad muffin at the local coffee shop, I might exclaim, "This muffin is as dry as a dirt road in summer!" Like the metaphor, a simile communicates meaning by inviting the listener to see that an object, item, or action is comparable to another in one or more ways.

As with other examples of the patterning play of words, the use of a metaphor or simile is rarely wasted in imaging a detail of minor importance. So when a storyteller shifts into this higher form of language, we as listeners will want to focus our attention not only on the language artistry but also on the subject being illustrated to determine its significance to the narrative.

This is clearly the case in Genesis 22 when the Lord seeks to reaffirm important promises given to Abraham. Following an incredible demonstration of faith during which Abraham had proven his willingness to sacrifice his son, Isaac, God affirmed for Abraham that his family would grow beyond his wildest estimation. Watch for the use of simile at work here that draws attention to the promise. The Lord said, "I will make your offspring as numerous as the stars of heaven and as the sand that is on the seashore" (Gen. 22:17). When the tribes of Israel came to Hebron to receive David as their king, they aligned their position with the one articulated by God. Here a metaphor helps emphasize the importance of David's leadership: "The LORD said to you: It is you who shall be shepherd of my people Israel, you who shall be ruler over Israel" (2 Sam. 5:2b). The tremendous wealth of King Solomon was difficult to communicate, so the storyteller resorts to a simile: "The king made silver as common in Jerusalem as stones, and made cedars as numerous as the sycamores of the Shephelah" (1 Kings 10:27).

The New Testament also has its share of metaphors and similes. In speaking of the pervasive influence of his followers, Jesus says, "You are the salt of the earth" (Mt. 5:13). Jesus also uses a simile to express his deep passion for saving the people of Jerusalem: "Jerusalem, Jerusalem, the city that kills the prophets and stones those who are sent to it! How often have I desired to gather your children together as a hen gathers her brood under her wings, and you were not willing" (Mt. 23:37). In the gospel of John we encounter one metaphor after another as Jesus describes his unique mission and character. Jesus says, "I am the gate for the sheep" (10:7); "I am the good shepherd" (10:11); and, "I am the vine, you are the branches" (15:5). Recalling that metaphor and simile will always be used to highlight a subject of importance, their use will both catch our attention and precipitate an investigation into the key role the subject is playing in the story.

Personification

Yet another tool in the hands of the wordsmith is personification. In this case, the storyteller provides an inanimate object with one or more personal traits, giving an inanimate object the ability to think, act, or even speak as if it were a human being.[14] Like the metaphor or simile, personification is not deployed casually but is designed to startle the reader into a deeper attentiveness and focus the listener's attention afresh on the point being made.

Several examples from Scripture will make this clear. As the Lord confronted Cain with his horrific act, a rhetorical question is followed by personification: "And the LORD said, 'What have you done? Listen; your brother's blood is crying out to me from the ground'" (Gen. 4:10)! Blood does not have the capacity to mumble, much less speak or cry out. Thus the Lord is not referring to an audible cry. But by commanding Cain to "listen" and by personifying the blood with the ability to cry out to the heavens, the author is focusing our attention on the horrific nature of this act in a way that ordinary language forms would not.

After the Israelites crossed into and conquered the promised land under Joshua's leadership, God's people gathered at Shechem to renew their commitment to the covenant. As they listened again to the terms of the agreement and voiced their commitment to it, Joshua set up a stone monument. Then, "Joshua said to all the people, 'See, this stone shall be a witness against us; for it heard all the words of the LORD that he spoke to us; therefore it shall be a witness against you, if you deal falsely with your God'" (Josh. 24:27). The inanimate stone monument neither had the ability to literally "hear" the people or the ability to speak as a "witness" of what they had said. But the personification of the stone monument, expressed three times in this verse, causes us to pause and to see the significance of the commitment the people are making.

Personification shows up again early in the book of Jonah. Throughout the first chapter of Jonah, the storyteller sculpts Jonah so that we view him in a very negative light. The divine storm grows, threatening to tear the trading ship apart, but Jonah has "gone down" into the bowels of the ship, and is asleep. By contrast, the heathen mariners are crying out to their gods and throwing cargo overboard, responding to the storm in the best way they know. What a contrast to Jonah! Then the biblical storyteller does something that many English translations obscure. In Jonah 1:4, the divine author imbues the ship with a human quality. In response to the storm, the narrator reports, "the ship was thinking about breaking apart" (author's translation). As the ship is assigned this human quality, it is elevated to the status of a "person" so that its response to the storm might be compared to the response of Jonah. That comparison makes one thing clear. Even this inanimate vessel knows more about responding to the storm in an appropriate way than does Jonah. Thus the personification of the ship participates in further degrading the reader's view of Jonah.

Finally, we also see personification surface in the word play of the New Testament. In the Sermon on the Mount, Jesus addresses the proper way in which gifts can be given to those in need. He notes that such charitable acts might be used to enhance one's own reputation. Consequently, Jesus encourages that, when giving such gifts, "do not sound a trumpet" (Mt. 6:2). Then he uses personification to drive the point home: "But when you give your alms, do not let your left hand know what your right hand is doing, so that your alms may be done in secret; and your Father who sees in secret will reward you" (Mt. 6:3–4). By themselves, our hands do not have the capacity for self-awareness. By personifying them in this way, the storyteller again summons the attention of the listener with this unusual language form, driving home the point being expressed.

Verbal Irony

Language can also be delivered "with a wink and nudge" to say more than or even the opposite of what has been said. This is verbal irony.[15] The use of ironic language may be intentional and strategic. The speech of Elijah delivered on Mount Carmel fits this category of ironic speech. During Elijah's day, the threat of Baal worship was very real. King Ahab and Queen Jezebel had actually welcomed Baal worship into their capital city to reside, not as a guest, but as a permanent member of the kingdom. So the Lord engineered a contest on Mount Carmel that pitted the prophets of Baal against the prophet of the Lord. The goal of the contest was to see which God would answer from heaven by fire. The Baal prophets went first—building their altar, preparing their sacrifices, and calling on Baal to prove his authenticity. This went on from morning until noon, a delay that already signaled the hopelessness of the cause. Intentional use of ironic language amplified the failure of this pagan deity: "At noon Elijah, mocked them, saying, 'Cry aloud! Surely he is a god; either he is meditating, or he has wandered away, or he is on a journey, or perhaps he is asleep and must be awakened'" (1 Kings 18:27). Taken out of context, this language of Elijah could be perceived as an attempt to defend Baal by providing excuses that legitimate his failure to respond. In context, the words are designed to have exactly the opposite affect. Far from defending this pagan deity, these ironic statements amplify the impotence and inadequacy of Baal.

This intentional use of ironic language stands in contrast to the irony expressed unintentionally by people like Nathanael, Caiaphas, and Pilate. These men all say much more about Jesus than they intended to say. As Jesus ministered in Galilee, he found and called Philip to divine service. Philip was so excited to find Jesus that he ran to tell Nathanael the good news. He had found the Messiah promised in the pages of the Hebrew Bible. When Nathanael heard that this Jesus was from Nazareth, he expressed his doubts. "Can anything good come out of Nazareth?" (Jn. 1:46). Of course, Nathanael used this rhetorical question to dismiss the possibility; but the insights already held by the reader transform this into an ironic affirmation, saying more about Jesus than Nathanael intended.

At the close of Jesus' ministry during Passion Week, we find many examples of verbal irony placed in the mouths of various characters. These speakers are often hostile to the cause of Jesus, but end up voicing some of the most memorable truths about him. Following Jesus' arrest, the reader of John is informed about an earlier statement of the high priest, Caiaphas. This opponent of Jesus "was the one who had advised the Jews that it was better to have one person die for the people" (John 18:14). Caiaphas was expressing his concerns about the Roman response to sedition in Jerusalem and advocating a position that would be better for the Sadducees as well. But the storyteller includes a reference to his statement because Caiaphas was speaking a greater truth than he realized.

Just a few verses later, it is the Roman governor's turn to speak ironic words. The unbelieving Jews who had gathered to denounce Jesus and call for his execution stood before Pilate. The governor brought Jesus before this crowd and announced, "Here is your King!" (Jn. 19:14). Neither Pilate nor his listeners were convinced of this ironic truth, but absolute truth it was.

Pilate handed Jesus over to Roman soldiers who had responsibility to break down the body and the will of Jesus in advance of his crucifixion. In an ironic act, they dress him as a king with a scarlet robe and a crown of thorns. Then they speak these words: "Hail, King of the Jews!" (Mt. 27:29). We say, "amen" to the great truth they speak in their ignorance. Thus verbal irony is deployed again and again by the divine storyteller during the story of Jesus' passion as a way of drawing our attention to powerful statements in the narrative that affirm his true identity and mission.

Rhetorical Questions

While most of the patterning play of words finds expression through declarative sentences, questions can also be employed as attention-getting devices. We use questions in a variety of ways. They may be used to get data from someone who is in the know: "How much snow will we get tomorrow?" We can use questions to solicit action from others. If the kids are falling behind schedule on a school morning, we may ask, "Isn't it almost time for the bus to pick you up?" But we can also use questions rhetorically. A rhetorical question is not seeking information or even calling for action as much as it is calling for deeper thought. In a narrative this kind of question is designed to call attention to the matter under discussion and to draw the listener into a moment of deeper reflection.[16]

The first example from Scripture concerns the day King Saul's failure as a ruler becomes most evident. God had directed Saul to destroy the Amalekites, a directive that included the destruction of all their livestock. After the battle was completed, Saul happily announced to Samuel, "May you be blessed by the LORD; I have carried out the command of the LORD" (1 Sam. 15:13). Samuel responds to this misguided declaration with a rhetorical question. "What then is this bleating of sheep in my ears, and the lowing of cattle that I hear?" (15:14). Saul attempts to explain away the presence of those animals, but Samuel was not looking for an explanation or further discussion. This rhetorical question was a statement that should have given Saul pause, as it does the listener. It calls attention to the failure of Saul in an artistic and dramatic way.

The divine storyteller also employs a rhetorical question at the close of the book of Jonah. In the first two chapters, the reader observes Jonah's disobedient flight from Nineveh and his time of reflection in the belly of the fish. Jonah appears to exit that fish with a new attitude and willingness to go to Nineveh. Jonah preaches so successfully in Nineveh that the entire city is brought to repentance. In response, the Lord repeals his judgment of destruction against this city. Jonah can hardly believe it. He is in no mood to celebrate this conversion, but, rather, points out that this repeal will make him look like a false prophet since the judgment he foretold will not fall on Nineveh. Jonah does not celebrate the repentance of sinners but instead voices concern for his own prophetic reputation. Following his angry tirade, Jonah takes a position well outside the city, certain that the Lord will alter his course of action again and destroy Nineveh. At this location, God provides Jonah with a plant that shelters him from the hot wind. But soon the Lord takes this plant away leaving Jonah to bake in the sun. This is the last straw. The man who was saved from drowning asks to die. The storyteller brings the story of Jonah to conclusion with the following statement and rhetorical question:

> Then the LORD said, "You are concerned about the bush, for which you did not labor and which you did not grow; it came into being in a night and perished in a night. And should I not be concerned about Nineveh, that great city, in which there are more than a hundred and twenty thousand persons who do not know their right hand from their left, and also many animals?" (Jon. 4:10–11)

The Lord uses this rhetorical question to return us to the enduring message of the book. It is a treatise on how (or how not) to be a missionary. Most of this treatise is delivered by showing the absence of the true mission spirit in Jonah. This question puts a laser-like focus on the quality most lacking in Jonah. He had failed to show love and concern for the lost. The final question not only emphasizes the importance of this quality, it also brings the matter to the reader for reflection in a way that a declarative sentence could not. Should we not be as concerned about others as the Lord is? We do not know how Jonah responded to this final question, but that is really not the function of the question in this story. It is the storyteller's call for the reader to reflect on this key truth.

Finally, Jesus also uses rhetorical questions at various times. When teaching his followers about the nature of proper prayer, he emphasized his Father's willingness to answer those requests by using a question. "Is there anyone among you who, if your child asks for a fish, will give a snake instead of a fish? Of if the child asks for an egg, will give a scorpion?" (Lk. 11:11–12). No, of course caring parents would never treat their child's request for food in such a way. But the rhetorical point being made follows naturally. If you as a parent know how to respond to requests from your children, the heavenly Father will certainly do what is right when God's children pray to God.

Conclusion

Language is the medium via which the storyteller shares the story with us. Yet as we have seen, the language the divine storyteller uses is far from ordinary. Here we have offered but a small sample of the patterning play of words evident throughout the stories of the Bible. In every case we have found that word play summons the listener's attention to key moments in the narrative or topics in the story related to its enduring meaning. That makes the patterning play of words not just an interesting artistic phenomenon in the text; it also makes this play of words a critical part of the storyteller's craft, yet another tool shaping the meaning of the story.

Notes

[1]Robert Alter, *The World of Biblical Literature* (New York: Basic Books, 1992), 43.

[2]David M. Gunn and Danna Nolan Fewell, *Narrative in the Hebrew Bible,* The Oxford Bible Series (Oxford: Oxford University Press, 1993), 3.

[3]E. W. Bullinger, Figures of Speech Used in the Bible, Explained and Illustrated (New York: E & J.B. Young, 1898).

[4]Shimon Bar-Efrat, *Narrative Art in the* Bible, JSOT Bible and Literature 17 (Sheffield: Almond Press, 1989), 198.

[5]E.W. Bullinger, *Figures of Speech Used in the Bible: Explained and Illustrated* (Grand Rapids: Baker Book House, 1968), vi.

[6]Meir Sternberg, *The Poetics of Biblical Narrative: Ideological Literature and the Drama of Reading,* Indiana Studies in Biblical Literature (Bloomington: Indiana University Press, 1985), 475.

[7]"Rhetorical Patterns," in *Dictionary of Biblical Imagery,* ed. Leland Ryken, James C. Wilhoit, and Tremper Longman III (Downers Grove, Ill.: InterVarsity Press, 1998), 722.

[8]Robert Alter, *The Art of Biblical Narrative* (New York: Basic Books, 1981), 88.

[9]Bar-Efrat, *Narrative Art in the Bible,* 201.

[10]Gunn and Fewell, *Narrative in the Hebrew Bible,* 148.

[11]Alter, *Art of Biblical Narrative,* 95.

[12]James L. Resseguie, *Narrative Criticism of the New Testament: An Introduction* (Grand Rapids: Baker Academic, 2005), 49; Leland Ryken, *How to Read the Bible as Literature* (Grand Rapids: Zondervan, 1984), 142.

[13]Bullinger, *Figures of Speech Used in the Bible,* 735.

[14]Ibid., 861.

[15]Bar-Efrat, *Narrative Art in the* Bible, 210; Gunn and Fewell, *Narrative in the Hebrew Bible,* 74; David Rhoads and Donald Michie, *Mark as Story: An Introduction to the Narrative of a Gospel* (Philadelphia: Fortress Press, 1982), 60.

[16]Rhoads and Michie, *Mark as Story,* 49; Bar-Efrat, *Narrative Art in the Bible,* 211.

PART TWO

The Storyteller's Geography

6

Narrative Geography Defined

Book titles create expectations. So in seeing the title *God as Storyteller,* you likely expected to read something about the divine author's use of characterization, the structuring of a plot, the role of the narrator, and the other dimensions of storytelling discussed in part one of this book. However, you probably did not expect to find a large number of pages dedicated to geography. We expect to learn about geography in a social studies class, within an interpretive center at a national park, or from the pages of a Bible atlas, but the connection between geography and storytelling is much less intuitive. So, the emphasis on the relationship between storytelling and geography found here makes the book you hold in your hands somewhat unique.

This author's love for the outdoors, coupled with his love for the Bible's literature, has led him to see an important, even vital, connection between the stories in the Bible, their message, and the storyteller's use of geography. This literary use of geography, which we call "narrative geography," will fill part two of this book.

Since the term "geography" is understood in various ways, this chapter will begin by defining all that this term entails for us. We will then note that the connection between geography and literature has already been made by those studying secular stories. The investigation of "regionalism" and "literary geography" will find brief introduction and illustration. Next, we will trace the historic link between geography and biblical studies. For more than a century, those interested in Bible history have studied the geography of Israel in a bid to better understand the events of Bible times. While narrative geography takes advantage of the wealth of information disclosed by historical geography, it is not the same as historical geography, for narrative geography works to reveal the literary role that geography may play when an event is placed in story form. This particular view will be defined and defended before we discuss a method that may be used to link the study of geography with narrative critical analysis.

Geography as a Discipline

For most people, the word *geography* immediately conjures images of maps. While maps are an indispensable part of the discipline of geography, they are only a very small part of what is a very large and integrated discipline. In 1963, William D. Pattison sought to define geographical study at the National Council for Geographic Education. His summary has frequently been quoted as the most helpful overview of the discipline currently in circulation. It breaks the study of geography into four overlapping disciplines, each of which makes a contribution to one another and to the whole field of geographical investigation. First of all, Pattison observes the contribution of *spatial tradition* to geography. This part of geographical analysis emphasizes collecting data and integrating that data on a map. All of us have made use of the spatial tradition of geography when we have consulted either a paper or electronic map when planning a trip. Pattison's second tradition is called *area studies.* Here researchers seek to characterize a "place," whether that is a small neighborhood or a nation. If you have read an article that compares the advantages of living in New York versus living in Chicago, or if you have seen a television program that provides an overview of a country like England or Ecuador, you have taken advantage of material collected by geographers doing area studies. Third, we have the *man-land tradition.* This tradition explores the relationship between people and place. Of course, this is a two-way street. The geography of a place impacts people; and people, in turn, have an impact on the place they inhabit. If the Midwest receives a large amount of snow this winter, geographers will study both the impact of that snow on the culture of the region and the way in which snow removal by that culture may impact the water quality of the local streams and rivers. Finally, the *earth-science tradition* encompasses all of physical geography with specialties like meteorology, glaciology, and mineralogy.[1] Even this quick look makes one thing crystal-clear: the discipline of geography is a far-flung and integrated study of our living space.

For our purposes, we will simplify things a bit and speak of geography in the way most biblical geographers address the topic. They break the study of biblical geography into two related areas of study: physical geography and human geography.[2] Physical geography focuses on features found on the surface of the earth and the processes that bring about changes in those features. This means that a biblical geographer will investigate and illustrate topics such as geology, topography, hydrology, climate, and forestation. By contrast, human geography or cultural geography addresses the interaction between humans and that physical geography. Biblical geographers will also be interested in topics like land use, political segmentation of the land, urbanization patterns, economics, roadways, and transportation.[3] These particulars of physical and human geography will become important to us in just a few minutes, as we study the geography, formally mentioned within a Bible story.

Regionalism and Literary Geography

Before we link that geography of the biblical world to the Bible's communication, we note that study of secular literature has already linked geography and literature. This appears under two categories of inquiry: regionalism and literary geography.

Regionalism is a style of narration noted for its "fidelity to a particular geographical area, the representation of its habits, speech, manners, history, folklore, and beliefs." A piece of literature is considered "regional" by definition if the action and personages of such a work cannot be moved to any other geographical setting without major loss or distortion.[4] The familiar stories of Mark Twain are well-suited for illustrating this point. The speech patterns we find in *Tom Sawyer,* the topics for conversation, the fears of the participants, and their beliefs are all closely connected to the southern banks of the Mississippi River.

We are not suggesting that the literary category of regionalism applies narrowly to the stories in the Bible. Regionalism, however, does honor two important premises that we wish to carry into our study of biblical stories. First, those who are telling the story are powerfully influenced by their own geographical realities. And second, storytellers may deploy geography within the narrative as part of the storytelling process.

The impact of geographical setting on authors is wonderfully captured in an essay by Kenneth Mitchell entitled, "Landscape and Literature." He compares the way different geographical settings impact the perceptions and presentations of authors from those regions. Mitchell turns to the literature of the island nation, Great Britain, to illustrate the point. The use of "island" as a metaphor and the notion of "insularity" occur much more frequently in the literature of Great Britain than they do in literature from other nations.[5] Mitchell observes the influence of geography on authors and their literature also when comparing the way in which Canadian literature and American literature portray the idea of frontier. Within American literature the frontier is something that can be pressed back and overpowered. By contrast, Canadian literature sees the frontier as terrifying, lethal, and impenetrable.[6] This difference in presentation coincides with the geographical realities associated with each of those nations. Thus storytellers living in specific geographical location are being influenced by geography that impacts their perceptions, and, in turn, these perceptions impact the way they tell their stories.

While this process may well occur without the storyteller being consciously aware of the process, the second premise of regionalism speaks of a strategic and intentional use of geography. Whether the storyteller is being directly impacted by the geography or not, the storyteller may formally nestle geographical references within the words of the story to impact the reading experience. The work of Willa Cather is frequently used to illustrate this strategic use of geography. In her novels, *O Pioneers* and *My Ántonia,* geography plays a key role in the storytelling process. The plains of Nebraska not only provide a setting for these provocative tales, but the land itself also becomes a character that plays a compelling role in reshaping the people who live on it.[7]

Analysts of European novels have also pursued writers' strategic use of geography. Persuaded by the premise that "what happens in a story depends a great deal on where it happens,"[8] Franco Moretti calls for greater attention to the phenomenon he calls "literary geography." Within his *Atlas of the European Novel, 1800–1900,* he sets the stage for what he hopes will become a larger historical atlas of literature. That movement would catalog geographical references in a novel or set of novels, chart those references, and analyze those references for patterns that impact the reading experience.[9]

Thus the idea of linking the study of geography and the study of literature is not new to the pages of this book. Within the study of secular literature, geography has been given its due. Analysts have observed and documented the critical connection between storytellers and their environment. They have noted further that storytellers may make a practice of deploying geography in a bid to shape the reading experience of those who enter their narratives.

Geography and the Bible

With this as a backdrop, we now turn to the Bible. And in doing so, we note that the study of geography and Bible study have a long history. We will begin with a look at the link between geography and Bible history and then summarize the previous links between biblical literature and geography.

History

When we investigate the link between geography and the Bible, it is not the literature of the Bible but the history of the Bible that has had the longest relationship with geography. Historical geographers have investigated the ways in which the geography of the Bible lands shaped and edited the events that lie behind the Bible stories themselves. The father of church history, Eusebius Pamphili, Bishop of Caesarea Maritima (ca. 260–ca. 339), may be the earliest of these historical geographers. In conjunction with his quest to better understand Bible history, he compiled a dictionary of Bible places, as he had come to know them, early in the fourth century. This compilation of place names is called the *Onomasticon.*[10] Despite its age, it continues to play a key role in identifying the locations of biblical events.

Later in the fourth century, Jerome himself used and translated a copy of the *Onomasticon,* as he explored Israel and set about translating the Hebrew Scriptures into Latin. The stories of the Bible came alive for Jerome as he read the stories in their geographical context. This experience led him to the following conclusion: "Just as those who have seen Athens understand Greek history better, and just as those who have seen Troy understand the words of the poet Virgil, thus one will comprehend the Holy Scriptures with a clearer understanding who has seen the land of Judah with his own eyes…"[11]

That compelling statement has been voiced by historical geographers through the centuries since the time of Jerome. While the specific language changes, the conviction remains the same. Within his classic book, *The Land of the Bible,* Yohanan Aharoni phrases it, "In the land of the Bible, geography and history are so deeply interwoven that neither can be really understood without the help of the other. Without an awareness of the stage, the action of the drama cannot be fully understood."[12]

Literature

While historical geography has had a long history in the church, the connection between geography and the literature of the Bible has only come into the scholarly light more recently. When surveying the various introductions to narrative criticism and the Bible, one is most likely to find geography mentioned briefly in connection with an introduction to the topic of setting.[13]

A few introductions to narrative criticism do place a greater emphasis on the role that geography may play in understanding a story.[14] Other than our own statements on the topic, Bar-Efrat makes the strongest declaration we have seen in print when he says, "Places in the narratives are not merely geographical facts, but are to be regarded as literary elements in which fundamental significance is embodied."[15] Unfortunately, even in this case, the topic is raised and then dropped within just a few pages, leaving the reader who wishes to integrate geography into a literary analysis of a Bible story both short on details and lacking a method for doing so.

Yairah Amit's introduction to narrative criticism devotes an entire chapter titled "Place, Story, and History" to the idea of geography and literature.[16] This chapter bounces between various ways in which she sees geography functioning within a biblical narrative. For example, Amit notes that geography may (1) be employed to give the story a more historical feel, (2) be removed from the story to give it more of a fictional feel,[17] (3) be deployed to explain why a certain place was named the way it was (etiology),[18] (4) become the main subject of a narrative, and (5) use place names typologically.[19] While this chapter presents helpful guidance to the one wishing to link geography to their study of a narrative, it addresses a variety of minor roles, leaving the impression that the contribution of a geographically sensitive reading will be small, even negligible. Even worse, the chapter fails to integrate the formal mention of geography with a discussion of its role in shaping the plot and characterization. In the end, Amit offers a hopeful start but leaves readers wishing to integrate geography into their reading of a Bible story longing for more than they have received.

Narrative Geography

Our own interests in both the Bible's geography and its literary qualities have led us to inquire more carefully into this topic. We call this form of investigation "narrative geography." It presumes that the divine storyteller is not including the formal mention of geography in a haphazard or careless way. Narrative geography assumes that the storyteller will strategically use, reuse, and nuance geography to impact the reading experience, particularly in shaping the meaning of a story through the role geography can play in the development of the plot and characterization.[20]

Rationale

The rationale for linking the study of geography to the narrative and to the meaning of a story is found at several levels: the central relationship of geography to the plan of salvation articulated in the Bible, the vivid and frequent use of geography throughout the biblical narratives, the precedent established by the study of geography in secular stories, and the productive—though limited—study of this topic to date.

First, the plan of salvation that lies at the heart of the Bible's communication clearly has an intimate connection to geography. As the Lord meets Abraham and tells him that his family will grow to become a great nation, he also informs Abraham that this nation will be given its own land. From that nation on that land, the messiah will be born (Gen. 12:1–9). This link between the promise of salvation and the promised land continues throughout the entire story of the Old Testament. The promise of the land is articulated again and again to Abraham and his descendants (Gen. 13:14–15; Gen. 15:17–20; Gen. 28:13–14, Gen. 35:12; Gen. 46:1–7). Given the enduring importance of this link between land and Messiah, we find direct mention of the land and allusion to the land casting its shadow over much of the Old Testament.

Lest we lose sight of this important connection in the New Testament, it surfaces very early in the gospel of Matthew within the question of the magi: "Where is the child who has been born king of the Jews?" (Mt. 2:2). Herod hustles to bring together his most learned advisors so that we can be reminded of something we should not have forgotten—that the Messiah would be born in Bethlehem (Micah 5:2). As Jesus left Bethlehem for Nazareth, Capernaum, and eventually Jerusalem, the promised land served as the backdrop for the rescue mission that would bring satisfaction for sin.

With that mission accomplished, Jesus' parting words at the time of his ascension articulate a vision that will take this gospel from the promised land to the world: "You will be my witnesses in Jerusalem, in all Judea and Samaria, and to the ends of the earth" (Acts 1:8). So the plan of salvation from beginning to end has a close connection with geography.

We then should not be surprised to find that the divine storyteller often makes vivid and detailed references to geography. This is another reason for us to integrate our literary reading of a text with greater geographical sensitivity. In his historical geography, George Adam Smith examines the various types of geographical data that find their way into the pages of our Bible. Smith himself becomes prosaic as he attempts to capture the nature of geography within the Bible's literature in a chapter entitled, "The Scenery of the Land and Its Reflection in the Bible."

> How vividly do these cries from Israel's mountains bring before us all that thirsty, broken land of crags and shelves, moors and gullies, with its mire and its rocks, its few summer brooks, its winter spates and heavy snows; the rustling of its woods, its gusts of wind, and its brush fires; its startled birds, when the sudden storms from the sea sweep up the gorges, and its glimpses of deer poised for a moment on the high sky-line of the hills.[21]

As we turn the pages of our Bible, we not only experience people, but place. The Bible may not be a geography book, but it is a book filled with geography.

Third, since the divine storyteller uses geography so widely, it seems prudent to follow the lead offered within the analysis of secular novels and pursue a form of literary geography. Recall that the key premise to regionalism is that a story in this literary category could not be moved from one geographical setting to another without doing significant harm to the narrative. In a similar vein, the geography found within Bible stories cannot be deleted or edited without dramatically affecting the communication process. George Adam Smith, though a historian, begins to sound like a literary scholar when he chides his listeners to pay careful attention to the geography found on the pages of our Bible:

> You see those details which are so characteristic of every Eastern landscape, the chaff and rolling thorns blown before the wind, the dirt cast out on the streets; the broken vessel by the well; the forsaken house, the dusty grave. Let us pay attention to all these, and we shall surely feel ourselves in the atmosphere and scenery in which David fought, and Elisha went, and Malachi saw the Sun of Righteousness arise with healing in his wings.[22]

Further validation for including the geography as part of narrative analysis is found in the helpful insights already produced by those who have explored this link. Various studies in both the Old and New Testament have yielded important validation. As Thomas Dozeman analyzed the story told in Ezra-Nehemiah, he concluded that geography was "crucial in the organization of the literature, in its thematic development, and in its influence on the reader."[23] In their narrative critical analysis of Mark, Rhoads and Michie link the structure of Mark's plot to geography.[24] As Gary Gilbert investigates the list of nations in Acts 2, he makes the following observation about Luke-Acts: "Geographical elements not only provide the narrative backdrop in which the action unfolds but also take center stage in expressing some of the most fundamental themes of the work."[25]

Several avenues of evidence conspire to reveal the critical importance that geography may play in the telling of a Bible story and to give us more than enough reason to pursue the study of narrative geography and a method via which to claim insights from it.

A Method for Narrative-Geographical Analysis

While various articles plucked from here and there help validate the connection between geography and narrative analysis, they do little by way of helping someone new to this area of inquiry know how to get started or how to proceed through what becomes an interdisciplinary maze requiring the use of literary, historical, archaeological, and geographical resources.

The only one who has proposed a method for pursuing literary or narrative geography in the secular arena is Moretti. Within his *Atlas of the European Novel, 1800–1900,* he suggests the following outline: (1) extract the geography from the text; (2) put the geography on a map; (3) analyze the map for insights.[26] This does offer us a starting point, but really lacks the detail and distinction necessary to study an ancient story that is birthed in a culture and climate far distant from most English readers in both time and place.

The suggested outline that follows is one that we have developed and refined over the last ten years of work on this topic. For those who wish to try their hand at narrative geography, it can serve as a starting point for such study. It consists of three steps. First, identify the formal references to geography within the narrative. Second, elevate your understanding of that geography. And third, integrate the geography into the previously noted categories of narrative analysis.

IDENTIFY THE FORMAL REFERENCES TO GEOGRAPHY

When reading a story, our eyes are most attracted to those details in the story that are familiar and intelligible to us. By contrast, we tend to read quickly past those words or references that are unfamiliar to us. Because geographical data is more likely to fall into the latter category, the first step in building a narrative-geographical analysis of a story is to mark all the formal references to geography within the narrative so that even those place names or phenomena that are more obscure stand out on the page. Look for the mention of city names, the names of countries, or regions. Examine the language of the story for topographical references to hills, valleys, mountain, rivers, and bodies of water. Highlight the references to hydrology and climate. Does the storyteller mention the season of the year, the temperature, or wind? Does the storyteller speak about springs, wells, cisterns, or other water delivery systems? Note any specific mention of trees or plants. Look for any mention of human geography: use of the land—mining, fishing, farming, or animal husbandry. And finally, mark the formal mention of roadways or modes of transportation.

ELEVATE YOUR UNDERSTANDING

The biblical storyteller often deploys geography within the narrative with an expectation that the listener will know more than the average person does today about the geographical realities of the past. Although Bar-Efrat encourages contemporary readers of biblical narrative to attend to matters of geography, he also acknowledges the potential disconnection modern readers may have from these realities:

> It is often difficult to comprehend fully what part is played by the places cited in biblical narrative because the narrator was addressing an audience which was familiar with them. This audience was able to ascribe significance to those spots which we cannot do today because of the distance in time and our inadequate knowledge of the geographical realities of the biblical period.[27]

This is clearly an issue and may well explain why we read so quickly past or misunderstand the geographical information placed into the stories.

At least a partial solution to this dilemma is available. While we will not be able to fully place ourselves in the same position as the initial listeners, we can approximate that knowledge by elevating our understanding of the geography at work in the story. Publications with varying purposes allow us access to knowledge that will be critical for properly understanding the geographical data we meet in a biblical story. We now offer our readers eight categories of material and examples of titles under each category that may serve as a starting point for investigating the geography we meet in a Bible story.

If a city or region is mentioned, our starting point will be a map. Because the original, local audience of these stories had a mental map on which to place toponyms such as Jericho, or Nazareth, or Assyria, or Samaria, we will benefit from improving our own orientation with a map. A variety of Bible atlases are available with high quality maps that will help us visually place a city or region in its context. We recommend the following atlases for your investigation.

Aharoni, Yohanan, Michael Avi-Yonah, Anson F. Rainey, and Ze'ev Safrai. *The Macmillan Bible Atlas.* 3d. ed. New York: Macmillan, 1993.

Beitzel, Barry J. *The Moody Atlas of Bible Lands.* Chicago: Moody Press, 1985.

Brisco, Thomas V. *Holman Bible Atlas* Nashville: Broadman and Holman, 1998.

Rasmussen, Carl G. *NIV Atlas of the Bible.* Grand Rapids: Zondervan, 1989.

Each of the atlases just mentioned also doubles as a historical geography. Historical geographies discuss the impact of geography on the events that lie behind the stories in the Bible. This material can be combined in an atlas or can be presented with less attention to the mapping of those events. As you consider a story within its historical setting, the following historical geographies will make a contribution by placing more emphasis on the way geography interacts with history but with fewer maps.

Aharoni, Yohanan. *The Land of the Bible: A Historical Geography.* Philadelphia: The Westminster Press, 1979.

Pfeiffer, Charles F., and Howard F. Vos. *Wycliffe Historical Geography of Bible Lands.* Chicago: Moody Press, 1967.

Turner, George. *Historical Geography of the Holy Land.* Grand Rapids: Baker Book House, 1973.

The geography of ancient Israel may also be presented to its readers according to a geographical rather than an historical outline. Such geographies will move through a region unit by unit, addressing both the physical and human geography in each.

Baly, Denis, *The Geography of the Bible.* London: Lutterworth Press, 1957.

Beck, John A. *The Land of Milk and Honey: An Introduction to the Geography of Israel.* St. Louis: Concordia Publishing House, 2006.

Orni, Efraim, and Elisha Efrat. *Geography of Israel.* 3d. ed. Philadelphia: The Jewish Publication Society of America, 1976.

Such geographies will be written with great breadth, which comes at the expense of some depth. Consequently, if your geographical needs are focused on a particular topic like hydrology or transportation, specialized titles may better serve your purposes.

Dorsey, David A. *The Roads and Highways of Ancient Israel.* Baltimore: The Johns Hopkins University Press, 1991.

Glueck, Nelson. *The River Jordan.* New York: McGraw-Hill, 1968.

Hareuveni, Nogah. *Tree and Shrub in Our Biblical Heritage.* Kiryat Ono, Israel: Neot Kedumim, 1984.

Issar, Arie. *Water Shall Flow from the Rock: Hydrology and Climate in the Lands of the Bible.* New York: Springer-Verlag, 1990.

Books that specialize in archaeology will also find their place in deepening our understanding of the Bible's geography. Since geography plays an important role in shaping culture and since archaeology is a prime source for learning more about ancient culture, topics related to human geography can be easily pursued in such publications.

Finegan, Jack. *The Archeology of the New Testament.* Princeton: Princeton University Press, 1992.

Hoerth, Alfred J. *Archaeology and the Old Testament.* Grand Rapids: Baker Books, 1998.

King, Philip J., and Lawrence E. Stager. *Life in Biblical Israel.* Library of Ancient Israel. Louisville: Westminster John Knox Press, 2001.

Mazar, Amihai. *Archaeology of the Land of the Bible: 10,000–586 B.C.E.* The Anchor Bible Reference Library. New York: Doubleday, 1992.

Murphy O'Connor, Jerome. *The Holy Land.* Oxford Archaeology Guides. Oxford: Oxford University Press, 1998.

Stern, Ephraim. *Archaeology of the Land of the Bible: The Assyrian, Babylonian, and Persian Periods 732–332 B.C.E.* The Anchor Bible Reference Library. New York: Doubleday, 2001.

Although some may regard the next group of titles as better linked with historical geography, I prefer to separate them because of the unique contribution they make. The nineteenth century was a time when exploration of the Holy Land took on a more scientific tone. These early explorers saw the land of Israel prior to its modernization, when the culture of the land was more closely linked to the time of the Bible than it is today. You will appreciate both their harrowing stories as well as their graphic descriptions of the places they visited.

Lynch, W.F. *Narrative of the United States' Expedition to the Jordan River and the Dead Sea.* Philadelphia: Lea and Blanchard, 1849.

Robinson, Edward. *Biblical Researches in Palestine and the Adjacent Regions 1838 and 1852.* 3 Vols. Jerusalem: Universitas Booksellers, 1970.

Smith, George A. *The Historical Geography of the Holy Land.* Reprint ed. New York: Harper and Row, 1966.

Thompson, William M. *The Land and the Book.* 3 Vols. London: T. Nelson and Sons, 1881.

Long before these nineteenth-century explorers arrived, many Christian pilgrims made their way to the Holy Land to visit the locations associated with the Bible stories they knew. Some of these pilgrims kept a record of their experiences. While these journals were not scientific studies of the geography and while they often favor traditional locations over locations with greater historical credibility, they can also provide us moderns with a look into how things were at a time to which we cannot return. You can read about the moving personal experiences and the geography they encountered in books like these.

Palestine Pilgrim's Text Society. 13 Vols. New York: AMS Press, 1971.

Schur, Nathan. *Twenty Centuries of Christian Pilgrimage to the Holy Land.* Tel Aviv: Dvir Publishing House, 1992.

Wilkinson, John. *Egeria's Travels in Palestine.* Warminster, England: Airs and Phillips, 1999.

Wilkinson, John. *Jerusalem Pilgrims Before the Crusades.* Jerusalem: Ariel, 1977.

Finally, consider the valuable articles that exist within various types of encyclopedias that are associated with biblical studies. By nature and design, encyclopedia articles will present topics in more abbreviated form. But even in their brevity, they may offer us the basics we need as well as being available in ways that other publications listed above may not.

- *The Anchor Bible Dictionary.*
- *Encyclopedia Judaica.*
- *The New Encyclopedia of Archaeological Investigation of the Holy Land.*
- *The Oxford Encyclopedia of Archaeology in the Near East.*
- *The Zondervan Pictorial Encyclopedia of the Bible.*

INTEGRATE THE GEOGRAPHY INTO THE NARRATIVE ANALYSIS

Once you have identified the formal geographical references in the story and have deepened your own understanding of those references, it is time to integrate that knowledge with your analysis of the storyteller's craft. Ask yourself questions like the following: Where has this place or this phenomena been discussed before in the Bible? What information or connotations do those earlier geographical references carry with them into the story before me? How is the geography mentioned in this story affecting my reading of the plot? How is the geography impacting the way in which I perceive and relate to the characters? By asking questions like these, you will be integrating geographical sensitivity into your reading of the Bible story. Once you start down this road, you be will be amazed both at how much geography finds its way into our Bible stories and at how important a role geography can play in shaping the fundamentals of a story.

Conclusion

Book titles create expectations about their contents. And while it is unlikely that you expected a discussion of geography in this book, we hope that you are leaving this chapter persuaded that geography may play a more important role in interpreting a Bible story than you anticipated. With a fresh awareness of what the discipline of geography entails, with an awareness that the storyteller may both be influenced by geography and influencing readers through geography, and with a method in hand, it is time to illustrate the role of geography as we seek meaning in the divine act of storytelling. The next chapter will do just that as it illustrates the process and product of narrative-geographical analysis.

Notes

[1]William D. Pattison, "The Four Traditions of Geography," *Journal of Geography* 63 (1964): 211–16.

[2]For an example, see C. Nicholas Raphael, "Geography and the Bible (Palestine)," in *Anchor Bible Dictionary,* ed. David Noel Freedman (New York: Doubleday, 1992), 5: 964–77.

[3]For an example, see Barry J. Beitzel, *The Moody Atlas of Bible Lands* (Chicago: Moody Press, 1985), 1–71.

[4]William Harmon and C. Hugh Holman, eds., *A Handbook to Literature,* 7th ed. (Upper Saddle River, N.J.: Prentice Hall, 1996), 435–36.

[5]Kenneth Mitchell, "Landscape and Literature," in *Geography and Literature: A Meeting of the Disciplines,* ed. William E. Mallory and Paul Simpson-Housley (Syracuse, N.Y.: Syracuse University Press, 1987), 24.

[6]Ibid., 26.

[7]Susan J. Rosowski, "Willa Cather and the Fatality of Place," in *Geography and Literature,* ed. Mallory and Simpson-Housley, 92. Floyd C. Watkins, *"My Ántonia:* Still, All Day Long, Nebraska," in *In Time and Place* (Athens: The University of Georgia Press, 1977), 73.

[8]Franco Moretti, *Atlas of the European Novel, 1800–1900* (London: Verso, 1998), 70.

[9]Ibid., 6.

[10]*The Onomasticon by Eusebius of Caesarea,* trans. G.S.P. Freeman-Grenville (Jerusalem: Carta), 2003.

[11]Jerome, as quoted in Yohanan Aharoni, *The Land of the Bible: A Historical Geography,* 2d. ed. (Philadelphia: The Westminster Press, 1979), x.

[12]Ibid., ix.

[13]For example, Adele Berlin, *Poetics and Interpretation of Biblical Narrative* (Winona Lake, Ind.: Eisenbrauns, 1994), 102–104; Mark Allan Powell, *What Is Narrative Criticism?* Guides to Historical Scholarship (Minneapolis: Fortress Press, 1990), 70–72.

[14]Leland Ryken, *How to Read the Bible as Literature* (Grand Rapids: Zondervan, 1984), 37; Tremper Longman III, "Biblical Narrative," in *A Complete Literary Guide to the Bible,* ed. Leland Ryken and Tremper Longman III (Grand Rapids: Zondervan, 1993), 75.

[15]Shimon Bar-Efrat, *Narrative Art in the Bible,* JSOT Bible and Literature 17 (Sheffield: Almond Press, 1989), 194.

[16]Yairah Amit, *Reading Biblical Narratives: Literary Criticism and the Hebrew Bible* (Minneapolis: Fortress Press, 2001), 115–25.

[17]Ibid., 119–21.

[18]Ibid., 122–23.

[19]Ibid., 123–24.

[20]John A. Beck, "The Storyteller and Narrative Geography," in *Translators as Storytellers: A Study in Septuagint Translation Technique,* Studies in Biblical Literature 25 (New York: Peter Lang, 2000), 165–96; John A. Beck, "Geography," in *Dictionary for Theological Interpretation of the Bible,* ed. Kevin J. Vanhoozer (Grand Rapids: Baker Academic Press, 2005), 253–56; John A. Beck, "Geography and the Narrative Shape of Numbers 13," *Bibliotheca Sacra* 157 (2000): 270–79; John A. Beck, "Faith in the Face of Famine: The Narrative-Geographical Function of Famine in Genesis," *Journal of Biblical Storytelling* 11 (2002): 58–66; John A. Beck, "Why Did Moses Strike Out? The Narrative-Geographical Shaping of Moses' Disqualification, Numbers 20:1–13," *Westminster Theological Journal* 65 (2003): 135–41; John A. Beck, "Geography as Irony: The Narrative-Geographical Shaping of Elijah's Duel with the Prophets of Baal, 1 Kings 18," *Scandinavian Journal of the Old Testament* 17 (2003): 291–301; John A. Beck, "The Narrative-Geographical Shaping of 1 Samuel 7:5–13," *Bibliotheca Sacra* 162 (2005): 299–309; John A. Beck, "Why Do Joshua's Readers Keep Crossing the River?

The Narrative-Geographical Shaping of Joshua 3–4," *Journal of the Evangelical Theological Society* 48 (2005): 689–99; John A. Beck, "David and Goliath, a Story of Place," *Westminster Theological Journal*, forthcoming.

[21]George Adam Smith, *The Historical Geography of the Holy Land,* 7th ed. (New York: Hodder and Stoughton, 1896), 97.

[22]Ibid., 100–101.

[23]Thomas B. Dozeman, "Geography and History in Herodotus and in Ezra-Nehemiah," *Journal of Biblical Literature* 122 (2003): 466.

[24]David Rhoads and Donald Michie, *Mark as Story: An Introduction to the Narrative of a Gospel* (Philadelphia: Fortress Press, 1982), 63.

[25]Gary Gilbert, "The List of Nations in Acts 2: Roman Propaganda and the Lukan Response," *Journal of Biblical Literature* 121 (2002): 497.

[26]Moretti, *Atlas of the European Novel,* 13.

[27]Bar-Efrat, *Narrative Art in the Bible,* 187.

7

Narrative Geography Illustrated

Narrative geography is the geography placed into a story by the storyteller to shape the literary experience of the reader. The previous chapter introduced this idea, placed it within the context of biblical studies, and discussed a method that might be used to lay bare the role of geography in the storytelling process. The goal of this chapter will be to illustrate how sensitivity to and understanding of geographical data in a story may contribute to our understanding of the plot and to our perceptions of the characters who participate in the unfolding of that plot.

These illustrations will flow from four different Bible stories: one from the New Testament and three from the Old Testament. The texts that follow were selected because the storyteller is making more aggressive use of geography within them and also because they illustrate various types of geography at work. In John 4, we learn about Jesus' meeting with a Samaritan woman at Jacob's well. Our analysis of this story will reveal the storyteller's strategic use of place names (*toponyms*). In Numbers 20, we will explore the role of geology and hydrology in the disqualification of Moses as he obtains water for the Israelites in a way that robs God of his glory. In Joshua 3–4, Joshua and the Israelite army prepare to cross the flood-swollen Jordan River en route to the promised land. This story will show how a geographical feature, the Jordan River, and the realities of ancient travel are summoned to boost the reputation of both Joshua and the Lord. Finally, we turn our attention to the climate of the promised land, particularly its vulnerability to drought. We will see that the divine author of Genesis makes mention of three specific famines that strike the promised land. As Abraham or his descendants are faced by the threat of these famines, their faith is demonstrated, for better or worse, as they weigh their decisions to leave the promised land in the face of such famine. While a comprehensive investigation of the geography in each of these stories would consume many more pages than we have dedicated to this chapter, we will selectively investigate the geography of these texts to illustrate the role narrative-geographical analysis can play in decoding storytelling process.

The Narrative-Geographical Use of Place Names in John 4:1–26

Humans habitually give bodies of water, villages, mountains, and other geographical features distinctive names. This simplifies our conversations, allowing us to refer to specific geographical features or cities with proper names such as "Chicago" or "Lake Michigan." Not surprisingly, the divine storyteller also uses this kind of shorthand in identifying locations. Turning through the pages of our Bible, we encounter references to Jericho, Mount Sinai, the Sea of Galilee, and so on. These proper names of places, or *toponyms,* may be the form of geography most easily identified in a set of Bible verses. But while references are easy to identify, modern readers may have great difficulty linking those proper names to a specific spot on the map, and find it nearly impossible to gather the connotations associated with a place name without deeper investigation.[1] For those willing to expend the energy in learning more about such places, the reward is well worth the effort, as we are about to see in the story of Jesus and the Samaritan woman at Jacob's Well. We will begin with a brief look at the plot of this story before examining the role that geography plays in advancing its cause.

The Plot

The plot of John 4:1–42 is built around the struggle to identify Jesus as the Messiah and the failure of those around him to believe that he is the Messiah. In the first scene (Jn. 4:1–16), the true identity of Jesus' is established, but only after Jesus has a lengthy conversation with the Samaritan woman. The first words that leave the Samaritan woman's mouth, and Jesus' response to her words, quickly move us to the topic of Jesus' identity:

> The Samaritan woman said to him, "How is that you, a Jew, ask a drink of me, a woman of Samaria?" (Jews do not share things in common with Samaritans.) Jesus answered her, "If you knew the gift of God, and who it is that is saying to you, 'Give me a drink,' you would have asked him, and he would have given you living water." (Jn. 4:9–10)

The further exchanges in this scene move the reader closer and closer to the revelation that we hear in the final two verses: "The woman said to him, 'I know that Messiah is coming' (who is called Christ). 'When he comes, he will proclaim all things to us.' Jesus said to her, 'I am he, the one who is speaking to you'" (Jn. 4:25–26). While the close of the first scene falls short of achieving the ultimate climax (achieved when the Samaritans boldly declare their belief that Jesus is the Savior of the world), this scene plays a very important role in setting the stage for that climax by getting Jesus' true identity out into the open.

Place Names in the Plot

In the exposition of John 4, the storyteller mentions a number of place names that make a significant contribution to the unfolding plot and revelation of Jesus' identity. In the first verses, we learn that Jesus is leaving the region of Judea to travel north toward the region of Galilee. The shortest and easiest route between those two regions would take Jesus through the intervening region of Samaria. But this point is far too important for the storyteller to leave to allusion. Thus the narrator formally mentions the fact, "But he [Jesus] had to go through Samaria. So he came to a Samaritan city named Sychar, near the plot of ground that Jacob had given to his son Joseph. Jacob's well was there, and Jesus, tired out by his journey, was sitting by the well" (Jn. 4:4–6). Note how the proper names narrow and refine the location, from the region of Samaria, to a village within Samaria (Sychar), to a specific location within the village (Jacob's well.) Given this amount of geographical precision, we may presume that the storyteller has an important role for geography to play in the story. We will now explore just what that role happens to be.

The first term, "Samaria," directs the reader to a portion of the mountainous region that lies in the middle of the promised land, west of the Jordan River.[2] While the economic viability of this region made it a more desirable place to live, the mention of Samaria carried with it a negative connotation for orthodox Jews living in Jesus' day. This negative connotation grew from historical events that had happened centuries before the details of our story unfold. When the Assyrian Empire defeated the forces of Israel and took command of this geographical area in the eighth century B.C.E., they exported the local, Jewish residents and imported new residents from other countries. These new residents brought with them a bloodline and religious ideology very different from the one God had planned for the promised land. When the Lord used wild animal attacks to make his displeasure known, the Assyrians sent a priest of the true God back into the country to teach them (2 Kings 17:24–28). Even this reintroduction of Israelite theology was not enough to save this part of the country from religious perversions. The author of 2 Kings laments the confused state of religious belief and practice in this area with these words: "So these nations worshiped the LORD, but also served their carved images; to this day their children and their children's children continue to do as their ancestors did" (2 Kings 17:41).

Eventually the residents of Samaria, with their mixed bloodlines and mixed theology, established their own religion based on the Torah of Moses.

Since they were not welcome at the temple of the Jews in Jerusalem, they built their own temple on Mount Gerizim just above the location of New Testament Sychar (alluded to in 2 Macc. 6:2). The flames of social stress that had already been evident in the Old Testament between the Jews and Samaritans (cf. Ezra 4) were further fanned by John Hyrcanus in the time between the Old and New Testaments. This Jewish king, who was expanding the holdings of his kingdom between the time of the Greek and Roman domination of the promised land, attacked the Samaritans and destroyed their temple. This, more than anything else, seems to have created the social rift between Jews and Samaritans that is referenced in gospel stories.

When the storyteller announces that Jesus is making a trip through "Samaria," the first response of the listener might be exactly the one that the woman and narrator articulate within the story itself: "'How is it that you, a Jew, ask a drink of me, a woman of Samaria?' (Jews do not share things in common with Samaritans.)" (John 4:9). At first blush, the geography does not seem to provide a very meaningful setting for an announcement of Jesus' messianic identity.

As the storyteller narrows the geographical setting from Samaria, to Sychar, to Jacob's well that negative connotation begins to evaporate. That is because the very geographical site where Jesus is meeting the Samaritan woman has a long and important connection to the promise of the Messiah, one that goes back many, many years, to well before the time of the Assyrians. To make that connection, readers of this story must see that the New Testament village of Sychar lies less than a mile from Old Testament Shechem, sharing a location at the base of Mount Gerizim and Mount Ebal.[3]

To stand between these two mountains is to stand at the very heart of the promised land. That becomes clear when we travel back in time to the days of Abraham. After Abraham leaves Haran at God's command and arrives in the promised land, the first place where the Lord appears to him is near Shechem (Gen. 12:6). On this important spot along the main north-south road following the watershed of the mountains, Abraham built an altar as a memorial to the incredible promises God had made to him here. His family would grow into a great nation. They would have this land as their own. From that nation on that land, the Messiah would be born. Subsequently, we read that Jacob purchased land in the vicinity of Shechem; and he also built an altar here, further marking the identity of this spot as critical to the divine promises made to this family. Given this powerful history with Abraham and Jacob, Shechem (the location of New Testament Sychar) would have an important and enduring relationship with the rescue plan that starred the Messiah.

The messianic connection of this area does not end with Abraham's family. Abraham and his family remained in the promised land until the time of Joseph, when they left the land for Egypt. After the long stay in

Egypt and Israel's reorganization as a covenant people at Mount Sinai, Joshua brought the Israelites back to the promised land. Following initial victories over Jericho and Ai, Joshua leads the people to Shechem, the setting for John 4. After building an altar on Mount Ebal, Joshua directs half the people to stand in front of Mount Gerizim and half to stand in front of Mount Ebal. Joshua then read the words of Moses to the people, reviewing their responsibilities as a covenant people in this promised land (Josh. 8:30–35).

Joshua brings the Israelites back to this city again after defeating the larger city-states within Canaan. Once the land was secured and divided among the various tribes of Israel, Joshua again assembles the Israelites at Shechem to review their history as bearers of the messianic hope and to witness the people's commitment to the mission (Josh. 24). While the history from the Assyrian invasion on bathes this region in a more negative light, and while the period between the Old and New Testament saw a growing disaffection between Jews and Samaritans, the earlier events associated with the family of Abraham and with Joshua surround the location of Shechem (Sychar) with positive messianic expectations.

Returning to the story in John 4, we note again the careful detail used to establish the setting for this story. Jesus and the Samaritan woman are meeting before Jacob's well at Sychar (Shechem). What a fitting place for a conversation about Jesus' identity as the Messiah! But the storyteller does not rush immediately into Jesus' self-revelation on this spot. The plot of this story moves slowly as the Samaritan woman cautiously and slowly explores the identification of Jesus. As we make that journey with her, it occurs to us that Jesus rarely said in so many words that he was the Messiah. While his actions often demonstrated his connection to the messianic promises, he rarely makes a formal claim to be the Messiah. The story before us is in an exception to that general rule.

The careful attention to the setting of this story suggests that the location of this announcement was not serendipitous but very strategic. Jesus could have declared himself to be the Messiah in any number of locations. Here at Sychar his words take on new power and new force. On this spot where Abraham first received his set of promises from the Lord, on the location where Abraham and Jacob both built memorial altars, on the spot where Joshua brought the people to review and focus on their role in the Messiah's mission not once but twice, the words of Jesus take on even deeper meaning. "The woman said to him, 'I know that Messiah is coming' (who is called Christ). 'When he comes, he will proclaim all things to us.' Jesus said to her, 'I am he, the one who is speaking to you'" (Jn. 4:25–26). Narrative geographical analysis has done its job. It has drawn our attention to the geographical details in the text. It has challenged us to learn more about the location and connotation of that geography. In the process, it has revealed the importance of those place names the storyteller used. While

Samaria might seem an unlikely location for this Messianic revelation, it is now clear that Sychar imbues the proclamation of Jesus with greater depth and meaning.

The Narrative-Geographical Use of Geology in Numbers 20:1–13

While place names may be the most frequent and obvious form of geography to appear within a Bible story, references to geology are more rare and difficult to decode. Nevertheless, the geology of the wilderness of Zin plays a critical role in explaining the story that highlights the disqualification of Moses to enter the promised land (Num. 20:1–13).[4] Following the Israelites extended stay in Egypt, God sent Moses as the leader who would bring them freedom from their captivity. He leads Israel through the water of the Red Sea, through various trials in the wilderness, and to the foot of Mount Sinai. The reader of Numbers has every reason to expect that this same Moses will lead God's people across the Jordan River into the promised land, bringing his lifelong quest to a close. But that expectation is suddenly disabled in the wilderness of Zin. What happens in the story we are about to study leads God to tell Moses that he has been disqualified as the leader who will bring God's people into the promised land. Our goal here will be to observe the role that geology plays in communicating the reason for this disqualification.

The Plot

As the storyteller begins, it appears as if this story's plot will revolve around the crisis caused by a lack of water and that the resolution of the crisis will come about as Moses provides water for the thirsty throngs of Israelites. When Moses strikes the rock bringing forth a rush of water, we presume that the crisis is over and that the story will wind down to a quiet close. Yet at just this moment, the voice of God announces a judgment that the listener did not see coming. Suddenly, the story is no longer revolving around the provision of water but about the topic of leadership.

Geology and the Plot

In the exposition of the story, the author tells us that these events are occurring in the wilderness of Zin. This region lies between Beer-sheba and Kadesh-Barnea, just north of the wilderness of Paran.[5] The topography, the lack of vegetation, and the lack of precipitation in this region conspire to make it a region hostile to human survival.[6] God used this geographical setting to test the Israelites. He allows a shortage of water to reach crisis proportions, all the while inviting the Israelites to trust the Lord's providing hand. But doubt and misgivings outpaced their faith. The people rose up against the divinely appointed leaders, pressing against them with threatening words: "Now there was no water for the congregation; so they gathered together against Moses and against Aaron" (Num. 20:2). They were convinced that they and their livestock would perish from lack of vegetation and water. "Why have you brought us up out of Egypt, to bring us to this wretched place? It is no place for grain, or figs, or vines, or pomegranates; and there is no water to drink" (Num. 20:5). The shortage of water in the harsh landscape of the wilderness of Zin appears to provide the crisis that needs resolution.

After consulting with the Lord, Moses and Aaron stepped before the crowd to provide a solution for the thirsty Israelites: "Then Moses lifted up his hand and struck the rock twice with his staff; water came out abundantly, and the congregation and their livestock drank" (Num. 20:11). Just as Moses had struck the rock at Rephidim (Exodus 17:6), providing water for the thirsty Israelites, so he now strikes the rock in the wilderness of Zin. His actions produce the expected results as water gushes from the rock, providing both mortals and animals with the much-needed water. Following this life-giving miracle, we might expect to hear words of repentance from people who had failed to trust their God; or, at the very least, we expect to hear words of thanks and celebration for God's loving kindness. But the people do not speak; God does. Coming to Moses, God speaks these fateful words, "Because you did not trust me, to show my holiness before the eyes of the Israelites, therefore you shall not bring this assembly into the land that I have given them" (20:12).

This unexpected condemnation places the topic of appropriate leadership on the table and sends the reader back into the story's details seeking an explanation for this surprising turn of events. When we reinvestigate those details, we notice that the Lord's instructions given to Moses were, in fact, not followed closely. While the striking of the rock recalls an earlier procedure used by Moses, God had not told Moses to strike the rock in this story. Here is the language we missed: "The LORD spoke to Moses saying, 'Take the staff, and assemble the congregation, you and your brother Aaron, and command the rock before their eyes to yield its water. Thus you shall bring water out of the rock for them; thus you shall provide drink for the congregation and their livestock'" (20:7–8). Moses was to speak to the rock.

How does the striking of the rock (as Moses had done at Rephidim) rather than speaking to the rock result in such a stern judgment? The answer to the question lies in the geology that distinguishes the story in Numbers 20 from the one in Exodus 17. First of all, we note something that English readers will have difficulty observing because English translations have not fully represented the unique geological language used in these verses. The storyteller has a variety of Hebrew words that might be used to describe a rock. In particular, three are evident in the Torah. One is the generic word for "stone" that carries no unique connotations. Another word for "rock" is typically used to distinguish the harder quartz and granite of the southern Sinai. The word here is used less frequently than the other two. It designates the softer and more porous stone of the wilderness of Zin.[7] Lest the reader miss the point being made through the geological reference, this word for the softer stone is not used just once but five times within the thirteen verses of this story. That repetition suggests that the divine storyteller sees something important about this "rock." In fact, this rock will give us the most helpful clue in understanding why Moses' act of striking the rock brought such a harsh judgment upon him.

To obtain this insight, we need to return briefly to the hydrology and rainfall in the region where this miracle occurred. The wilderness of Zin totals only about four inches of rain per year at the higher elevations.[8] The water that does not evaporate or immediately run off the surface is pressed downward by gravity through the soft, upper courses of limestone found in the wilderness of Zin. When this seeping moisture encounters a harder layer of limestone, it begins to travel laterally along the seam between soft and hard limestone, exiting as a spring on the sides of rising terrain.[9] Thus water naturally flows from rock in this region.

Since the seeping water dissolves some of the softer limestone through which it passes, it is not water alone that exits from the rock, but a mixture of water and chalk. The warm desert air immediately begins to evaporate the water from this mixture. The chalk that is left, following this evaporation, begins to crystallize at the exit point, shutting off the flow of water exiting the rock. A mineral cap can completely stop the flow of water from the rock. Although the water stops flowing, the water from successive seasons of rain continues to collect behind this mineral cap under increasing hydrologic pressure. This hidden water supply awaits the hand of the wise water seeker, who only needs to give the mineral cap a mighty blow to release the liquid treasure lying behind it. To this day, those who know the geology in this region can cause water to flow from a rock.[10]

The geology associated with the companion story of Exodus 17 is very different from the geology just described. When the people came to Moses with water needs near Rephidim (Ex. 17), they were experiencing thirst in a land graced by the impermeable red granite of the southern Sinai wilderness. This rock sheds water rather than absorbing it. Thus the mightiest of blows landed upon the rock at Rephidim would not have produced a small cup of water through natural means or human ingenuity. In this geological context, God instructs Moses to strike the rock (Ex. 17:6). Water flowed from the rock, making it apparent to all that God deserved the glory for the extraordinary miracle accomplished here.

That same technique deployed in the wilderness of Zin could lead the observers to a very different conclusion. The porous rock of the wilderness of Zin might have looked dry, but it contained stored water that the wise reader of the rock could release. For this reason, God changed tactics. Moses was not to "strike" the rock as he had done earlier at Rephidim; rather, he was to "speak" to the rock. The miraculous flow of water that followed would then have a clear and unmistakable link to the command and power of their God. Whether out of fear of failure or out of fear for his own life, Moses resorted to a Bedouin trick he may have learned while living in this wilderness earlier in his life. In doing so, he not only disobeyed a direct command from his superior but also opened the door for misunderstanding, since it appeared that he had brought about this water deliverance through his own shrewd actions. Rather than directing attention to the Lord's intervention, he directed attention to himself.

So a story that appears to be about the provision of water is really a story about leadership. Not even the Moses, the man who spoke with God face to face, would be permitted to take honor at the expense of the Lord. Thus Moses' imprudent action disqualified this great leader from bringing his lifelong quest to its conclusion. The divine storyteller leaves us with a message about leadership: the actions and words of God's leaders must always give glory to God. This message only becomes clear when we understand how the storyteller made use of geography in this story.

The Narrative-Geographical Use of a Feature in Joshua 3–4

A third form of geography that the storyteller may deploy within the narrative is the geographical feature. In Joshua 3–4, the features that dominate the narrative are the Jordan River and the transportation issues involved in crossing it. As the divine storyteller describes the Israelites' entry into the promised land, formal mention of the Jordan River and of the crossing of the Jordan River meets the reader's eyes again and again. The notion of "crossing" occurs twenty-one times within this story. Mention of "the Jordan" occurs no less than twenty-eight times in these two chapters (more than once every two verses, on average).[11]

As the book of Joshua opens, two very important changes have occurred since the disqualification of Moses. Moses has died, and Joshua has risen as the newly appointed leader of God's people on the march. We also note that Israel's entrance into the promised land is no longer a remote hope but an imminent reality. The people of the promise are encamped on the plains of Moab on the east side of the Jordan River, ready to cross the Jordan River and enter the promised land. In the first chapter of Joshua, the storyteller allows us to hear the commissioning speech that the Lord gives at the time Joshua takes the reins of leadership. We also hear Joshua's words of encouragement to the people. In the second chapter, we learn of the reconnaissance mission Joshua directs at the city of Jericho. All this ultimately leads to the chapters of interest to us here (3–4), where the preparations for the river crossing and the actual crossing itself are detailed.

Characterization

The sheer number of verses dedicated to this story makes it clear that the crossing of the Jordan River is an important event in the mind of God.

The story could have been told in a much more abbreviated fashion. The events of that day and the retelling of the events of that day were to have an enduring impact both on the way that the people perceived Joshua and the way they perceived the Lord. The storyteller articulates both intentions in clear and unmistakable language. In speaking with Joshua, the Lord says, "This day I will begin to exalt you in the sight of all Israel, so that they may know that I will be with you as I was with Moses" (Josh. 3:7). In his speech to the Israelites, Joshua says that this day's events will raise their awareness of God's powerful presence among them: "By this you shall know that among you is the living God who without fail will drive out from before you the Canaanites, Hittites, Hivites, Perizzites, Girgashites, Amorites, and Jebusites" (Josh. 3:10). Just as the characterization of Joshua and the Lord were enhanced via this event, so the narrative account of the event is to produce the same results among those who hear it (Josh. 4:14 and 4:24). Given the frequent and persistent references to the Jordan River, we will now explore how this geography participates in accomplishing those goals for the storyteller. We will begin by examining the geographical realities of crossing the Jordan River and its connotations before turning our attention to the way the storyteller has used this geography to enhance the reputation of Joshua and the Lord.

Crossing the Jordan River

One could enter the promised land without crossing the Jordan River either by pushing through the Negev in the south or past the flanks of Mount Hermon in the north. But each of these entry points had their own risks, problems, and complications. Nevertheless, they remain out of view in our story because the Lord had a plan for the Israelites to enter their inheritance from their encampment just northeast of the Dead Sea on the plains of Moab. This entry point, opposite the city of Jericho, made it imperative for the Israelite army to physically cross the Jordan River.

While our first thought might be that Joshua would look for a bridge, this was not an option for the Israelites. Bridges did not become a part of the transportation system in this region for centuries. To live in the world of Joshua meant to live within its limitations. Joshua and his army would have to wade and swim across the river preferably at a natural ford. Such fords were typically found where a tributary joined the river being crossed. At such locations, silt carried down stream by the tributary would enter the main river and make the river shallower.[12] This is exactly what we find at the location of Joshua's crossing point opposite Jericho where the Wadi Qilt enters the Jordan.

The geography informs us not only how the river would be crossed but also indicates that this crossing would be extremely dangerous. This narrator alludes to these dangers by saying, "Now the Jordan overflows all its banks throughout the time of harvest" (Josh. 3:15a). This may not seem like a critical observation at first blush, but it heightens the complexity and danger of the crossing significantly. At other times of the year, one could expect to cross the ford opposite Jericho by wading through water that was three to four feet deep. During the spring flooding, the water at this ford would have been ten to twelve feet deep and up to one hundred and forty feet wide.[13] During this season, the riverbanks giving access to the river would have been a mire, making each step toward the river proper a comical struggle to negotiate mud that might be several feet deep.

The greatest risk to life and limb would not necessarily have been the depth of the river or the muddy banks, but rather the swiftness of the river's current. We get some appreciation for the hydrologic power of the current from the American explorer William Lynch. Standing on the bow of his boat in the nineteenth century, Lynch described his experience running the river with these words. "With its tumultuous rush, the river hurried us onward and we knew not what the next moment would bring forth—whether it would dash us upon a rock or plunge us down a cataract."[14] The same concerns for the swiftness of the current existed for the early Christian pilgrims who came to be baptized in the Jordan River. Despite the leaders' efforts to give these pilgrims a safe and meaningful experience, each year some were "carried away by the rapid stream and perished."[15]

When we become aware of these geographical realities, we can better understand why ancient travelers dreaded the portion of their trip that involved a crossing of the Jordan River. In a letter dating to the thirteenth century B.C.E., one such traveler lists various problems associated with travel in ancient Israel. Chief among those concerns was nothing less than the danger associated with crossing the Jordan River.[16] While we may not think twice about crossing a river on our way to the store, the biblical authors viewed crossing the flooding Jordan River as a heroic act (1 Chr. 12:15). So, by studying the geography formally included by the storyteller in this story from Joshua, we have learned a bit more about how the river would be crossed and the inherent risks associated with the crossing. Each time the word "Jordan" returns to the storyteller's lips, the geographically informed reader is reminded again and again of these matters. This crossing would be difficult, time consuming, and risky.

The Characterization of Joshua and the Lord

This now leads us to inquire about how this information plays a role in accomplishing the storyteller's stated goals of enhancing the people's perception of both Joshua and the Lord. If Moses had still been alive, the people would have been looking in his direction at this crucial time. But Moses was dead. The untested leader, Joshua, now stood before them on the banks of the roiling river.

Everyone knew that the advancing army must cross the river, but the logistical challenges of making that crossing must have given Joshua great pause. Carl von Clausewitz was a nineteenth-century Prussian military strategist. He wrote a book entitled *On War* that continues to be consulted and studied by those involved in military planning. Clausewitz details a variety of challenges the nineteenth-century generals faced, including an entire chapter dedicated to the topic of crossing a river. Because of the significant risks associated with a river crossing while in a combat setting, he says, "No general will place himself in such a position unless he can count on substantial moral and material superiority."[17]

Joshua knew the risks before him. The river crossing would not happen quickly. Given the depth of the water and mud on the banks that can be as deep as a horse's knees,[18] the advance across the river would be painfully slow leaving the soldiers who were crossing the river vulnerable to attack from the residents on the western shore. Should a retreat become necessary, the water and the mud would again slow the process, leaving dozens of soldiers stranded and vulnerable. He had to face the question of how many individuals might be lost to drowning in the swift, zigzag current that compromised footing and pulled one into the deepest part of the river.[19]

Great leaders can be defined in connection with the great challenges they overcome. Assyrian generals boasted about their crossing of the Tigris and Euphrates Rivers, listing such crossings among their greatest achievements.[20] Within the Bible itself, we find that Moses was lifted in the eyes of the people as God used him to create a path through the water of the Red Sea (Ex. 14:31).

Now the storyteller puts all eyes on Joshua. The Israelites rocked nervously from one foot to another, contemplating the perils of the river crossing for three days. The storyteller recreates some of that drama by formally mentioning the Jordan River over and over again in the lengthy lead-up to the crossing itself.

Then, from the mouth of Joshua, the solution arises. Of course, it is the Lord who provides the miracle. His divine hand causes the water to stop flowing and allows the Israelite army to cross over on dry ground. But in this narrative we hear Joshua's voice more often than the Lord's.[21] Joshua directs the people to prepare, tells them what to expect, and brings them to the riverbank. Then, suddenly, the difficulty of the crossing, the time of exposure during the crossing, and the risk all evaporate with the water. Since the solution is mediated through the leadership of Joshua, the people respond as the Lord had intended. "On that day the LORD exalted Joshua in the sight of all Israel; and they stood in awe of him, as they stood in awe of Moses, all the days of his life" (Josh. 4:14). Thus the repetition of the word "Jordan" by the storyteller redirects the reader again and again to the problem facing the Israelite army on the march so that we might more fully celebrate the mortal leader who provides the solution to those problems.

As the characterization of Joshua is impacted by the geography in this story, so that geography also impacts the characterization of the Lord. The geographical motif of a water obstacle confronting the Israelites clearly recalls the days of the Exodus and the crossing of the Red Sea. The use of similar vocabulary used to describe the two water miracles (Exodus 3 and Joshua 3–4) creates a link between these two stories.[22] But this link is too important to leave to subtle allusion. The storyteller formally makes this connection by saying, "For the LORD your God dried up the waters of the Jordan for you until you crossed over, as the LORD your God did to the Red Sea, which he dried up for us until we crossed over." (Josh. 4:23). On his own, Joshua lacked the power and skills to remove all the difficulty and danger associated with the river crossing. But the unlimited power of their God made all things possible. The sequel is to have the same affect on the Israelites as the original. In both cases, the miraculous removal of the water obstacle leads the people to an awe-filled respect for the Lord (Ex. 14:31 and Josh. 4:24).

Not merely the power demonstrated in drying up of the river but also the faithfulness of God is celebrated in this story. The storyteller's repetition of "Jordan" recalls not just the Red Sea crossing but the array of promises associated with the land that lay just across the river from the Israelite camp. The Jordan River is mentioned 165 times in the Old Testament. Of those, 117 are associated with the notion of border.[23] This connotation is particularly prominent in the five books of the Torah. In Numbers, God identifies the Jordan River as the border to the promised land (Num. 33:48–51; 34:12). In Deuteronomy, "Jordan" appears twenty-seven times in references that remind the people again and again that they will be crossing the Jordan River to enter the land of their inheritance (Deut. 2:29; 3:27; 4:26; 9:1; 11:31; 12:10; 27:2; 30:18; 31:13; 32:47). As the storyteller opens the account of Joshua, we get no farther than the second sentence before the word "Jordan" surfaces in connection with the commissioning of Joshua. "My servant Moses is dead. Now proceed to cross the Jordan, you and all this people, into the land that I am giving to them, to the Israelites" (Josh. 1:2). Thus the reader has been conditioned through previous mention of the Jordan River to associate this river and particularly the crossing of the Jordan River with God's promise to give the land of Canaan to this nation.

As the storyteller repeats the word "Jordan" again and again in this narrative, the reader is brought to see the water not just as an obstacle to the military assault, but as a border to the promised land. God had removed a water obstacle from the path of the Israelites as they departed the land of Egypt. Now as a rhetorical bookend, God removes the water obstacle that hinders their entrance into a land long promised to the Israelites. God has been faithful to God's word. Who could not celebrate the great things God has done? The stone memorial established at the point of the crossing was to be an ongoing reminder that God had kept God's promise in a dramatic way. The story that captured details of that event endures in a way those stones did not, "so that all the peoples of the earth may know that the hand of the LORD is mighty, and so that you may fear the LORD your God forever" (Josh. 4:24).

So again we have seen how the storyteller's formal use of geography directs the impact of the narrative. By attending to the geography in this story, we may come to more fully appreciate the fact that the Jordan River represented both a threatening obstacle and an important boundary for the Israelites. The stress placed on this geographical feature and its connotations plays a significant role in accomplishing the goals of the story, to enhance the character of Joshua, and to glorify the faithfulness and power of God.

The Narrative-Geographical Use of Famine in Genesis

Our final illustration of the use of geography by the storyteller involves the climate of Israel and particularly the threat of famine in the promised land.[24] The divine storyteller makes use of famine in three stories from Genesis: one about Abram (Abraham), one about Isaac, and one about Jacob. These men and their families were all living within the promised land. While this land certainly appeared to be a very rich and diverse land to those who entered it after living for decades in the wilderness, the land of milk and honey has a very fragile ecosystem largely devoid of the natural resources modern readers might take for granted.[25] This land is so destitute in regards to natural resources that it becomes a land that cultivates and inspires faith. That reason alone may have caused the Lord to select this land rather than another to be the place where God's covenant people would live.[26] The narratives about Abraham and his descendants tell a story of faith and struggle. As we are about to see, the horrifying realities of famine put faith in tension with perceived reality. On the one hand, these men had God's directive to live in the land. On the other hand, their very survival seemed to depend on their leaving the land. In this tension their faith is tested and comes to light.

Characterization

The decision to migrate or to remain in the land was a decision with far-reaching consequences. The decision to remain put every member of the family in harm's way. The decision to migrate meant disrupting the rhythm of the family lifestyle and leaving the security of a land that was known. For Abraham's family the stakes were even higher. God had promised Abraham that his family would become a great nation and would live in this land. The rescue plan that would bring salvation for all people depended on the presence of Abraham's family in this land. Thus each time a famine threatened the region, each person had a chance to demonstrate faith in action. That is not to say that an act of migrating or staying could be easily characterized as right or wrong. As the storyteller shares the stories of Abraham, Isaac, and Jacob with us, we observe the way in which they made the decision to stay or migrate. That information participates in the characterization of their faith as demonstrated in the face of famine. In what follows, we will again expand our understanding of the climate in the promised land and the intrusion of famine. Then, using that enhanced geographical knowledge, we will consider the way in which the storyteller illuminates their decisions to stay or migrate from the promised land.

Climate and Famine

To appreciate the mention of famine in these stories means to appreciate the issue of water in this land. All of us have a need for fresh water, but the land of Canaan is very stingy in paying out this natural resource to its residents. By contrast to the average citizen of the United States, with a per capita availability of 10,000 cubic meters (2.6 million gallons) of water, the resident of ancient Israel likely had considerably less than 460 cubic meters available.[27] The less water available to residents of a country, the less buffering they have when drought strikes.

An interruption in the rainfall cycle was the most likely cause of the famines we read about in Genesis. In contrast to other cultures around them, the residents of Canaan enjoyed a precipitation-based hydrology rather than a river- or lake-based hydrology.[28] This means that the fresh water the family of Abraham enjoyed was drawn from cisterns, wells, and springs that had a direct connection to the annual rainfall cycle. The Lord wanted to be sure that the Israelites knew of this unique feature of the promised land. By contrast to the river-based hydrology they had experienced in Egypt, they would come to depend on the rain that the Lord provided in their new home:

> For the land that you are about to enter to occupy is not like the land of Egypt, from which you have come, where you sow your seed and irrigate by foot like a vegetable garden. But the land you are crossing over to occupy is a land of hills and valleys, watered by rain from the sky. (Deut. 11:10–11)

The seasonal rainfall cycle follows a somewhat predictable pattern in the promised land related to the summer and winter seasons. The summer season lasts from mid-June through mid-September. While this is a season of high humidity, the atmosphere is dominated by high pressure, a condition that discourages the formation of clouds and precludes the necessary dynamic for rain to develop. Consequently, during the summer season, no rain will fall.[29]

By the time October rolls around, a change in the jet stream begins to change the dynamics of the atmosphere. During the winter season, a series of low-pressure areas will cross the borders of Israel, bringing with them the promise of both clouds and much-needed rainfall. From October through April, the land will experience the early, middle, and late rains referred to in Deuteronomy 11:14. Each season of rain will make its unique contribution to the agricultural and pastoral life of Israel's residents: softening the soil for planting, watering the maturing plants, lifting the water table for the springs, filling wells and cisterns. Since the promised land has a rain-based hydrology, it requires the consistency of this winter season to guarantee the well being of its residents.[30]

Still, the integrity of the annual rainfall cycle is not guaranteed. "Years of drought and famine run like a scarlet thread through the ancient history of Palestine."[31] If the seasonal rainfall is mistimed, if the total rainfall is less than expected, or if the rain fails all together, then the pastures will lack vitality, the grain fields will wither, and the water sources will go dry. For those of us accustomed to the predictable flow of water from our faucets, it is difficult to know how deeply this matter impacted the thinking and well being of those living in the biblical world. Perhaps Jeremiah offers the most helpful window into these conditions. Note the broad and profound impact that drought brings to the land:

> The word of the LORD that came to Jeremiah concerning the drought:
> Judah mourns and her gates languish; they lie in gloom on the ground,
>> and the cry of Jerusalem goes up.
> Her nobles send their servants for water;
>> they come to the cisterns,
> they find no water,
>> they return with their vessels empty.
> They are ashamed and dismayed
>> and cover their heads,
> because the ground is cracked.
>> Because there has been no rain on the land
> the farmers are dismayed;
>> they cover their heads.
> Even the doe in the field forsakes her newborn fawn
>> because there is no grass.
> The wild asses stand on the bare heights,
>> they pant for air like jackals;
> their eyes fail because
>> there is no herbage. (Jer. 14:1–6)

Other biblical authors speak about the related maladies of disease (1 Kings 8:37), pestilence, plague (Deut. 32:24), and the complete collapse of morality (2 Kings 6:25–29). This window into the culture of the biblical world suggests that famine was among the most dreadful and most feared events that confronted the residents of ancient Israel. When families in ancient Israel faced famine, they had to make a decision. Either they would remain in the land and try to ride out the famine, or they would migrate to a land untouched by the shortage of water and food.

Famine and the Characterization of Abraham, Isaac, and Jacob

It is now time to carry those insights into the literary shaping of Genesis, as the divine storyteller narrates three stories related to the matter of famine in the promised land. The tension in each narrative is created by opposing pressures. On the one hand was the pressure to leave this land to avoid the hardship, pain, and even death that famine brought. This pressure was amplified even more in the southern reaches of the country, where Abraham, Isaac, and Jacob resided, since the famine would always be more severe there than in the north. On the other hand was the pressure to remain in the land because of the promises the Lord had made to Abraham, his son, and his grandson. That promise is given directly to Abraham in Genesis 12:6, to Isaac in Genesis 22:17–18 and 26:3–4, and to Jacob in 28:13–14. They could not mistake God's intentions on this point. These men and their families belonged in the land of Canaan. To leave this land compromised the intentions of God to bring the messiah into the world through this family and within the borders of this land.

While not every event from the lives of these men finds its way into the pages of Genesis, three stories related to famines do. That makes the famines mentioned in Genesis a literary motif that invites the listener to bring these stories into one another's company for comparison. When we do, it becomes apparent that the decision of each individual reflects on them at a stage in their faith journey. Since the storyteller has given this formal invitation, we will now compare the experiences of Abraham, Isaac, and Jacob as they exercise their faith in the face of famine.

The story of Abram (the future Abraham) begins to take on shape and detail in the first verses of Genesis 12. God summoned him to leave his homeland and move to a new home. Upon his arrival in Shechem, the Lord affirmed that he had arrived in the land where he was to live (12:6–7). Abram continued his journey southward through Bethel until arriving in the southern portion of the promised land, the Negev (Negeb in NRSV). Every expectation of the reader at this point is that Abram would remain in this land awaiting the fulfillment of the other promises God had made him in connection with this land. We do not know how much real time passes between 12:9 and 12:10, but in the brief time it takes the reader to pass between these verses, we observe a shocking change in circumstances. "Now there was a famine in the land. So Abram went down to Egypt to reside there as an alien, for the famine was severe in the land" (12:10).

In the space of half a verse, the storyteller brings us to a point of tension in Abram's life. Should he stay or should he go? In the place where we might expect to hear that Abram is wrestling with this decision or where we might expect to hear him pouring out his concerns in prayer, we hear instead that he has evacuated the promised land. In the space of less than a verse, we are rushed from the famine-stricken Canaan to the security of Egypt, where the Nile River provides the promise of uninterrupted fresh water no matter whether it rains or not.

What does this retreat from the promised land suggest about Abram's faith commitment? Some have sought to characterize this decision as one that grieved Abraham deeply.[32] Others observe that he was responding to circumstances that lay outside his control, and so defend his decision as entirely appropriate given the circumstances.[33] But we have to wonder if the storyteller intends for us to jump in and rescue the character of Abram quite so quickly. All that follows in the closing verses of this chapter, particularly Abram's willingness to surrender his wife Sarai to the bedroom of Pharaoh, shows a decided lack of faith on Abram's part. It rather appears that Abram's hasty retreat from the promised land betrays a lack of faith. He quickly abandons this fragile but critical homeland without report of reflection, prayer, or thought.

As the storyteller advances the narrative beyond the time of Abraham, we find that his son, Isaac, faces a similar circumstance. The first words of Genesis 26 are designed to draw the listener back to Genesis 12. "Now there was a famine in the land, besides the former famine that had occurred in the days of Abraham" (26:1a). The storyteller expects us to be listening carefully. We are not only to make the link with Abraham but also wonder how Isaac might respond to this time of tension. Would the son have learned a lesson from his father and avoid the risks associated with leaving the promised land for Egypt, or would he also be drawn by the siren song of the Nile's ever-flowing stream? It takes less than a verse to answer the question. Isaac strikes out for Egypt just like his father. Once again there is no pause for reflection, no struggle in prayer, only sudden and shocking retreat from the land that means everything for the plan that will rescue the world from sin.

At Gerar, the Lord interrupts Isaac's flight south and orders him to remain in the land. "Do not go down to Egypt; settle in the land that I shall show you" (26:2). He reminds Isaac of all that is at stake by reviewing the connection between this land, famine-stricken as it was, with the promise of the messiah.

> Reside in this land as an alien, and I will be with you, and will bless you; for to you and to your descendants I will give all these lands, and I will fulfill the oath that I swore to your father Abraham. I will make your offspring as numerous as the stars of heaven, and will give to your offspring all these lands; and all the nations of the earth shall gain blessing for themselves through your offspring. (Gen. 26:3–4).

Isaac stumbles in his faith (26:7) . Like Abraham, he portrays his wife as his sister. But eventually he gets it right. He terminates his flight to Egypt and begins to dig a series of wells (26:18–22), each one closer to Beer-sheba, where a final well marked a return to his faith roots (26:32). So once again famine illuminates character as we see what kind of faith Isaac had when confronted by famine in the promised land.

Finally, we encounter Isaac's son, Jacob. His experience with famine is set within the larger story of Joseph found in Genesis 37–50. The ups and downs of Joseph's life wrenched him from the promised land bringing him to Egypt first as a slave, only to later become a royal advisor. No famine was in view at first—only the jealousy of his brothers and their plotting to be rid of him. But Joseph's change in status is directly connected to his decoding of Pharaoh's dream that predicted the coming of a seven-year famine in the region (41:27). When that famine became a reality, it set the world around Jacob into motion. "Moreover, all the world came to Joseph in Egypt to buy grain, because the famine became severe throughout the world" (41:57). In particular, the storyteller informs us that this famine was also creating hardship in Canaan (42:5: 43:1). Joseph now invites his father and his family to come and live with him in Egypt. Once again, careful listeners are expected to wonder: Would Jacob take his family to Egypt as his grandfather had and as his father intended to do?

As the need for food and love for Joseph pulled powerfully on Jacob, urging him to move to Egypt with all haste, we find the decision to leave the promised land portrayed in a very different way than it had been portrayed in the narratives of Abram or Isaac. Jacob does not rush from the land. In fact, he gets as far as Beer-sheba, the southern boundary of this land, where he stops. Before setting so much as a foot outside the land, he hesitates, takes time to worship, and questions whether or not a famine or even reunion with his long-lost son would justify his departure from Canaan. A tradition preserved in the *Book of Jubilees* says Jacob had decided to remain in the promised land and invite Joseph to come and visit him there (44:3). While only a tradition, the spirit of that tradition appears to have merit. Jacob was so hesitant to leave the promised land that God had to put in an appearance to make it happen. God speaks to Jacob in a vision: "I am the God of your fathers, the God of Abraham and Isaac. Do not fear to go down to Egypt, because I will make you into a great people there. I shall go down with you, and I shall bring you (back) and you will be buried in this land. And Joseph will place his hand upon your eyes" Do not fear. Go down to Egypt (44:5b-6).[34] Despite the severity of the famine, Jacob presumed that the God who commanded his presence in this land would also preserve his presence in this land. He would stay put. It took a personal message from God that affirmed his right to leave the land—and, even more importantly, that assured him his family would return to the land–before this man of faith would leave. In contrast to Abram and Isaac, this is truly faith in the face of famine.

Thus we see that the land of Canaan was not merely a home for the Patriarchs. It was also a forum in which their faith was tested and revealed. The divine storyteller makes use of a natural phenomenon, famine, to create the setting where Abram, Isaac, and Jacob each have a chance to give a testimony to their faith. Only when we know the great perils that accompany famine in this region and see the literary link between each of these stories can we appreciate the strategic use of geography in the storyteller's craft, a strategy that reveals faith in the face of famine.

Conclusion

Each story we studied above contains many other geographical references. But even in this *selective* sample, it becomes apparent that the storyteller will deploy geography in a narrative that shapes the plot, characterization, and meaning of that story. We can only hope that this small sample might sensitize you to the use of geography in Bible stories and whet your appetite for learning more about that geography. Most importantly, we hope that it may lead you to inquire more closely into the ways in which the divine storyteller uses geography to shape our understanding of these stories.

Notes

[1] For a helpful discussion on the use of place names in the Bible, see the chapter entitled, "The Study of Toponomy," in Yohanan Aharoni, *The Land of the Bible: A Historical Geography* (Philadelphia: The Westminster Press, 1979), 105–30.

[2] John A. Beck, *The Land of Milk and Honey: An Introduction to the Geography of Israel* (St. Louis: Concordia Publishing House, 2006), 50–51.

[3] Carl G. Rasmussen, *NIV Atlas of the Bible* (Grand Rapids: Zondervan, 1989), 170.

[4] For a more complete study of the geographical shaping of this text, see John A. Beck, "Why Did Moses Strike Out? The Narrative-Geographical Shaping of Moses' Disqualification Numbers 20:1–13," *Westminster Theological Journal* 65 (2003): 135–41.

[5] Aharoni, *Land of the Bible,* 31.

[6] Beck, *Land of Milk and Honey,* 130–31; Barry J. Beitzel, *The Moody Atlas of Bible Lands* (Chicago: Moody Press, 1985), 37.

[7] For a more complete discussion of this distinction, see Beck, "Why Did Moses Strike Out?" 139–40.

[8] Efraim Orni and Elisha Efrat, *Geography of Israel,* 3d. ed. (Philadelphia: The Jewish Publication Society of America), 27.

[9] Arie Issar, *Water Shall Flow from the Rock: Hydrology and Climate in the Lands of the Bible* (New York: Springer, 1990), 119.

[10] Ibid., 121. I am personally indebted to Dr. James Martin of Bible World Seminars, who first suggested this explanation to me during our time in this wilderness.

[11] For a more complete discussion of the geography at work in these chapters, see John A. Beck, "Why Do Joshua's Readers Keep Crossing the River? The Narrative-Geographical Shaping of Joshua 3–4," *Journal of the Evangelical Theological Society* 48:4 (2005): 689–99.

[12] Menashe Har-el, "The Pride of the Jordan," *Biblical Archaeologist* 41 (June 1978): 69. The crossings of the Jordan River that we read about in the Old Testament consistently happen at such fords (Gen. 32:22–23; Judg. 3:28; 7:24; 8:4; 12:5–6; 2 Sam. 17:16, 22; 19:18).

[13]Carl Ritter, *The Comparative Geography of Palestine and the Sinaitic Peninsula* (New York: Greenwood, 1968), 4.51–53.

[14]William F. Lynch, *Narrative of the United States' Expedition to the Jordan River and the Dead Sea* (Philadelphia: Lea and Blanchard, 1849), 255.

[15]Ritter, *Comparative Geography of Palestine and the Sinaitic Peninsula*, 3.40.

[16]James B. Prichard, ed., *Ancient Near Eastern Texts Relating to the Old Testament*, 2d ed. (Princeton: Princeton University Press, 1955), 477.

[17]Carl von Clausewitz, *On War* (Princeton: Princeton University Press, 1976), 532–33.

[18]J.W. Mendenhall, *Echoes of Palestine* (New York: Philips and Hunt, 1888), 103.

[19]George A. Smith, *The Historical Geography of the Holy Land* (New York: Harper and Row, 1966), 313.

[20]John van Seters, "Joshua's Campaign of Canaan and Near Eastern Historiography," *Scandinavian Journal of the Old Testament* 2 (1990), 6–7.

[21]The direct speech of the Lord is heard in 11 percent of the text while the direct speech of Joshua is heard in 27 percent of the text.

[22]For a more detailed discussion of these vocabulary choices, see Beck, "Why Do Joshua's Readers Keep Crossing the River?" 698.

[23]Henry O. Thompson, "Jordan River," in *Anchor Bible Dictionary,* ed. David Noel Freedman (New York: Doubleday, 1992), 3.954.

[24]For a more complete treatment of this topic, see John A. Beck, "Faith in the Face of Famine: The Narrative Geographical Function of Famine in Genesis," *The Journal of Biblical Storytelling* 11(2001): 58–66.

[25]Beck, *Land of Milk and Honey,* 26–27.

[26]Beitzel, *The Moody Atlas of Bible Lands,* 27.

[27]These numbers reflect the modern per capita water availability for the United States and Israel. Priit J. Vesilind, "Water, the Middle East's Critical Resource," *National Geographic* (May 1993): 48.

[28]The Sea of Galilee was a source of fresh water for those living in the lake basin. But its elevation (or lack thereof) at 700 feet below sea level prevented transportation of that water for use in other areas.

[29]For a more complete summary of the summer season in Israel, see Beck, *Land of Milk and Honey,* 155–57.

[30]For a more complete summary of the winter season in Israel, see ibid., 158–59.

[31]Aharoni, *Land of the Bible,* 14.

[32]Umberto Cassuto, *A Commentary on the Book of Genesis,* vol. 2 (Jerusalem: Magnes Press, 1964), 346.

[33]Gordon J. Wenham, *Genesis 1–15,* Word Biblical Commentary, vol. 1 (Waco, Tex.: Word Books, 1987), 287; Robert Davidson, *Genesis 12–50* (Cambridge: Cambridge University Press, 1979), 24.

[34]O. S. Wintermute, "Jubilees," in *The Old Testament Pseudepigrapha,* ed. J. H. Charlesworth (New York: Doubleday, 1985), 135.

PART THREE

The Storyteller's Meaning

8

A Method for Seeking Meaning in Biblical Narrative

While all forms of reading use the same physical processes, we do not read all types of printed material in exactly the same way. For example, a contract that will receive our signature gets a slow, painstaking reading. Our eyes strain to digest every single word, weighing the nuance of every phrase and sentence in that document. On the other end of the spectrum, our reading literally moves to freeway speed when our eyes catch a billboard alongside the freeway. Needless to say, we do not read a contract and a billboard in exactly the same way.

Between these two extremes lies most of the reading we do. Even in this middle ground, we observe differences in our reading style. We use one style when catching up on world events in the weekly news magazine. Another style takes over as we reread the pages of our favorite novel. One size simply does not fit all when it comes to our reading. So what reading style or method may offer the most promise when seeking meaning in a biblical narrative? We have spoken about the storyteller's craft; now we will speak about the reader's craft used when seeking meaning in a Bible story.

The method for reading a story will be directed by the goals the storyteller has for the reader. When we read to our children from a storybook or when we pick up the novel that fills our relaxation time, we read quickly and lightly. In many respects, that seems appropriate. Stories that are meant to entertain are not written to be read like a contract. The storyteller wants us to leave our conscious world for a time to join the world of the characters in the story. Nothing would please the storyteller more than if we completely lost ourselves in the telling only to awaken minutes, if not hours, later unaware of the passage of real time in our lives or the unfolding of events around our reading chair.

While the stories of the Bible are entertaining, the storyteller did not tell them specifically to entertain. The storyteller or writer wants to teach us about God and about ourselves. If we read those stories in exactly the same way we read a children's story, we may find ourselves entertained but not edified. That edification is more likely to come when we actively and intentionally read a Bible story with a method designed to reveal its meaning. By reading the first chapters of this book, you have begun that journey. Where the change in the naming of a character may not have caught your eye, now you note its impact on the characterization of that person. Your reading will have gained a greater sensitivity to the way the divine storyteller manipulates time or strategically places a metaphor that calls attention to the message of the story. Your Bible reading may even have grown to see that the divine storyteller will use geography to shape readers. But this chapter is designed to take you a step beyond these random observations.

This chapter offers Bible readers a step-by-step method for reading a Bible story to capture its meaning. This method will take us first to those portions of the story most likely to reveal the topic of the story and the point of view being expressed on that topic. We will then back away to observe how other components of the story wrap around that meaning to make it more vivid and certain. The first portion of this analysis will take us directly to the design of the plot, while the second portion will lead us to explore the characterization, as well as the artful use of time, setting, word play, and geography. Using a step-by-step approach promises a more organized inquiry into the meaning of a story.

Such an approach may give off auras of artificiality. In some respects, it is like taking an internal combustion engine apart and laying out all the individual parts on our workbench. Of course, engines are not designed to function while lying in pieces on a workbench. Neither are stories. If I want to understand how that engine works, I may have to disassemble it for a time and examine its parts. We need to turn the carburetor over in our hands. We need to see what a cylinder and its rings look like. We need to see the connections between the alternator, starter, and battery to understand their working relationship. In the same way, I am proposing that we systematically disassemble the story to appreciate how each of the parts contributes to the meaningful function of the whole. This treatment of a narrative may appear somewhat artificial, but it can clarify the role of every detail in accomplishing the greater goal the storyteller has for that narrative.

Berlin cautions that the application of a method of analysis can lead to a mechanical and lifeless criticism.[1] This is a fair concern. If we disassemble the story and study its components, we must not leave it on the workbench in a pile of disassociated parts. We must reassemble it. Failure to reassemble the parts would rob the story of its vitality, animation, and flow. One could argue for an equal risk of missing the message completely if we fail to slow and even pause our reading of a story to analyze its components. So with these cautions in view, we offer a method for defining the reader's craft to better see the meaning in a biblical narrative.[2]

Step One: Set Aside What You Already Know

If you have read this far, you are most likely an experienced Bible reader. This creates a liability that needs to be addressed. You have met the story you are studying before and have some familiarity with the characters and the plot. You may have preconditioned views about what the story means. Take the story of Jonah as an example. A number of details about the plot and characters are already floating about in your subconscious. You know Jonah. You recall the boat, the great fish, and the shelter in which he sat. In your mind, you may already believe this story will be one about missionary efforts to the lost. This knowledge and presupposition is not bad in and of itself, but it can put us in a reading position that *leads* the story where we want it to go, paying attention only to those details that will support our views of what we believe the story should be saying.

A second issue in this regard is the matter of parallel accounts. In many instances with a gospel account, one historical event may have given birth to parallel stories found in different books. For example, consider the calling of the first disciples by Jesus in Matthew 4:18–22; Mark 1:16–20; Luke 5:1–11; and John 1:35–42. One question we must face in those instances is whether we should blend each of those parallel accounts into a hypothetical narrative for analysis or whether we should treat each narrative as an independent entity deserving its own investigation. Our commitment is to the latter course of action. Because each individual story has its own unique narrative components as well as a discrete literary context, each is deserving of its own inquiry. While we may profitably explore the parallel accounts in an attempt to reconstruct the historical event behind the narrative, our goal is to respect the literary independence of each gospel account. The same event may be placed in story form by multiple gospel writers to deliver the same message, but that is not necessarily the case. Consequently, when we seek to limit our preconceptions about a story upon entering it, this will also mean setting aside the information we might know or could gain about the event from parallel accounts.[3]

While it is impossible to completely eliminate all our prior knowledge and preconceptions about the story, it is helpful to acknowledge they exist and then do what we can to limit the influence of what we already know. By setting aside these presuppositions, we will be able to approach the story with fresh eyes and ears. Our goal is not to lead the story where we want it to go but to have the story lead us to the place where it is going.

Step Two: Read around the Story

Before engaging in the details of the narrative that lie at the focus of our interests, it is helpful to get a sense of that narrative's literary context, reading the story in light of the family of stories that surround it. Questions like these will help us put the story into that larger context. What had happened in the larger story world just before the narrative we are reading? What happens immediately after the story we have in view? What is the literary tone and focus of the book as a whole? What unique contribution to the whole book does this particular story promise to make?

Perhaps the best way to achieve a greater sense of literary context is to read the entire book in one sitting. If time or interest prevents you from actualizing that option, another way to get a general sense for the literary quality and focus of a book is through the use of an introduction found in a Bible handbook or study Bible. The information you find there may be complemented by a resource that specifically addresses the literary quality of the Bible book in which the story resides. This type of literary introduction can be found in a book such as *A Complete Literary Guide to the Bible.*[4] By reading around the story in one or more of these ways, you will be better prepared to hear the story as presented in its larger literary context.

Step Three: Read the Story Slowly Several Times

The third step in this process calls for us to read the story slowly over and over again. This should not be a quick skim of the details but a series of slow readings that carry your eyes from the first sentence to the last. This is not the time to distract your reading experience with thoughts about characterization or narrative geography. This is about meeting the story as it was told. If you encounter something interesting or unique, resist the urge to stop and linger. There will be time for that later. The one goal you have during this reading and rereading of the story is to obtain control of all the story details. You will know where the story is happening, when it is happening, the names of the participants in the plot, and the general direction that the story flows. By committing to this step, you will leave with knowledge of the story details and also a sense for the story as a whole.

Step Four: Identify the Structure of the Story

Step four begins a more analytical approach to the story. It is time to read the story again, but this time the goal is to identify the profile of the plot and its components. Here it can be helpful either to physically mark the story on the page or to draw a diagram that links the various parts of the plot to the verses in the story. Recall that a narrative typically begins with an exposition that provides the necessary background for the story. This is where we meet the participants whom we will shadow through the story, discover the location of the action, and even find out the time of day. The storyteller will then move quickly to put the crisis or conflict before our eyes. Identify the verse or verses that raise the unanswered question, that describe the moral predicament, or that define an inaccurate perception. Once you have identified the crisis, look ahead in the storyline for further complications that delay resolution and even call into question the ability of resolution to occur. Then look for the climactic moment. This is the fulcrum of the story. A step in one direction leads back toward the crisis, while a step in the other direction leads toward conclusion. Remember that resolutions that are either incomplete or completely unhelpful may separate the crisis from one or a series of climactic moments. Eventually these false climaxes will lead to an ultimate turning point in the story, marked by falling tension as the story transitions to resolution and then on to conclusion. You will have achieved the goal of this step when you have a clear profile of the story's plot in view, one that lays bear the rising tension, climax, and falling tension in the story.

Step Five: Identify the Topic and Point of View

Once you have gained the obtained intimacy with the story through the first four steps, you have come to the critical moment of positing a meaning for the story. It is best to handle this in two distinct steps. The first is identifying what topic lies at the heart of the story. For example, is this a story about God, about suffering, about relationships, about sin, or about death? Once you have identified the topic around which the story revolves, you can determine what the storyteller is saying about that topic. Now, remember, meaning is not the same as the topic. Meaning also requires the particular point of view taken on a topic, imbuing the story with enduring value. For example, if I identify the topic of a story as "sin," I have really not yet arrived at the meaning of the story, for the topic of "sin" could be used to communicate a variety of lessons. The story could be teaching that sin creates hardship, or that sin can cause even the strong to stumble, or that sin is forgiven. Good preaching and good teaching, in particular, demand that we do more than simply talk about the topic introduced in the story. Any topic encompasses many facets, all of which may serve as a wonderful theme for a sermon. But our goal is to talk about the topic in the same way the storyteller did, communicating the point of view on the topic the story portrays.

The search for the topic and the divine point of view on that topic require us to return to the story once again. This time we will be reading the story carefully with an eye toward identifying the topic of the story and the point of view expressed on that topic. Certain portions of the story are more likely to carry those clues than others. Begin with the plot diagram obtained from the story in the previous step. Focus on the crisis to see what topic that places before the reader of this particular story. Then consider the resolution of the story and how the divine storyteller uses that resolution to articulate a particular point of view on the topic. Here it is helpful to physically write down two sentences that will help clarify your thinking. The first sentence will answer the question: What is this story about? The answer to this question will be the topic. The second question will press on toward its meaning: What is the storyteller saying about that topic? This will result in an initial identification of the story's point of view on that topic, or the story's enduring meaning.

This initial identification of the story's meaning can be tested by looking for supporting evidence in other key locations within the narrative. For example, in returning to the story again, pay particular attention to the direct speech of the main character. Often the storyteller will summarize the topic about which the story revolves and articulate the meaning in a well-crafted "punch line" delivered by the main character in the story.[5] If no specific speech of the character seems helpful, watch the main character closely as he or she moves through the story. Topic and meaning can also be linked to a change we observe in the main character.[6] This could be a change in understanding, a change in action, or a change in faith. In that connection, the story may revolve around a choice the character makes either to act or not act, to speak, or to remain silent.[7]

You may use several other locations in the story to validate your initial observation on the story's meaning. Read the story again looking for repeated words, phrases, or actions. Do any of those correspond with your proposed meaning of the story? We have also noted that storytellers will slow down the time within the story to make their point. Does the point of the story's slowest movement correspond with your premise about the meaning? Finally, although it is rare, the storyteller may use the voice of the narrator to most clearly summarize and articulate the meaning of the story. At the conclusion of the fifth step, you will have come to a tentative conclusion on the topic and meaning of the story.

Step Six: Divide the Story into Scenes

Once you have taken step five, it is now possible to determine how each of the scenes within the story functions to create focus on the topic, give it definition, and advance its meaning. Again it may help to physically mark the text so that the division between the scenes is clearly apparent. A scene break will occur whenever we observe a change in time, a change in setting, or significant change in actors on the story stage. Remember that a typical scene will take shape around two characters. As one or both participants leave the story stage, we may mark the passage of one scene to the next.

Once you have marked out the scenes, read each one in light of the meaning you have posited for the narrative. Walter Kaiser suggests that the relevance of each scene may be linked to its role in answering one of six questions: who, what, when, where, why, how?[8] If we have determined that the story before us is talking about salvation, and if we have proposed that the story was composed to teach us that salvation comes to all people regardless of their nationality or ethnicity, a scene within the narrative may be dedicated to answering questions such as the following: Who makes this salvation possible? What do others need to do to obtain this salvation? When did this salvation become available? Where do I have to live to get this salvation? Why does God extend salvation to everyone? The answers to questions like these will help us see the story in a new light as its details become united around the story's meaning. If we have accurately identified the meaning of the story, then we will be able to accurately identify the role of each scene in delivering that message.

Step Seven: Explore the Artistic Presentation of People and Events in Time and Place

The final step in the process is to read the story again to understand how various dimensions of the storyteller's craft participate in the artful delivery of that meaning. Pay particular attention to the characters. Divide them into two groups: main characters and supporting characters. Then ask the questions that will illuminate how the main characters are introduced to us: What do they say? What do they do? What is said about them? How do their speech and actions compare with the speech and actions of others? What do we know of their appearance? How are they named?

After isolating the characters and examining the way the storyteller introduces them to us, isolate the voice of the narrator to see what role that voice plays in shaping our response to the details of the story and its meaning. Remember that the narrator is the voice of the storyteller within the story. The storyteller may be using the narrator to make aggressive statements about the point of view communicated in the story.

Changes in time and setting can also be isolated and investigated. You may already have considered such changes and their role in breaking the story into scenes. Now pay particular attention to the way in which the storyteller has conditioned our experience with time. Note the places where the passage of time slows to create emphasis. Look for events that have been related out of historical sequence. Watch for any specific mention of time that plays a role in telling the story. Note the various settings–geographical, architectural, and social. Consider how those settings may highlight or change the impact of the speech and actions of the characters.

We have seen that geographical data can also be used as part of the storytelling process. Isolate any specific mention of geography, whether that be place names, topography, geology, climate, etc.; learn what you can about the geography; and then consider the narrative-geographical function of that language in the story.

Finally, read the story again. Mark any forms of word play that stand out. The most frequent involve: repetition, metaphor, simile, personification, irony, and rhetorical questions. Consider again how these particular devices contribute to the beauty and meaning of the story before you.

As we consider the various dimensions of the storyteller's craft evident in the story before us, we will not only heighten our sensitivity to the artful way in which the story is told, but we will also be working to validate our sense of the story's meaning. Coherence is evidence of a successful analysis. For example, if the storyteller's deployment of characterization, use of time, and the patterning play of words all support our proposed meaning for the story, we will have discovered internal support of our conviction. Too many unexplained discrepancies will require us to rethink our proposal. But coherence and fit will help validate our conclusion.

Conclusion

While all forms of reading use the same physiological processes, we do not read all types of printed material in exactly the same way. When we read a Bible story for meaning, that type of reading will also have its own unique qualities. We have just provided an overview of a reading plan that can carry us through a step-by-step process for reading a story in pursuit of its meaning. This means setting aside what we already know about the story to let the story's details lead us toward the story's meaning. It means reading around the story with the goal of understanding the literary context from which the story follows. It means carefully reading the story as a literary unit to control the details contained with the story. It means identifying the plot structure and using that plot structure to posit a topic and point of view for the story. It means dividing the story into scenes and assessing the contribution of each scene to the message of the story. And it means exploring the artful delivery of that story so that we might appreciate the ways in which the storyteller has used various storytelling techniques to draw our attention to the topic of the story and deliver its meaning. While all such methods fall far short of perfection, this one offers a starting point in developing your own method of reading a Bible story for its meaning.

Notes

[1]Adele Berlin, "Characterization in Biblical Narrative: David's Wives," in *Beyond Form Criticism: Essays in Old Testament Literary Criticism,* ed. Paul R. House (Winona Lake, Ind.: Eisenbrauns, 1992), 219.

[2]The method discussed here is our own but will reflect the influence of others who have forwarded a complete or partial method of analysis in this area. In particular, we acknowledge our indebtedness to the writings of Walter Kaiser and Leland Ryken. Walter C. Kaiser Jr., *Preaching and Teaching from the Old Testament: A Guide for the Church* (Grand Rapids: Baker Academic, 2003); Leland Ryken, *How to Read the Bible as Literature* (Grand Rapids: Zondervan, 1984).

[3]While this particular matter occurs less frequently in the Old Testament, the same would apply in those cases where an event is placed into story form by more than one author. For example, we note that the death of King Saul receives very different treatment in two parallel accounts (1 Sam. 31 and 1 Chr. 10). Each of those narratives would best be

treated as a discrete literary entity with the potential of delivering a different meaning to the story.

[4]Leland Ryken and Tremper Longman III, eds., *A Complete Literary Guide to the Bible* (Grand Rapids: Zondervan, 1993).

[5]Walter C. Kaiser Jr., "Preaching from Historical Narrative Texts of the Old Testament," in *Giving the Sense,* ed. David M. Howard Jr. and Michael A. Grisanti (Grand Rapids: Kregel, 2003), 447.

[6]Ryken, *How to Read the Bible as Literature,* 60.

[7]Ibid., 52.

[8]Kaiser, *Preaching and Teaching from the Old Testament,* 56.

9

Seeking Meaning in the Story of David and Goliath

The story of David and Goliath is one of the Bible's most entertaining and treasured stories. Bible study groups have discussed it, sermons have talked about it, and the media have borrowed it to characterize the unexpected victory of the underdog. Because of its popularity and rich literary qualities, we have made it our Old Testament text for illustrating the method of analysis outlined in the previous chapter. This method calls for us as readers to actively pursue the subtle and not so subtle ways in which the divine storyteller is manipulating our perspective, leading us to see the world as he does.

Our journey into the story of David and Goliath will walk the seven-step path presented in the previous chapter.

As we follow those steps, we will find ourselves led to the focal point and message of the story. Once we have achieved a sense of the story's intended direction, this outline will help us appreciate how the storyteller carefully selected content and form to enhance and affirm that message for the reader.

While these matters occupy our time, please note that this chapter is also restrained by two important limitations. First, it is not designed to be a complete commentary on 1 Samuel 17. Such an undertaking would require the application of more than one method of analysis and would demand that the author interact more aggressively with the work of other scholars who have addressed the shape and meaning of the story before us. By contrast, what follows is a summary of the insights gained when the story is read using our step-by-step method. Second, as an illustration of narrative criticism, even this narrative-critical study is incomplete. We have limited our discussion to those components of the story that promise to make the most powerful and meaningful contribution to this illustration. Toward that end and with a prayer for the Holy Spirit's guidance, we now enter the story of David and Goliath as readers seeking its meaning.

Step One: Set Aside What You Already Know

We already know a great deal about the story directly before us. At one level that familiarity can be very helpful, permitting easier entry into the story. But this familiarity can also be a grave liability. What we know of Goliath, David, Saul, and the plot of this story may cause us to read this story less attentively, reading past or even ignoring details that will become an important part of its interpretation. Our previous experience with this story may also contaminate our attempts to make a fresh reading of the story, one that sets aside for a time the preconceptions we have about what the story means.

Consequently, the first challenge we have in applying this method of analysis is to temporarily set aside what we already know or believe we know about the story. That is not to say that our preconceptions are wrong. It is to say that the story deserves a fresh look, one that calls for us to listen to the story as if we were hearing it for the first time.

Step Two: Read around the Story

Once we have acknowledged the risk of previous encounter with this story and have made a commitment to limit the power and impact of our previous experiences, it is time to read around the story. Recall that no Bible story is meant to live within a vacuum. Every story resides within a larger family of stories that provide a literary context. Thus the second step in the process is to read around the story so that we may enter the story of David and Goliath aware of the larger story from which it flows. In the case of David and Goliath, we see that this story has important roots that tap into the leadership crisis described in the earlier chapters of 1 Samuel and that extend back into the time of the Judges. We will consider how that larger story sets the stage for our reading of 1 Samuel 17.

Judges

The core of Judges is found in chapters 3–17, where we meet a series of narratives that portray the time between Joshua and the rise of Samuel. As Joshua sent off the individual tribes of Israel to consolidate their hold on the territory each had been given, he reminded them of their commitment to remain faithful to the Lord. They were the covenant people of God with a unique mission. Because they had this unique mission, God had also prescribed that they live a distinctive lifestyle. As the people of Israel prepared their meals, made their garments, planted their crops, and worshiped their God, they distinguished themselves from those living around them. They were to live the unique lifestyle prescribed by the Lord. Joshua encouraged the Israelites to remain faithful to their covenant with God and to hold dearly to their distinctive role in the world.

The book of Judges documents the incredible struggle the Israelites had in doing just that. The introduction to Judges outlines a tragic cycle (2:10–19) that the reader encounters again and again in the stories of this book. The cycle begins as the Israelites assimilate into the thinking of their heathen neighbors, living their lifestyle and worshiping their gods. In God's passion for holiness, the Lord empowers local nations and people to oppress Israel to bring about a change. It works. This oppression brings the people to repentance as they cry out to the Lord for help. He hears the cry of his people and then raises a deliverer, a judge, who leads the people to freedom from this oppression. The victory ushers in a time of greater obedience and peace before the cycle begins afresh. This is the cycle, in full or in part, that shapes the presentation of the core stories in Judges (chapters 3–16).

As they spin around and around in this cycle, the tribes of Israel are not united under a single leader but directed by various judges who arise for a time and then leave the story stage. Some of these leaders have the potential for sustained greatness, but one after the other sees his or her life close without realizing a politically unified Israel or a sustained desire within Israel to serve the Lord. In the end, we leave these stories unconvinced that we have met the next Moses or Joshua.

As disappointing as the core of the book is, the Book of Judges closes with a set of stories (17–21) even more disturbing than those that precede them. The moral corruption, social chaos, and civil war that we read about here are unmatched in other pages of the Bible. We have seen a few bright and hopeful moments earlier in the book, but these last stories do not even mention a single leader worthy of our confidence. Lest the reader has missed this pervasive crisis in leadership that so troubles the divine author, the book itself closes with an observation on the times that drives the point home: "In those days there was no king in Israel; all the people did what was right in their own eyes" (Judg. 21:25).

1 Samuel

With this lament over the state of leadership in Israel, we enter the pages of 1 Samuel. While we hope for quick improvement, the storyteller introduces us to more of the same. While piety remains alive in the hearts of common people such as Hannah (1 Sam. 1), the leaders of Israel display anything but such heartfelt piety. The low morality and lack of effective leadership found among the priests is documented in graphic detail (2:12–17, 22–25). By the time we reach chapter three, we have all but abandoned hope. At just this moment, we meet Samuel. Like Hannah his mother, this boy demonstrates a faith in the Lord and a passion to hear God speak, attributes long absent from Israel's leadership. As this young man grows to become a prophet, judge, and reformer, Samuel takes the Israelites to a spiritual place we have not seen them occupy for quite some time. They abandon false gods and recommit themselves to the path the Lord has placed before them.

The building hope that surged through the early stories of Samuel does not endure as a legacy through his sons (8:1–3). The failure of Samuel's sons to lead as Samuel did brings the people to agitate for a king, as all the other nations have (8:4–5). Samuel comes to understand that this is part of a larger divine plan meant to infuse the leadership of Israel with the power to unify the nation around their covenant mission. So Samuel anoints Saul, Israel's first king, initiating the era of the monarchy (1 Sam. 9–10).

The promising start to Saul's monarchy decays quickly. When God approved the rule of a king over Israel, he was not abdicating his own role as Israel's king. The king of God's people was not to be like the other kings of the land. Israel's king would live a life of obedience to the covenant God had made with Israel and would do all he could to advance the interests of the Lord (Deut. 17:14–20). Saul's failure to be that kind of king destines him for downfall. From one story to the next, Saul begins to look more and more like the pagan kings of the region. Although forbidden to offer sacrifice, Saul usurps this role limited to those of the priestly family (13:9). He erects a monument to aggrandize his accomplishments (15:12). Ultimately, he demonstrates his arrogance by defying a direct command from the Lord (15:7–23). As we observe Saul moving farther and farther from his spiritual base, we find Israel sliding once again into a leadership crisis.

Because Saul fails in such dramatic ways, the Lord steps away from Saul and begins the process of putting a new leader on the throne of Israel. A divine hand guides Samuel to the family of Jesse in Bethlehem, where he is directed to anoint a king whose "heart" is in the right place (16:7). That man is David. Saul appears to know nothing of this new appointment, and so ironically summons David to his royal court where he functions both as musician and armor bearer (16:14–23). This is the literary context that lies immediately ahead of the story of David and Goliath.

The Tension

By reading around the story, two related tensions have surfaced that will inform our reading of the story before us. First of all, leadership has been a persistent problem since the death of Joshua. The book of Judges records the uneven and troubling pattern of leadership, lamenting both the lack of centralized leadership and lack of sustained godly leadership. The first chapters of Samuel show that this leadership crisis has continued, directing us pointedly to one question: Not just *what* person, but *what kind of* person is best suited to pull Israel out of its spiritual spiral?

The second tension we carry into the story of David and Goliath is also related to leadership: Who is in charge? We have a sitting king, Saul, now rejected by the Lord; and we have an anointed king, David, about whom we know almost nothing. Questions abound. Is Saul really done, or will he repent and find restoration? Who is David, and how is he different from Saul? Is David the solution or simply another failure waiting to take shape? Readers will carry these questions into the story of David and Goliath—questions about leaders and leadership. Thus an awareness of the literary context will participate in directing our reading of 1 Samuel 17.

Step Three: Read the Story Slowly Several Times

With the issues of the larger context for the story in view, this is the time for us to read through the story of David and Goliath (1 Sam. 17) slowly, several times. Recall that this is not the time to stop or even pause at a unique metaphor, nor is it the time to reflect on the way in which Goliath is characterized through the narrator's physical description. The goal is to sharpen your awareness of the story's details as you listen from the very first words to the last. Once we have read the story as a whole and have a sense for the way the details flow together to construct the whole, we can more effectively disassemble it. After having read through the story of David and Goliath slowly several times, please return to the next portion of this chapter for a discussion of the plot structure.

Step Four: Identify the Structure of the Story

The more haphazard way in which we meet people, observe actions, and hear conversations in our day-to-day life stands in sharp contrast to the carefully structured way in which we meet such matters within a Bible story. Each story has a beginning, middle, and ending that contributes to the flow and focus of the whole. In our fourth step, we will work to identify that plot structure in the narrative. In particular, this means identifying the verses that comprise the exposition, introduce the crisis, present the complications, arrive at the climax, and establish the resolution of the story.[1]

Exposition 1 (17:1–7)

Predictably, the first verses of chapter 17 serve as an exposition. In verses 1–7, the storyteller provides the details we need to effectively enter the core of the story. The setting for the story is the Elah Valley, where most of the events will occur.[2] The participants include Saul and Goliath, as well as a large number of Philistine soldiers and a cast of Israelite soldiers. We note that the personal names given to Goliath and Saul indicate that they will play a more central role in the story, while the nameless Philistine and Israelite soldiers will function as agents. Of course, the person missing from this exposition is the newly anointed David. His introduction is reserved for a later time.

The Crisis (16:8–11)

The first person to speak in the story is Goliath. The storyteller uses the words of this heathen champion to establish the crisis requiring resolution.

As readers of 1 Samuel, we have been sensitized to the leadership crisis that existed in Israel. That point has not gone unnoticed in the Philistine world. The first words of this giant cut quickly to the heart of the matter. He calls for Israel to identify a leader from among them who will champion the cause of God's people:

> "Why have you come out to draw up for battle? Am I not a Philistine and are you not servants of Saul? Choose a man for yourselves, and let him come down to me. If he is able to fight with me and kill me, then we will be your servants; but if I prevail against him and kill him, then you shall be our servants and serve us…Today I defy the ranks of Israel! Give me a man, that we may fight together." (1 Sam. 17:8–10)

Immediately, the crisis in leadership that plays at the heart of this story is before us. The reaction to Goliath's challenge brings anything but hope to the reader. He calls for Israel to identify a leader, but the reaction of God's people points up the crisis: "When Saul and all Israel heard these words of the Philistine, they were dismayed and greatly afraid" (1 Sam. 16:11). Thus the brazen challenge of Goliath does not create the leadership crisis in Israel. It simply calls our attention to it. Despite the abusive language of this heathen fighter, he speaks the truth. Israel has no leader willing to take up the divine cause.

Exposition 2 (17:12–16)

Of course, one very important person is missing from the story. While the storyteller introduces us to Saul and Goliath in the first exposition, David remains out of the picture. We had met him in the previous chapter, but David's presence is unfelt through the first eleven verses of this story. His introduction is saved for a second exposition found in verses 12–16. This exposition tells us that David was the son of Jesse from Bethlehem, that he had seven brothers, and that David was the youngest of them. The storyteller does not say in so many words that David is the anointed king of God's people, but in the second exposition, several of the details allude back to David's anointing–the reference to Bethlehem (cf. 16:4), to Jesse's sons (cf. 16:6–11), to Eliab (cf. 16:6), and to David's role as shepherd (cf. 16:11). Through these allusions and by delaying the introduction of David until after we hear the challenge of Goliath, the storyteller puts a spotlight on David. Our expectation is that he will do something to address the crisis Goliath articulated.

Complications

The storyteller could have moved us quickly to the climax of the story, but rather allows the tension to build through various complications. Goliath has drawn our attention to the crisis. Either Saul or David may provide the answer to that crisis. In our quest to understand the qualities that make up a leader of God's people and in our search for such a leader in this story, we meet complications that draw us into deeper and more attentive thought on these topics.

The first complication is associated with Saul. The reader of 1 Samuel has been conditioned to expect that the king will demonstrate leadership in just such a situation as this. When the people had asked Samuel for a king, they specifically did so with this expectation. The king would go before them and fight their battles (1 Sam. 8:20). Here was Saul's opportunity to reassert himself as an appropriate leader. But his slide from grace continues. Saul does not address the challenge, nor does he inspire those around him to fight with courage (17:11). So the expected leader fails to function as a leader, creating a complication that delays resolution of the crisis.

David is the other person who has a shot at greatness in this story, but his rise to prominence as a leader does not take a direct path. The storyteller places several complications in our path, which lead us to question both his motives and his ability. When David comes to the battlefront, the storyteller allows us to hear a conversation in which David inquires about the personal reward awaiting the man who steps forward to fight with Goliath (17:26). This makes us wonder if David is as self-invested as Saul, and is simply another anointed leader destined to fail. Moments later, his oldest brother, Eliab, impugns the presence of David by suggesting that presumption, an evil heart, and a morbid curiosity have motivated David to come to the front lines (17:28). Eliab would certainly know David better than we do. If he is accurately describing David, then we have to wonder if David has the qualities God demands of his leaders.

When David ultimately casts himself in the role of leader, his abilities as well as his motives come into question. Saul looks at David and bemoans his immaturity and lack of experience. "You are not able to go against this Philistine to fight with him; for you are just a boy, and he has been a warrior from his youth" (17:33). While Saul may have a vested interest in keeping David out of the limelight, we wonder if his assessment as an experienced general might not have some merit. Finally, we note Goliath's perception of David. As David steps onto the valley floor to accept the challenge, Goliath's words betray a complete distain for this combatant (17:41–42), punctuated by, "Am I a dog, that you come to me with sticks?" (17:43) Thus the crisis that centers on leadership in Israel is not quickly resolved in this narrative. Both Saul and David are identified as potential leaders, yet we encounter significant reservations about each that complicate the resolution of the matter.

Climax (17:40–51)

Once we reach the climax of the story, the narrative pace increases. By verse 40, we see David reaching for five smooth stones. Following an exchange between Goliath and David, David accelerates into a dead run, heading directly for the experienced warrior, and dispatches him with one, well-placed shot from his sling. That sling shot that disables the Philistine champion allows David to finish him off. Suddenly all the questions about leadership and leadership qualities are answered. David's words and actions show us the true nature of a leader whose heart is in the right place.

Resolution and Conclusion (17:52–54)

David's victory marks the turning point in the story. The resolution and conclusion confirm the effectiveness of David's leadership and show the results of it. Not only is the precipitator of the Philistine threat gone, his fellow soldiers are in retreat hotly pursued by the newly inspired Israelite soldiers. The Philistine presence has been removed from the land. As an ultimate statement of their defeat, the Israelites raid and pillage the Philistine camp. The final verse once again puts the name of David before us as the key player who resolves the leadership crisis in Israel. "David took the head of the Philistine and brought it to Jerusalem; but he put his armor in his tent" (17:54).

Step Five: Identify the Topic and Point of View

While more than one topic may find its way into the storyteller's presentation, typically one topic will rise above the others and may be identified as the key topic of the narrative. Our review of the literary context helped us to see that leadership was a key issue elevated to prominence in the book of Judges and persisting into the early chapters of Samuel. As readers of 1 Samuel, we are on the lookout for any information that might inform this topic. Thus it is legitimate to inspect the story of David and Goliath for language that addresses leadership. When we do, we find that the divine storyteller places this matter at the heart of the story. The language of Goliath makes it unmistakably clear that Israel needs a royal champion who will lead the people (17:8–10).

Identifying the meaning of the story is more than merely identifying the topic. We need to push beyond the topic to the particular point of view on the topic expressed in the story. In doing so, it becomes clear that this story not only seeks to identify who will now lead God's people in the battle with the Philistines. Beyond that, the storyteller addresses the true nature of godly leadership.

Just a few verses before the story of David and Goliath, the Lord has encouraged us to think about leadership in a new way. God directed Samuel to anoint the next king of Israel, but cautioned him about the allure of appearance or height. God was interested in the heart (16:7), but the details of what it meant for a leader to have the right kind of heart are lacking. This story serves as an illustration of what it means for a leader to have his heart in the right place. David wages war against a seemingly undefeatable foe. He succeeds as a leader because he recognizes a divine presence and power on the battlefield that others do not. Nowhere in the story does that become clearer than in a lengthy speech that shows where his heart is on this day. Note in particular the faith illustrated in the opening and closing sentences. Standing before the awesome Philistine fighting machine, David says:

> "You come to me with sword and spear and javelin; but I come to you in the name of the LORD of hosts, the God of the armies of Israel, whom you have defied. This very day the LORD will deliver you into my hand, and I will strike you down and cut off your head; and I will give the dead bodies of the Philistine army this very day to the birds of the air and to the wild animals of the earth, so that all the earth may know that there is a God in Israel, and that all this assembly may know that the LORD does not save by sword and spear; for the battle is the LORD's and he will give you into our hand." (17:45–47)

At every step of this declaration, David's trust in the Lord and what the Lord will do distinguishes his approach to leadership.

We have entered the story expecting to learn more about what constitutes effective leadership and to find out who that effective leader will be. The storyteller does not disappoint us. Through it all, this narrative articulates one view on leadership. Effective leaders are those who demonstrate an absolute trust in God's presence and power in the face of seemingly insurmountable challenges. Assuming for the moment that we have correctly followed the evidence in the story leading to this meaning, we will examine the other literary components of the narrative to confirm our suspicion and to see how the storyteller has carefully woven that thesis into the narrative.

Step Six: Divide the Story into Scenes

This message found within the story of David and Goliath unfolds slowly and deliberately through a series of scenes. The next step in our analysis will be to identify the various scenes deployed in the story and inquire into the way each advances the cause of the plot and the meaning of the story.

The first scene follows the initial exposition and is housed within verses 8–11. Goliath stands before Saul and the Israelites, announcing his challenge. He calls for a leader to arise and fight him. As we noted above, this language of Goliath allows the crisis to become obvious. Who will that leader be? And, more importantly, what will that leader be like? The answer to these questions becomes more critical and the crisis more poignant as our eyes travel to the final sentence in the scene. The narrator steps to the stage and observes the reaction of Saul and his soldiers: "They were dismayed and greatly afraid" (17:11).

The second scene follows the second exposition and covers verses 17–18. We are transported to Bethlehem and allowed to hear Jesse speak with his son, David. This scene tells us what motivated David to leave his family and travel to the battlefield. Here the storyteller is very careful to note that David did not make the decision to travel to the Elah Valley on his own. Rather he was directed to go by his father. What is more, David did not go with the intention of using this stage to propel his political career forward. Rather, his father sent him to deliver some food and to return with news of his brothers' well being. Ironically, the man who would lead Israel to victory this day begins his day with a very unassuming assignment.

The transformation of David from delivery boy to armed champion begins to occur in scene three (17:20–30), although this transition is slow and not without its complications. After dropping off the supplies with the keeper of the baggage, David personally hears the challenge of Goliath and observes the reaction of the Israelite soldiers. He then enters a conversation with a nameless group of soldiers. The topic of the conversation shows the extremes to which the king has gone to arouse a leader from within the ranks of the soldiers: "The king will greatly enrich the man who kills him, and will give him his daughter and make his family free in Israel" (17:25). This shows that Saul fully recognized the gravity of the situation. He is absolutely desperate to find a volunteer willing to take the challenge of Goliath. But despite all the incentives he placed on the table, Saul failed to inspire even one taker.

In this scene, David asks the men to repeat what they had said about the bonus Saul offered, making us wonder about his motives. Lest we had failed to do so, his oldest brother, Eliab, steps into the conversation, angrily attacking both David's motives and character: "Why have you come down? With whom have you left those few sheep in the wilderness? I know your presumption and the evil of your heart; for you have come down just to see the battle" (17:28). By the close of scene three, questions still encircle David's character.

Scene four (17:31–39) records the conversations between Saul and David. Here the storyteller gives us our first opportunity to see these two men together in the same physical location in this particular story. This is the second most important scene in the story, a scene that gives us the opportunity to compare the responses of Saul and David to the leadership crisis before them. Saul is all business and logic. When David says he is willing to fight, Saul initially tries to discourage him, citing his youth and lack of experience in the face of the Philistine veteran. When that fails, Saul offers an ironic prayer: "Go, and may the LORD be with you!" (17:37). He then attempts to equip David with some of the King's own armor. Given Saul's size (1 Sam. 9:2), our expectations are realized. His extra-large armor was not going to fit the more modest size of young David. Given his lack of faith in God, Saul could only hope to delay what was sure to be an inevitable slaughter.

In contrast to Saul, the character and nature of David as leader become clearly evident for the first time in this scene. Rather than reacting with fear and misgivings to the challenge of Goliath, David speaks these confident words: "Let no one's heart fail because of him; your servant will go and fight with this Philistine" (17:32). No one in the story, not even Saul, has dared to speak these words of faith. Lest we think this confidence of David is born of youthful naiveté, David goes on give reason for his trust in this Higher Power: "The LORD, who saved me from the paw of the lion and from the paw of the bear, will save me from the hand of this Philistine" (17:37). For the first time on this battleground, we are hearing the words of a leader who trusts in the Lord, and are receiving tangible evidence of what it means to be a leader of God who has his heart in the right place. Thus this scene heightens our expectation that David will lead the way instead of Saul. But the climax of the story is yet to come.

Finally, in the fifth scene the storyteller allows the crisis of the story to rise through its various complications to the climax. Scene five (17:40–51) puts David and Goliath on center stage. During this scene two important qualities of David are highlighted: his wisdom and his faith. Brought into harmony, these two qualities show us what a leader of God can be and demonstrate that David, rather than Saul, will lead God's people into their future. The scene opens with David selecting stones from the wadi and approaching the battle line with his sling in hand. David would not bristle with armor like Goliath, but his choice of weapon tells us something very important about David. He is approaching this engagement with great wisdom. Every offensive weapon that Goliath brought with him to the valley floor had a limited killing range. David recognized that he would put himself at great risk should he enter that killing zone. Consequently, he selects and eventually uses a weapon with sufficient range and power to disable Goliath without getting close enough to Goliath that his weapons would be a threat. The details offered in the description of David's preparation clearly are designed to highlight the intelligence of this leader.

Intelligence alone would not lead to success. The storyteller makes certain that this scene not only communicates David's wisdom but also his faith. David first meets the words of Goliath. The Philistine champion disdains David. He had asked for a leader, a champion from Israel to fight with him. All he gets is a lightly armed, inexperienced young man. Goliath promises that David's body will become food for the local animals within minutes. That is the last thing Goliath will say in our hearing. In fact, the disdainful speech of Goliath only sets up the incredible speech of David, in which he articulates his absolute trust in the Lord. In this public speech delivered within earshot of both Goliath and the Israelites, David shows us his faith and illustrates what it means to be a leader who has the right kind of heart. While soldiers of the heathen world rely on their weapons, the true king of Israel approaches challenges with faith in the Lord.

Once David's speech is done, the details of the engagement are handled in quick fashion. The slung stone of David finds its way past all the defensive armor of the Philistine, disabling the Philistine champion long before he has a chance to attack David with spear or sword. He crumples to the ground. The formidable war machine, now vulnerable, is dispatched by his own sword. As Goliath draws his last breath, we are able to catch our first breath since the scene had begun. We know both what a leader of Israel looks like and who that leader will be.

From this scene, the story moves quickly to its resolution and conclusion, affirming all that we have learned already (17:52–54). The leadership of David inspires the soldiers of Israel in precisely the way the leadership of Saul had not. The Philistines are driven from the land, and the final verse again puts David on the page as the leader of God's people. So through five unfolding scenes, the storyteller has led us to the intended conclusion. The questions about leadership that began in Judges and that carried through the early chapters of 1 Samuel have been answered. We know that an effective leader of God's people is one who has his heart in the right place. We have seen that David rather than Saul deserves to sit on the royal throne of Israel.

Step Seven: Explore the Artistic Presentation of People and Events in Time and Place

By examining the larger components of the narrative, we have learned a great deal about the way in which the storyteller has shaped our experience with this day in the life of David. We will now reenter the story looking more closely at the artful ways in which the storyteller has delivered the narrative and enhanced its message. Once again our examination of these details will not be comprehensive. We will address the storyteller's carefully selected language in terms of characterization, the use of time, geography, and the patterning play of words.

Characterization

The successful delivery of the plot means that we must meet and interact with three primary characters in the story: Goliath, Saul, and David. We will spend a few moments with each of these characters, examining some of the ways in which the storyteller has shaped our impressions of them.

GOLIATH

While the story is really about Saul and David, Goliath receives a considerable amount of space in the story. The frequent use of his personal name lifts him above the other Philistine soldiers, calling us as listeners to pay more careful attention to him. Two other appellations are also worthy of note. In two instances, he is called a "champion" (17:4, 23), naming that further distinguishes him from his compatriots and informs us of his capabilities. If we were choosing up sides for a fight, Goliath is the guy we want on our team—that is, until David names him for what he is truly is, "this uncircumcised Philistine" (17:26, 36).

In the characterization of Goliath, the storyteller gives him one of the most detailed physical descriptions we find in the entire Bible (17:4–7). Since such a description is rare, the reader is summoned to pay special attention to it. Leaning in for a closer look, we are struck by the size of this man, by the number of weapons slung about him, and by the sheer weight of those weapons. As we move our eyes from one threatening aspect of this fighter to the next, we are left with one unmistakable conclusion: it would take a man of wisdom, courage, and deep faith in God to meet his challenge.

Appearances aside, the language of Goliath betrays his greatest weakness. David sees it when he calls him an "uncircumcised Philistine." This man lies outside the people of God and lacks a personal relationship with the true Deity. This fact becomes more certain as the storyteller allows us to hear Goliath himself speak. In everything he says, Goliath fails to take into account God's presence and power. This lack of faith is subtly present in his first speech, when he defies the ranks of Israel to provide a leader (17:8–10). In his second speech, Goliath articulates his worldview most clearly. Cursing David by his own gods, Goliath quickly articulates a plan of action that takes into account neither the power of his own gods nor the presence of the one eternal God. It is all about Goliath. His confidence is in his weapons, his skill, and his strength.

If we had met Goliath personally, we may have found some things we liked about him. But the storyteller allows us to develop no affection for this fighter. He lives outside the people of God not only by birth but by declaration as well. He does not live to advance the kingdom of God but to defy and destroy it. By characterizing Goliath in this way, the narrator makes him become a problem to be solved in this narrative, a problem that only a true leader of Israel could solve.

SAUL

Saul has been on the stage in the preceding chapters of Samuel for some time. We know enough about him to be confused about him. Will he repent and resume effective leadership of God's people, or will God's rejection of him be sustained? Despite our reservations about him, he remains the reigning leader of Israel and the one expected to resolve the problem associated with the Philistine intrusion. Saul's personal name occurs sixteen times in the story. Every mention of his name occurs in the first thirty-nine verses, before the climax of the story is reached. As soon as David steps onto the battlefield, Saul's name and presence completely disappear from the story, along with any expectation that he will somehow find courage in the example of David to lead as one should. In only one instance is reference made to the "king" (17:25). This is in a discussion, not of what the king will do personally in fighting Goliath, but what the king will do for the one who steps up to lead in this way.

The absence of a royal title is complemented by the lack of royal actions. Rather than what Saul does, what he fails to do captures our attention. He himself does not stand to fight Goliath, he fails to inspire action in the other soldiers, and he fails to articulate any sort of plan to bring the matter to resolution. His inaction stands at the forefront of his characterization. Twice the storyteller informs us that the Israelite soldiers, including Saul, were dismayed and greatly afraid of Goliath (17:11, 24). As we noted earlier, this is anything but the kind of man the Israelites expected in their king (8:20). In fact, the only "positive" action we see Saul taking is a half-hearted effort to arm David for the battle (17:38–39). Even this effort ends in failure.

Saul not only fails to act much in this narrative; he also fails to say much. When he does speak, what is most apparent is his lack of faith. When David boldly announces his trust in the Lord (17:32), we are ready to respond with a loud "Amen." Saul does not follow our lead. David's confession of faith does not jolt Saul into reassessing his own perspective. Instead, he responds negatively, focusing only on David's age and lack of experience in a bid to discourage David from thinking that his actions could live up to his lofty ideals: "You are not able to go against this Philistine to fight with him; for you are just a boy, and he has been a warrior from his youth" (17:33).

Saul is given one last chance to speak in this story. Taken out of context, his final words might seem to express a hint of faith: "Go, and may the LORD be with you!" (17:37). But the storyteller seemingly presents this statement to us not as a turning point in Saul's characterization but as the final nail in his coffin. Saul said it, but he really did not own this language. He speaks these final words not so much in faith as in desperation. Thus, in a burst of irony, Saul's closing words have touched on exactly what David has that Saul lacks, a faith in God's presence.

DAVID

The individual who receives the most complete and complex characterization by the storyteller is David. With the exception of a few questions raised about his motives and character in scene three, the storyteller is bent on showing us not only what qualities are housed within a great leader but also that David has them.

David's personal name occurs more often than any other in the story, solidifying his position as the main character in the story. Although his personal name does not appear until the twelfth verse of the story, it occurs twice as often as the name of Saul, sustaining its presence throughout the story long after the name of Saul is discontinued. Again and again, the storyteller reminds us of David's presence and importance through this characterization technique.

David's actions in the face of the Philistine threat also rise well above those of Saul. When we meet David, he is taking care of the family sheep and running back and forth to the Elah Valley with supplies and news (17:14–15). While a small thing, it is worth noting that each time he is given a new responsibility, he carefully delegates his old responsibility to another person. When he leaves the sheep, he places them into the hands of an alternate shepherd (17:20). When he leaves the provisions he was carrying to the Elah Valley, he leaves them in the hands of "the keeper of the baggage" (17:22). In a quiet way, the storyteller is noting that David is a responsible man. While this may not be the only or even the most important quality of leadership, it is one that attracts our support as readers.

But these more ordinary actions are the last ordinary things we hear about David. Before long we see him carefully selecting five smooth stones from the wadi with sling in hand (17:40). While Saul has done nothing, David is clearly doing something. As Saul and the Israelites stand paralyzed before Goliath, David "runs quickly" to meet the challenger (17:48). Time then slows as the details of David's shot and its consequences are recounted. "David put his hand in his bag, took out a stone, slung it, and struck the Philistine on his forehead; the stone sank into his forehead, and he fell face down on the ground" (17:49). This is not the end, although verse 50 does say the stone killed Goliath. But David is running again, making sure the deed is done. Standing over the incapacitated warrior, he delivers the insurance deathblow with the very sword that threatened Israel (17:51). Throughout this scene David is depicted as a man of action constantly in motion. Those detailed actions stand in striking contrast to the inaction of Saul noted above.

David is characterized as wise, as responsible, as active, but most importantly he is characterized as a man of faith. Here the speeches of David rise above all contenders. Recall that Saul is virtually silent. When he speaks, Saul can only mutter misgivings and resignation. By contrast, David again and again gives profound speeches that articulate his trust in the Lord. He alone among the Israelites gives voice to the incongruity of a heathen warrior defying Israel: "For who is this uncircumcised Philistine that he should defy the armies of the living God?" (17:26b). David alone voices his willingness to fight: "Let no one's heart fail because of him; your servant will go and fight with this Philistine" (17:32). That is only the warm up for the longer speeches we find in 17:34–37 and 17:45–47. As we move toward the climax of the story, his speeches get longer and become filled with more details that articulate the depth of his relationship to the Lord. By sheer repetition and length of his speech, David makes it clear that he is no Saul. In them, we clearly see not only what a leader of God's people looks like, we also see that David is in fact that leader. Goliath counted on his weapons and skills. Saul despaired of David's weapons, experience, and skills. In doing so, both Saul and Goliath failed to take into account the power and presence of the Lord. David did not. He declared he did this so "this assembly may know that the LORD does not save by sword and spear; for the battle is the LORD's and he will give you [Goliath] into our hand" (17:47).

So through careful characterization of the participants, the storyteller has shaped our impressions of these three men. Goliath is the godless challenger. Saul is the king of Israel who lacks the wisdom and faith to lead. David is the man of wisdom and faith who rises to lead God's people in their moment of need.

Time and Setting

The storyteller not only controls our experience with the characters in the narrative but also our experience with time and location. We will now take a closer look at how those topics make their contribution to the story and the delivery of its meaning.

TIME

The matter of time is handled subtly throughout the story. On one occasion, very explicit mention of time is worthy of note. On a quick and light read of the story, we may be left with the impression that Goliath came out to make his unthinkable challenge to the Israelite army just once. In verse 16, the storyteller tells us that this challenge had been issued and reissued to the Israelites twice a day for "forty days." Before David arrives on the scene, this challenge has fallen from the mouth of Goliath at least eighty times! Mention of the forty days makes the whole matter even more embarrassing for Saul and the Israelite army, increasing the tension within the narrative.

By contrast to the summary fashion in which those forty days pass, two scenes in this story are presented with considerable detail, dramatically slowing the passage of time. In scene four, dialogue slows the pace of time, creating emphasis on the exchange taking place between Saul and David. By using this technique, the storyteller invites us to linger longer here and to listen more carefully to what is said as Saul and David exchange verbal observations on the state of this crisis in Israel. Time also slows in scene five. At the climatic moment of the narrative, the storyteller uses both dialogue and more detailed description of the participants' actions to slow the passage of time. Since this scene contains the climax of the story, revealing the nature of true leadership, it is fitting that we spend more of our reading time here.

SETTING

The first verses of the exposition carefully articulate the setting of the story. Because of the great amount of geographical detail we find in the description of the setting, we will return to discuss it in the section on narrative geography that follows. For the moment, we note that all the events of this story occur outdoors and most of them occur in association with the Elah Valley, with the Israelite army occupying one ridge and the Philistine army occupying the other ridge (17:2–3). This last detail suggests that we are witnessing an event that is occurring within a natural amphitheater. While the details of some Bible stories occur in spaces as private as one's own bedroom, this story occurs in a very public venue. The disparaging challenges of Goliath are shouted for all to hear from this stage, a public stage that also betrays Saul's lack of leadership. In the same way, this public arena showcases the words and actions of David. It is no wonder that the storyteller provides us with these details of the setting. Hundreds are enabled to witness and eventually recount the story for the benefit of those not here on this day.

Narrative Geography

While the setting for the story gives us a sense for the public venue, we find more geographical language at work here than would be necessary to accomplish that goal. Space prevents us from treating all twenty geographical references that occur in this story, but we will focus energy on the geographical details presented in the exposition of the story.[3]

> Now the Philistines gathered their army for battle; they gathered at Socoh, which belongs to Judah, and encamped between Socoh and Azekah, in Ephes-dammim. Saul and the Israelites gathered and encamped in the valley of Elah, and formed ranks against the Philistines. The Philistines stood on the mountain on the one side, and Israel stood on the mountain on the other side. And there came out from the camp of the Philistines a champion named Goliath, of Gath. (1 Sam. 17:1–4a)

The amount of detail goes well beyond what would be necessary for the mere establishing of the story's setting. That is our clue to press on with a deeper investigation of the narrative-geographical strategy the storyteller puts to work.

First, we note the mention of three cities. A map reveals that these three cities are associated with the Elah Valley. The Elah Valley is an east-west valley that stretches between the home of the Philistines on the coastal plain and the home of the Israelites in the Judean hills. Gath was the Philistine fort that guarded access to this valley on the western (Philistine) side of the valley.[4] Azekah lies on a ridge in the middle of this valley. Socoh lies east of Azekah.[5] Ephes-dammim is the name of the S-shaped valley that lies between Socoh and Azekah.

With this mental map in mind, we see how the storyteller superimposes this story on that map. The Philistine forces have penetrated deeply into the Elah Valley, establishing their camp in Ephes-dammim. This means that the Israelite army has been pushed to the far eastern segment of the valley with their backs against the rising terrain of the central mountains. Thus as Goliath steps forward to make his challenge, he does so at a time when the Israelite army is already in a very precarious position. The Elah Valley is all but lost.

The geographical detail not only shows how precarious a position the Israelite army holds, but also reminds us of what is at stake in the loss of this valley. The Elah Valley is part of the Judean Shephelah that extends from the Aijalon Valley southward for thirty miles. The Hebrew name, Shephelah, alludes to the "humble" elevation of the hills. By contrast to the mountains just east of them, the Shephelah hills rise to little more than 1,200 feet above the valley floor. These hills form east-west ridges separated by east-west valleys that are from six to ten miles in width. The Elah Valley itself is very characteristic of the Judean Shephelah. This wide u-shaped valley connects the heartland of the Philistines on the coastal plain with the heartland of the Israelites in the central mountains. As the writer opens the story of David and Goliath, this connecting-link valley has all but been lost.

But how would the people living in the mountains just above those valleys have interpreted that fact? To gain that perspective, we need to press even more deeply into an understanding of the economic and national securities issues in view. As with the other valleys in the Judean Shephelah, the Elah Valley had much to offer economically.

Trees are part of that economic formula. On the low ridges of this valley, we find the sycamore and terebinth trees. The abundant sycamore (1 Kings 10:27; 2 Chr. 1:15 and 9:27) produced a low-quality fig. Yet it is not the tree's fig but its wood which made it so valuable to those in the hills of Judah. Given the general lack of wood in the area, residents employed other construction materials when building their homes and shelters—generally fieldstones and mud bricks. But it was difficult to build a structure without spanning the walls with wood so that a roof could be put into place. Here the sycamore limbs came into use. They were not used to frame walls, but their light weight made them ideal roof rafters.[6] The other tree, the terebinth, produced turpentine, a brownish-yellow resin collected and used for caulking, shellacking wall paintings, and in the mummification process.[7] Thus the trees growing on the ridges of the Elah Valley promised to bring economic profits to those who controlled them.

The valley proper also made an economic contribution to those who controlled it. Here sufficient rainfall and rich soils produced strong grain fields.[8] The potential of such agricultural fields stands in marked contrast to the fields available in the hill country. In Judah, the steep mountainsides plunge into narrow V-shaped valleys that contain very little room for grain agriculture. This forces the residents to invest significant effort in building and maintaining terraced fields on the sides of the mountains.[9] No one who expended energy on agriculture in the Judean hills would miss the incredible value of the wide, natural fields lying just to their west. Thus the potential for harvesting construction grade lumber and for harvesting wheat fields made the Elah Valley very desirable land to hold.

Economic desirability fueled a desire for this land, but national security made the fight for this land absolutely necessary. The Israelites lived in the mountains of Judah that rise well over 3,000 feet. The elevation and ruggedness of these mountains provide its residents with a secure isolation from those living on the coastal plain who must fight uphill to get to them. But the east-west valleys of the Judean Shephelah—and the Elah Valley in particular—form an "Achilles' heel." These easily accessed valley floors lead to ridges that lead directly into the natural transportation routes in the hill country. That makes valleys like the Elah Valley a military buffer zone lying between the Philistines on the coastal plain and the Israelites living in the hills to their east. If control of such a valley is lost, the door for infiltration lies wide open. Thus the economic value of the Elah Valley and its critical role as a buffer zone make it not just desirable but necessary for the Israelites to control. If there were a valley worth fighting for, this is it.

With this enhanced awareness of the geography, it is time to again return to the strategic use of geography by the storyteller. Even before we meet David or Saul or Goliath in this narrative, we are told that a battle is occurring for control of the Elah Valley. This ramps up the crisis on its own. But the storyteller goes on to say that the Philistines are encamped deeply in the valley, with Saul and his forces pressed into the eastern portion of the valley. Those details portray a national security crisis of incredible proportions. The Elah Valley, which brings with it great economic value and the promise of security to those living in the Judean mountains, has all but been lost to the Philistines. If there were a time for a leader to rise within Israel, this is it. Armed with these insights, the listener will be able to watch the response of both David and Saul against a new backdrop. The physical setting indicates that this is an apt proving ground for leadership.

The Patterning Play of Words

The final dimension of the storytelling craft we will consider is the patterning play of words. The story of David and Goliath is filled with many figures of speech. Once again, space will limit us to highlighting a few of the examples, noting how they contribute to the story. We will look at several examples of repetition in the story, one instance of irony, and a series of questions exchanged between David and his oldest brother.

REPETITION

Repetition is a favorite tool in the hands of the divine storyteller, and the story of David and Goliath has no shortage of repetition within it. We will look at three examples. As Goliath steps forward to announce his challenge, note how frequently he deploys the word *servant* (or *serve*) in his speech:

"Why have you come out to draw up for battle? Am I not a Philistine and are you not *servants* of Saul? Choose a man for yourselves, and let him come down to me. If he is able to fight with me and kill me, then we will be your *servants*; but if I prevail against him and kill him, then you shall be our *servants* and *serve us*." (1 Sam. 17:8–9)

As Goliath calls for a leader to arise within Israel to fight with him, he uses language that points up the lack of leadership he sees before him. By repeating the idea of servitude again and again, he makes the point that he is looking at servants who will always be servants serving someone. No leaders are in sight.

As the Israelites respond to Goliath's challenge, we find repetition at work again defining and emphasizing the response of the Israelites. Immediately after the challenge, the narrator reports the response: "When Saul and all Israel heard these words of the Philistine, they were dismayed and greatly afraid" (17:11). Shortly after David arrives on the scene, Goliath bellows his challenge again. The narrator reports the same response. "All the Israelites, when they saw the man, fled from him and were very much afraid" (17:24). The repetition of this language, "greatly" or "very much afraid," indicates that this is the status quo in the Israelites' camp. Since faith mitigates fear, we see a helpless lack of faith paralyzing the army under Saul's leadership. Only David breaks the chain of fear by declaring, "Let no one's heart fail because of him; your servant will go and fight with this Philistine" (17:32). While the repeated response of fear heightens the nature of the crisis, David's breaking of this chain signals the rise of a leader in Israel.

The third example of repetition is associated with the storyteller's formal mention of "Philistine" or "Philistines" throughout the narrative. It may not strike us on a casual read of these fifty-four verses. When we go back and count, we find the word *Philistine* (or *Philistines*) repeated thirty-eight times, more than once in every two verses on average. This repetition subtly but persistently announces the problem again and again. From the Israelite perspective, the Philistines are in exactly the wrong place, a place that threatens both the Israelites' economic well-being and their national security. This refrain takes on a new meaning when we arrive at verse 52.

Once David has defeated Goliath, the repetition of Philistine continues, but with an entirely different purpose: "The troops of Israel and Judah rose up with a shout and pursued the Philistines as far as Gath and the gates of Ekron, so that the wounded Philistines fell on the way from Shaaraim as far as Gath and Ekron" (17:52). Specific mention is made of Gath and Ekron because these cities lie outside the Elah Valley. Under the leadership of David, the Israelite army rallies and drives the Philistines from the Elah Valley. While the repetition of the word *Philistine* had previously had the overtone of defeat, the repetition now signals a victory, for only the bodies of dead and dying Philistines are left in the location that is so precious to the Israelites. When a real leader arises, the enemy fails and falls.

IRONY

Irony also makes its contribution to the story of David and Goliath. Although Saul would certainly have said more than what the storyteller has allowed us to hear in his meeting with David in scene four, we are only allowed to hear him speak a couple of sentences. One of those sentences is a pointed case of verbal irony where Saul speaks a much greater truth than he knows, and speaks it at his own expense. After a powerful and heartfelt speech comes to us from the lips of David (vv. 32–37a), Saul responds, "Go, and may the LORD be with you!" (17:37b) When taken from its context, this language is a wonderful prayer and blessing. But the reader of this story is unable to hear the positive in this language. Saul has given us no reason to expect that he has suddenly developed a confidence in the Lord's presence. That leads us to hear these words as words spoken in resignation. They are also ironic in that they place a finger directly on what will give David success when Saul has failed. Neither Saul's armor nor David's sling, but the presence of the Lord makes the difference in this battle. Thus the rejected king of Israel who has lost his faith in God's presence and blessing ironically identifies the very difference between himself and David that allows David's fortunes to rise in this story.

RHETORICAL QUESTIONS

In reading scene three, yet another form of word play becomes evident as we meet a dialogue filled with questions and counter-questions. After Goliath again makes his presence known, the Israelite soldiers ask the first rhetorical question, "Have you seen this man who has come up?" (17:25) Of course, how could anyone have missed him! That is their point. David acknowledges his awareness of Goliath's challenge by asking a factual question: "What shall be done for the man who kills this Philistine, and takes away the reproach from Israel?" (17:26a) As David seeks clarification, his oldest brother reads it as impudence. Eliab fires off two rhetorical questions designed to strike back at his upstart sibling: "Why have you come down? With whom have you left those few sheep in the wilderness?" (17:28) Perhaps covering for his own lack of courage and still stinging from David's anointing at the hand of Samuel, Eliab uses these questions to suggest David is presumptuous and irresponsible. These questions force the reader to think about David's motives and character, offering a bit of complication to the hero's arrival. Feeling the sting of Eliab's questions, David asks the final question of the scene. "What have I done now? It was only a question" (17:29). David's final direct quote of the scene proclaims the purity of his motives. But is David getting it right? Had he come to the battlefront in a bid to obtain glory, riches, and fame? Would his leadership be compromised by self-interest and self-pride? The following scenes will answer that question for us. But through a series of rhetorical questions, the divine storyteller has challenged us to become critical thinkers evaluating both the sitting ruler of Israel and his anointed successor.

Conclusion

While you have likely heard the story of David and Goliath before, it is unlikely that you have thought about the various ways in which the divine storyteller has shaped our meeting of this event. By following through a formal set of steps, we have been able to reverse the building process and examine various components that have shaped our reading of this story. In doing so, we have come to conclude that this story is about leadership, and particularly points us to the fact that a true leader of God's people is one who leads with full faith and confidence in the Lord's presence even when faced with what appears to be an insurmountable obstacle. Every scene and every detail makes its contribution to the revelation of that fact and the reality that it is David rather than Saul who has the right heart for leading God's people.

Notes

[1]In reviewing the details of chapter 17, it has become clear to this author that a narrative break occurs at verse 54. Verse 54 marks the conclusion to the crisis of the story. Verses 55–58 seem to serve as an appendix to the story whose contents live outside the narrative frame of verses 1–54. Thus this analysis will focus on the narrative content, structure, and meaning of verses 1–54.

[2]We note that in these early verses a significant amount of geographical detail is provided. We will address this detail and its contribution to the story in the narrative-geographical segment of this discussion.

[3]A more complete discussion of the narrative geography at work in this story may be found in John A. Beck, "David and Goliath, a Story of Place," *Westminster Theological Journal,* forthcoming.

[4]Ephraim Stern, "Zafit, Tel," in *The New Encyclopedia of Archaeological Investigation of the Holy Land,* ed. Ephraim Stern (Jerusalem: The Israel Exploration Society and Carta, 1993), 4: 1522.

[5]David A. Dorsey, *The Roads and Highways of Ancient Israel* (Baltimore: The Johns Hopkins University Press, 1991), 189–90.

[6]Aharon Kempinski and Ronny Reich, *The Architecture of Ancient Israel* (Jerusalem: The Israel Exploration Society, 1992), 7.

[7]Philip J. King and Lawrence E. Stager, *Life in Biblical Israel,* Library of Ancient Israel (Louisville: Westminster John Knox Press, 2001), 109.

[8]Amihai Mazar, *Archaeology of the Land of the Bible 10,000–586 B.C.E.* (New York: Doubleday, 1992), 4.

[9]John A. Beck, *The Land of Milk and Honey: An Introduction to the Geography of Israel* (St. Louis: Concordia Publishing House, 2006).

10

Seeking Meaning in Jesus' Stay in Samaria *(John 4)*

The second detailed illustration of the storyteller's craft transports us from the time of David to the time of Jesus. Here we join Jesus as he interacts with the Samaritan woman at Jacob's well and as he draws the citizens of Sychar to acknowledge him as the Savior (Jn. 4:1–42). By applying the method of analysis defined in chapter eight, our understanding of the story's details, our appreciation for the artistry of its composition, and our comprehension of its meaning will grow dramatically.

This analysis, similar to that in the previous chapter, is not meant to be a complete commentary on this story, nor should it be considered a comprehensive treatment of its narrative qualities. We will follow the seven-step approach to illustrate the insights that may be gained through a narrative-critical analysis of the story. We will once again discover how the artful presentation of the plot, the process of characterization, the use of time, narrative geography, and the patterning play of words conspire to hold our attention and to direct our response to the story. Once again we pray that the Holy Spirit might sensitize our ears and eyes so that, guided by our method, we might engage this story in a deliberate, detailed, and thoughtful way.

Step One: Set Aside What You Already Know

Our first goal is to once again limit the power of our preconceptions so that any previous knowledge of the story's details or any understanding of the story's meaning might be set aside for the moment. This will permit the particulars of the narrative to seize our attention and lead us into the experience the storyteller intends for us.

Since a gospel account lies before us, we need to inquire if this particular story from the life of Jesus is represented in more than one gospel, for one historical event frequently gives rise to two or more parallel gospel accounts. If that were the case, our goal would be to restrict our analysis to the details and presentation style of just one gospel account, rather than attempting to merge multiple presentations into a hybrid story for analysis. A quick check of our study Bible indicates that only John records this story from Jesus' ministry for us. Thus we need not worry about the risk of conflating accounts.

The other potential preconception we need to address in regard to John 4 is where to place the close of the story unit. Those familiar with this story may be inclined to end at verse 26. This story might well be called, "The Story of Jesus and the Samaritan Woman at Jacob's Well." Our approach will extend the narrative unit, delaying the close of the story until we reach verse 42. Our motive for doing so is related both to the subject matter and to the construction of the story that will be discussed in the pages ahead. Here we note that the early verses of John 4 move Jesus into a Samaritan context. Not until verse 43 does this larger story change audience and location, moving Jesus into Galilee. By extending the close of the story to verse 42, we find that the interaction between Jesus and the Samaritan woman is only the first scene of a larger story. With that larger story in view, we can entitle this particular narrative, "The Samaritans of Sychar Discover Jesus' True Identity."

Step Two: Read around the Story

With this check of our presuppositions complete and the story boundary established, we can take the second step. Honoring the fact that this story of Jesus in Samaria is not an autonomous narrative but one that flows from its literary setting, our goal is to better understand the general direction of John's gospel and the stories that lead up to the presentation in John 4.

John's gospel provides a direct and clear statement about its purpose. John's report on the life and ministry of Jesus, by John's own admission, has been selective (Jn. 20:30–31). This account of Jesus' life took the form that it did to accomplish one significant outcome: "But these are written so that you may come to believe that Jesus is the Messiah, the Son of God, and that through believing you may have life in his name" (20:31). John is not agenda neutral in his selection and presentation of these events. He wants people to believe that Jesus is the Messiah so that they too might have eternal life.

In the stories that lead up to John 4, we see this agenda at work. The book itself begins with a profound prologue (1:1–18) that boldly proclaims the eternal heritage of Jesus, the Messiah, who took on the flesh of mortals. The divine storyteller then directs our attention to the work and words of John the Baptist. John clearly shuns the title of Messiah, asserting that he is only the transition figure who prepares the way for the Messiah (1:19–28). When Jesus comes into the physical presence of John, he points in Jesus' direction and announces, "Here is the Lamb of God who takes away the sin of the world!" (1:29). After recounting the details of the miracles associated with Jesus' baptism, John adds, "And I myself have seen and have testified that this is the Son of God" (1:34).

While John the Baptist is the first to say it, he is not the only one who sees that Jesus is the long-awaited Messiah. When Andrew comes to know Jesus, he runs to find his brother, Peter. Breathless, he blurts out, "We have found the Messiah" (1:41). We do not escape the first chapter of John's gospel without being confronted again and again with the premise that lies at the heart of this gospel. Through his own language in the prologue and through the language of others, the divine storyteller proclaims that Jesus is the promised Messiah.

As persuasive as the gospel of John has been to this point, a second theme emerges that indicates not everyone was finding it so easy to accept John's premise.[1] This gospel is also filled with stories of people who struggle, doubt, and even entirely reject the notion of Jesus as Messiah. For example, when Philip comes to Nathanael with the news that he has found the one that Moses wrote about, Nathanael brushes this news off with a disdainful question: "Can anything good come out of Nazareth?" (1:46). Only after he meets Jesus does Nathanael affirm the premise of this gospel: "Rabbi, you are the Son of God! You are the King of Israel!" (1:49).

Nicodemus and the disciples of John also struggle in their bid to understand and believe that the kingdom of God has come to earth. Nicodemus comes to Jesus during the night. He affirms that Jesus must be a great teacher given the miraculous signs that he can do. As Jesus attempts to lead Nicodemus into a deeper understanding of his identity and mission, this teacher of Israel struggles to comprehend it all: "Jesus answered him, 'Very truly, I tell you, no one can see the kingdom of God without being born from above.' Nicodemus said to him, 'How can anyone be born after having grown old? Can one enter a second time into the mother's womb and be born?'" (3:3–4). Finally, the storyteller brings to us the confusion evident in John the Baptist's disciples. These disciples were concerned that this Jesus was drawing crowds to himself and away from their teacher (3:26). The patient teaching of John again asserts the theme of the gospel, marking the distinctive origins of Jesus: "The one who comes from above is above all; the one who is of the earth belongs to the earth and speaks about earthly things. The one who comes from heaven is above all" (Jn. 3:31).

Thus in the chapters that lead up to our narrative in John 4, we observe two themes played and replayed again and again. We find various individuals announcing in clear and striking language that Jesus is the promised Messiah. And we find individuals from various social camps and categories struggling in their attempts to understand and to believe that Jesus is the promised Messiah. Since the goal of this gospel is to build a greater and deeper clarity on this topic, the reader entering John 4 may well expect to see attention given to these two themes as well.

Step Three: Read the Story Slowly Several Times

With the larger literary setting of the story in view, it is time to become intimate with the details of John 4:1–42. Read the story through several times in a location where external interruptions will be kept to a minimum. The goal here is for us to become familiar with the details of the story. During these readings, our eyes may be drawn to unique components of the characterization process. We may be tempted to pause upon encountering the formal mention of time or setting. A particular form of word play may invite further reflection. For the moment, shun the temptation to stop reading and reflect. There will be opportunity to do that later. Read the entire story as an interacting unit and allow the storyteller to touch you with the narrative as naturally as possible.

Step Four: Identify the Structure of the Story

The details of this story, like the rest of the stories in the Bible, do not flow haphazardly but participate in a structure meant to claim and retain our interest as listeners. In the fourth step, we will look for the structure of the story to get a sense of how it flows from exposition to crisis to resolution.

Our experience with this event from Jesus' life begins with six verses of exposition. True to form, this exposition delivers information on the setting, characters, and time of day before allowing us to enter the first scene of the story. The exposition first addresses the matter of setting, noting that Jesus has initiated a change in location. The stories leading up to John 4 are set in Judea. Now Jesus is on the move with his sights set on Galilee (4:3). Within the real world of the events, this move from south to north in Israel would have entailed a trip through the intervening region of Samaria. This larger region will be the home for the story that follows. But the exposition does not stop here. Through a series of steps the storyteller further narrows the setting. The camera zooms in, and our focus moves from the region of Samaria to the city of Sychar and eventually to a water source just outside of Sychar. In this clearly defined spot during the noon hour, the physically tired Jesus is joined by a second individual, a Samaritan woman who has come to draw water.

With these details of setting, time, and characters in place, the dialogue begins between Jesus and the Samaritan woman. It does not take us long to reach the crisis that lies at the heart of this story. Jesus asks for a drink of water. When the woman questions the propriety of the request, identifying Jesus as an ordinary Jewish man, Jesus articulates the crisis: "If you knew the gift of God, and who it is that is saying to you, 'Give me a drink,' you would have asked him, and he would have given you living water" (4:10).

As we have seen so often in the narratives leading up to this story, we find yet another person struggling to understand just who Jesus is.

In contrast to many of the other stories in the preceding chapters, this crisis of understanding is not resolved quickly but played upon through the following verses, complicated at one turn and then the next. In the first scene, the woman sees Jesus as only a Jewish man who needs a drink of water. When she hesitates to lower her jar into the well for him, Jesus turns the tables on the Samaritan woman and offers to give her a drink. She responds with a glib, rhetorical question that deflects Jesus' attempts to help her: "Sir, you have no bucket, and the well is deep. Where do you get that living water" (4:11)? Undaunted, Jesus presses on with the metaphor, offering her water that will become a spring of water welling up to eternal life. Once again, the woman does not find the speaker or the message credible. The words of her reply could be read as a pious request, or they could ring with sarcasm: "Sir, give me this water, so that I may never be thirsty or have to keep coming here to draw water" (4:15). Though she has been given a personal audience with the Messiah, the Samaritan woman cannot get past Jesus' ordinary appearance. She sees him only as a thirsty Jewish man–and a strange one at that–offering water he cannot deliver.

The complication to the crisis continues as Jesus gets personal. He broaches the topic of her marital status, showing that he has intimate knowledge of her personal life. The Samaritan woman is taken aback both by the topic and by his knowledge of her personal affairs. She offers a new identification that comes closer to Jesus' true identity, yet is still short of the mark. Formerly Jesus was only a "Jew" looking for a drink of water (4:9). Now she says, "Sir, I see that you are a prophet" (4:19). This identification of Jesus shows that the woman has grown in her understanding of the presence before her, but the crisis continues, for she has yet to see him as the Messiah.

The Samaritan woman quickly turns the conversation away from the less comfortable topic of her martial status to the more general topic of the differences between Jews and Samaritans, particularly in regards to how they worship. She is confused by the claims and counter-claims made by Jews and Samaritans, one claiming Jerusalem as the only appropriate worship site and the other Mount Gerizim (4:20). By quoting Jesus, the storyteller again asserts the crisis of knowledge: "You worship what you do not know, we worship what we know, for salvation is from the Jews" (4:22). Confronted more directly by her lack of knowledge, the poor woman has had enough. In desperation, she blurts out that she does know one thing: "I know that Messiah is coming... When he comes, he will proclaim all things to us" (4:25). In an incredible moment of irony, the very word "Messiah" crosses her lips. Yet even this becomes a further complication in the plot since she has only indicated her belief in a coming Messiah, not her belief that Jesus is one and the same.

The plot then appears to be on the verge of its climatic moment, for Jesus announces, "I am he, the one who is speaking to you." We would expect such an explicit statement to be the highpoint in the story. Jesus has declared himself to be the very Messiah whom this woman claims to seek. But this Messianic declaration becomes a false climax in this narrative, skipping like a stone off smooth water. Although the Samaritan woman has heard it, she has not believed it. She leaves Jesus' presence intrigued, but struggling with belief. The climax of the story and the resolution that follows will only come when Jesus' true identity is accepted in faith. That has yet to happen. The Samaritan woman leaves the well and returns to the residents of Sychar, wondering if she has just met the Messiah or an imposter. She goes to her fellow residents in Sychar to discuss the matter with them. In that context, she says, "Come and see a man who told me everything I have ever done! He cannot be the Messiah, can he?" (4:29).

As this question hangs in the air, the storyteller redirects our attention away from the city and back to the well, where a further complication arises. Jesus is at the well with his disciples. They take their turn in demonstrating a lack of understanding both about Jesus' identity and mission. The disciples had left Jesus at the well while they went to buy food. Upon returning, they encourage him to eat. Jesus' response is terse and to the point: "I have food to eat that you do not know about" (4:32). The food Jesus is talking about is his mission work. As is shown in his words that follow, the disciples did not think the Samaritans and the city of Sychar to be an important mission stop. Thus they, too, demonstrate a lack of knowledge that further complicates resolution to the story.

Just when we are about to throw our hands up in despair assuming that no one is going to get it, the storyteller brings us to the climax and conclusion of the narrative. While it has been a long and painful task to follow the struggles of the Samaritan woman and the disciples as they demonstrate a lack of understanding, we are about to find relief. Following all the failures to understand and Jesus' repeated declarations that people do not know, we finally reach the turning point, the climax, and the conclusion of the narrative. The people in Sychar have been intrigued enough by the woman's testimony that they invite Jesus to spend some time with them, so he stays two days. At the conclusion of this time with Jesus, the people of Sychar give voice to the conviction we have been longing to hear: "They said to the woman, 'It is no longer because of what you said that we believe, for we have heard for ourselves, and we know that this is truly the Savior of the world'" (4:42). Thus following the exposition, the storyteller leads us through the event in a very structured way. Misunderstanding of who Jesus is and what he has to say stands as the crisis to be resolved. Through a variety of complications that include experiments in identification of this man, the storyteller finally leads us to the Samaritans' declaration of Jesus' true identity.

Step Five: Identify the Topic and Point of View

The topic of this story and the point of view being expressed on that topic are closely linked both to the self-stated purpose of John's gospel as well as to the plot we have just discussed. The topic of this story is the identity of Jesus. God had appeared to mortals prior to the time of Jesus in ways that brought no mistaking of his presence. Formerly, when God stepped through the threshold of eternity onto the stage of God's created world, the arrival was announced with an array of visible and audible indicators: pillars of cloud, fire, thunder, and a booming voice. In stark contrast to what this world had experienced before, Jesus slipped quietly into this world. Born in an animal shelter, he lived in a place where he would have received little attention from the religious leaders of his day. For most of his life, he blended in with the locals.

Because Jesus looked so much like everyone else, this story takes up the topic of Jesus' true identity, taking the point of view that Jesus is the Messiah, the Savior promised in the Old Testament. Through a series of experimental identifications and by weaving through various cultural obstacles, the storyteller draws us to adopt the language of the residents of Sychar: "We have heard for ourselves, and we know that this is truly the Savior of the world" (4:42). Thus the topic and point of view in this story conform very closely to the self-stated purpose for the entire book, which John articulates in 20:31. The topic is Jesus' identity. The point of view expressed on the topic is that Jesus is the promised Messiah, deserving of our faith.

Step Six: Divide the Story into Scenes

With a clear sense of the narrative structure, topic, and point of view in hand, it is time to divide the story into scenes and consider the role each scene plays in accomplishing the storyteller's goal. Following the exposition, the story comes to us in four scenes. Each scene change is marked by a change in location and participants. Scene one is the longest of the scenes (4:7–27). It occurs at Jacob's well, recording the conversation between Jesus and the Samaritan woman. Scene two (4:28–30) is a short scene that occurs within Sychar summarizing the testimony that the Samaritan woman gave to the people in the city. Scene three (4:31–38) occurs at the same time as scene two, but returns us to Jacob's well for a conversation between Jesus and the disciples. Finally, scene four (4:39–42) takes us back into the city, where it summarizes the experience that the residents of Sychar had with Jesus.

Scene One

The first scene of this story is the longest, recording the conversation between Jesus and the Samaritan woman in great detail. When Jesus asks the woman if she will use her jar to draw a drink of water for him, the Samaritan woman responds by pointing out the social obstacles that make this simple request seem less than appropriate. She calls Jesus "a Jew" and identifies herself as a "woman of Samaria" (4:9). Both her gender and her regional affiliation would normally have precluded any further interaction between the two. But Jesus uses her observation that he is "a Jew" to continue a conversation that takes us quickly to the crisis in this story, the inability of people to fully understand his true identity. Jesus seizes upon a word that will become a key concept in this story, the one for "to know." "If you *knew* the gift of God, and who it is that is saying to you, 'Give me a drink'…" (4:10). This is the problem. She does not know; and others in this story will follow her lead, failing to fully comprehend Jesus' true identity.

The scene does not stop here. The storyteller allows us to observe as this woman experiments with language that works ever closer to the accurate identification of Jesus. With sarcasm in her voice she asks if Jesus thinks that he is greater than the famous Jacob (4:12). When Jesus presses too close to home, identifying issues that surround her marital status, she says, "Sir, I see that you are a prophet" (4:19). Confronted again and again by her lack of knowledge, the Samaritan woman insists that she knows one thing for sure: "I know that Messiah is coming" (4:25). Thus throughout this conversation recorded for us from scene one, the listener is participating with her in the process of experimental identification, getting closer and closer to Jesus' true identity every step of the way.

The scene draws to a close with a thunderbolt. Jesus does something that he did very infrequently during his earthly ministry. He says in just so many words that he, in fact, is the Messiah. When the woman expresses her hope that the arrival of the Messiah will finally bring clarity to so many of the religious issues being debated between the Jews and Samaritans, Jesus says to her, "I am he, the one who is speaking to you" (4:26). While such a powerful testimony would make a fitting climax to the story, here it serves to be but a false climax, for the woman leaves Jesus, mesmerized by his depth of knowledge and intrigued by his statements; yet she does not affirm Jesus as the Savior.

Scene Two

The second scene (4:28–30) transports us from the well into the city of Sychar. Changes have begun to occur in the Samaritan woman, but she remains skeptical. The storyteller does not give us access to all that she said to the residents of Sychar, but does record two sentences that reflect her response to Jesus' claim that he was the Messiah. One the one hand, she knows that there is something special about this person. Although they had never met before, he knew intimate details of her personal life that both made her uncomfortable and curious about him. She said, "Come and see a man who told me everything I have ever done!" (4:29a) But her identification falls short of full faith and confidence. This becomes apparent in the second part of the quote: "He cannot be the Messiah, can he?" (4:29b). Thus this scene fails to bring the plot full circle to its conclusion. It shows us that the Samaritan woman has been touched by her exchange with Jesus, but she is still reluctant to assign him the title of Messiah. So we are left to wait a bit longer as the storyteller draws us forward, looking for the moment when the identity of Jesus will be fully affirmed.

Scene Three

Scene three gives us some hope that this might occur. The storyteller returns us to Jacob's well and a dialogue between Jesus and the disciples. The Samaritan woman has left the stage and takes with her the uncertainty about Jesus that has plagued the story from the start. Now as Jesus' disciples join him at the well, we are hopeful that they will have it right. But that is not the case.

Earlier, the narrator had told us that the disciples had left Jesus at the well while they went to purchase some food (4:8). On their return, they encourage Jesus to "eat something" (4:31). At this moment, the storyteller reasserts the lack-of-understanding theme that has dominated the story so far. Jesus says, "I have food to eat that you do not know about" (4:32). Of course, Jesus was using "food" as a metaphor for the important work that had engaged his time while they were away. But the disciples miss the point. They exchange confused glances and mutter, "Surely no one has brought him something to eat?" (4:33).

Jesus attempts to repair their misunderstanding with yet another metaphor using imagery borrowed from the agricultural cycle in Israel: "Do you not say, 'Four months more, then comes the harvest'? But I tell you, look around you, and see how the fields are ripe for harvesting" (4:35). In doing so, Jesus is addressing a criticism that was subtly introduced into the story at the close of scene one. When the disciples returned to the well, they were unsettled by what they saw: "They were astonished that he was speaking with a woman, but no one said, 'What do you want?' or, 'Why are you speaking with her?'" (4:27). Because the disciples did not fully understand that Jesus was the Messiah who was sent to redeem people from all walks of life, no matter what their ancestry might be, they thought it inappropriate for him to be speaking with this Samaritan woman. Although they did not give voice to their complaint, Jesus knew about it. Here he addresses their lack of understanding with a metaphor that says the gospel is meant even for the people of Samaria. So while we enter scene three hopeful that the disciples will express understanding of Jesus' true identity and mission, we leave disappointed. Even they fail to articulate the words that the listener has been longing to hear.

Scene Four

The storyteller has left us with diminishing hope that the people in this story will understand his true identity. Scene four changes all of that. This time it is back to the city of Sychar. After hearing the testimony of the Samaritan woman, the residents of Sychar believe in Jesus and invite him to remain with them. They wondered, as the woman had, how it was possible for Jesus to know the personal details of this woman's life even though he had not met her (4:39–40). The testimony of the Samaritan woman, even tainted by her own uncertainty, had opened the door for further discussions with Jesus. While the storyteller glosses over all the detailed conversations that would have occurred during Jesus' two days in Sychar, we do know the results of that time together. This scene provides the climax, resolution, and conclusion of the story all in just a few words. From the moment Jesus begins his conversation with the woman at the well, we have been moving through a series of experimental identifications and through a series of misunderstandings. Those complications have only invited us to press on in the quest to find someone who really gets it. The residents of Sychar do. From this unlikely source we get one of the most profound statements of faith found in the gospel of John: "It is no longer because of what you [the Samaritan woman] said that we believe, for we have heard for ourselves, and we know that this is truly the Savior of the world" (4:42).

Step Seven: Explore the Artistic Presentation of People and Events in Time and Place

This story, like so many others in our Bible, is filled with the techniques and art forms that betray a master storyteller at work. Once again, our look into the artful ways used by this storyteller to deliver this narrative will not be comprehensive but will illustrate how this composer has shaped our experience with this story. We will spend a few moments with characterization, time depiction, setting, narrative geography, and the patterning play of words as an illustration of the storyteller's craft and its contribution to the meaning of this story.

Characterization

The story of Jesus in Samaria has two main characters and two groups of people that form dialogue partners with them. We have Jesus, the Samaritan woman, the disciples, and the residents of Sychar. In looking at the techniques used to introduce these individuals and groups to us, we note that there is little action recorded in this story, no physical descriptions of the participants, and no overt statements by the narrator that would shape our perception of these groups. Rather, the primary way in which we meet the participants in this plot is through the process of naming and through citing the direct speech of the characters. We will examine those two methods of characterization to unveil the manner in which the storyteller invites us to know Jesus and the Samaritan woman.

JESUS

We would expect that Jesus would stand out as a prominent figure in the story, and we are not disappointed. Through the use of naming techniques and direct quotations of Jesus, he occupies the story's center of interest. When we examine the details of the story, we see that Jesus is identified by the personal name, "Jesus," more than ten times. What is even more striking is that Jesus is the only individual in the story who is given a personal name. This fact alone draws us to him as the main character in the narrative.

Apart from his personal name, Jesus is also assigned two important appellations that further shape our impressions of him. We note that he calls himself "the gift of God" (4:10) and acknowledges that he is the "Messiah" (4:25–26). These very powerful titles that Jesus uses for himself reveal his true identity. But at the same time we find our impressions of Jesus confirmed in these titles, we also feel ourselves drawn more deeply into the plot as others fail to adopt and understand the implications of those titles.

The other appellations given to Jesus are assigned by various participants in the story and reflect their misunderstandings and struggles with Jesus' identity. The Samaritan woman calls him "a Jew" (4:9), "a prophet" (4:19), "a man" (4:29), and possibly "the Messiah" (4:29). The disciples call him "rabbi" (4:31). Finally, the residents of the city announce that he is "the Savior of the world" (4:42). Thus the naming of Jesus functions both to increase the tension within the plot and ultimately to provide the climax and resolution to the crisis.

The direct speech of Jesus is the second key to his characterization in this story. We note that both the amount of speech permitted him and the more exalted quality of that language serve to set him apart from others whose voices we hear. His direct speech fills more than one-third of the verses in this story, making his voice the one heard much more frequently than any other. Beyond the quantity of speech, the quality of his speeches and the content of his speeches set him apart from any mortal in the story. Jesus is the only one to use metaphor. He calls the gospel message "a spring of water gushing up to eternal life" (4:14). He tells his disciples, "I have food to eat that you do not know about" (4:32), likening the pressing business of his ministry to food. Jesus offers a lengthy agricultural metaphor that discusses the nature of his mission: "Do you not say, 'Four months more, then comes the harvest'? But I tell you, look around you, and see how the fields are ripe for harvesting" (4:35).

In addition to his use of metaphor, Jesus' speech is also distinguished by a depth of knowledge unparalleled in the words of other characters. He knows the private, sultry side of the Samaritan woman's personal life. He takes a dispute about where it is appropriate to worship (Mount Zion or Mount Gerizim) and resolves it in a way no mortal had dared to speak: "But the hour is coming, and is now here, when true worshipers will worship the Father in spirit and truth, for the Father seeks such as these to worship him. God is spirit, and those who worship him must worship in spirit and truth" (4:23–24). Thus, in both the insights that his speeches deliver and in the loftier quality of his language, the speeches of Jesus set him apart as someone who is special and unique. Not just the names and titles given to Jesus but also his own speeches demonstrate his true identity.

SAMARITAN WOMAN

The other character who finds herself in the spotlight more than any other in this story is the Samaritan woman. She is mentioned in scenes one, two, and four, occupying the stage with Jesus during the lengthy dialogue that occurs in the first scene. Unlike Jesus, whom the reader has met in the stories leading up to John 4, this is our first meeting with this woman. Consequently, as listeners we are going to lean in for a closer look at her naming, her speech, speech about her, and her actions.

While other women Jesus meets in the Bible are given personal names, such as Mary and Martha, this woman remains nameless. Those deprived of a name often find themselves consigned to play a minor role in the story. That is clearly not the case here. So how does her namelessness function in this story? Her lack of personal name forces us to attend to the other labels given to her. The narrator calls her "a Samaritan woman" (e.g. 4:7, 9). She calls herself "a woman of Samaria" (4:9). In all other cases she is identified as "the woman," "a woman," or simply as "woman." The appellations that stand out reference her gender and ethnicity. She is a Samaritan and a woman. Given the social context of this meeting, the audience who would hear this story in the first century would likely have very low expectations for her. Yet she tantalizes the reader again and again in her quest to find language that appropriately identifies this man at the city well.

After Jesus, the Samaritan woman gets the second-most speaking time in the story. While her speeches do not rise to the heights of the language assigned to Jesus, they do play an important role in the story. Through those speeches we see her experimenting with various ways of identifying Jesus. As the plot moves forward, a developing clarity in her language parallels her movement toward spiritual clarity. At first, she sees Jesus as an ordinary Jewish man (4:9), then "a prophet" (4:19), and finally the Samaritan woman is entertaining the possibility that he is the promised "Messiah" (4:29). She is a seeker, longing for the coming of the Messiah so that this Savior might lead her to better understanding of herself and her purpose in life, something that her own religious leaders have failed to do.

As Jesus speaks to her, we learn that this is a woman with a questionable past (and present):

Jesus said to her, "Go, call your husband and come back." The woman answered him, "I have no husband." Jesus said to her, "You are right in saying, 'I have no husband'; for you have had five husbands, and the one you have now is not your husband. What you have said is true!" (4:16–18)

The details of her previous and current relationships make it clear that this woman is living in sin. Like other "sinners" whom Jesus meets, we are not inclined to shun her. The details of her life revealed by Jesus show her to be a woman truly in need of assistance and direction. Well over her head in this word battle with Jesus, we pity her in her ignorance and pray that she might be led to faith.

The final dimension of her characterization occurs with the mention of two actions. The first time we meet this woman we hear that she is coming to draw water (4:7). This is the task that occupies the core of her day. After her conversation with Jesus, life begins to change. That change is signaled by the mention of a subsequent action—or, rather, an omission thereof: "Then the woman *left her water jar* and went back to the city" (4:28, author's emphasis). This is a small detail that could easily have been unmentioned. Its presence shows that the Samaritan woman is filled with a new passion. She had come to draw water, but now abandons both the tools and the particulars of this task. Before she does anything else, she needs to come to clarity on Jesus' identity. In contrast to the disciples who seem uninterested in the larger mission field before them, this woman is not only on the path to faith, she is speaking with her neighbors about Jesus.

Time and Setting

This story also aptly illustrates the way in which the divine storyteller may exploit our experience with time and setting. When we read through the story again, carefully noting the specific ways in which the storyteller deploys this information in the narrative, we are able to make some important observations about their participation in the narrative as well.

TIME

The passage of time is varied significantly from one scene to the next. Time passes very slowly in scene one, very quickly in scene two, slows a bit for scene three, and moves quickly again through scene four. Perhaps the greatest contrast in this technique is evident in comparing scenes one and two. Dialogue dominates the storytelling in scene one, which houses the direct speech of Jesus and the Samaritan woman. Given that more than one-half of our reading time is spent in this scene, we come to recognize that this exchange is very important to the storyteller. The inspired author wants to be certain that we hear Jesus articulate and rearticulate the problem of understanding. In this dialogue we also hear the Samaritan woman experiment with various ways of assigning an identity to Jesus. The passage of time in the second scene is drastically different. In this scene, the woman travels back into the city, speaks with the people in the city at some length, and heads back to the well with residents of Sychar in tow. All of this occurs in less than one minute of reading time! Since most of the work in developing the crisis and complications to the plot has filled scene one, time is permitted to pass more quickly in scene two.

The storyteller can also employ specific mention of time to direct our reading experience. We note two references here. In the exposition of the story, we are told that the woman is coming out to draw water at noon (4:6b). While this may not strike us as unusual in our context, it is very unusual in the context of the ancient world of Israel. More difficult labor was not done during the warmest part of the day, thus the work of drawing and transporting water was better left for the morning or evening hours, when it was cooler. The mention of "noon" by the storyteller does a couple of things for the reader sensitive to this matter. On the one hand, it raises the question of why this woman was coming to the well at midday to draw water. Did her marital situation, reported later in scene one, create social stigma that kept her from mingling with the others as they came to the well in the cooler hours of the day? We cannot know this for sure. But one thing is certain. The hour of the day guaranteed that Jesus and the woman would be alone at the well and would carry on the conversation of scene one without interruption even though they were at a very public location.

Scene four contains a second explicit reference to time. When the residents of Sychar began to listen to Jesus, they pressed for him to remain with them. We know that Jesus honored that request, for the narrator then tells us that Jesus remained with them for two days (4:40). This stands in striking contrast to the reception that he had received among some of his fellow countrymen in Judea, who were more than happy to have him move along. The story allows most of those two days to pass without any comment, but this time reference does say something about Jesus' commitment to this group of people. He was on his way to Galilee, where he had important work to do among his fellow Jews. Yet the spiritual needs of Jews in Galilee were not more important than the spiritual needs of Samaritans in Sychar. A two-day visit allows people to come to clarity on Jesus' identity, to ask questions, and to build a relationship. This personal time with Jesus brings the residents of Sychar to make the bold confession that stands as the climax of this story (4:42).

SETTING

In the exposition of the story, we also meet a great deal of detail related to the setting of the story. Trouble in Judea with the Pharisees leads Jesus to make a travel decision: "He [Jesus] left Judea and started back to Galilee. But he had to go through Samaria" (4:3–4). Here the storyteller mentions the three districts into which Israel had been divided. Judea is the district in the southern portion of Israel where Jerusalem is found. The District of Galilee lies in the northern portion of Israel, west of the Sea of Galilee. Samaria is the district that lies between the two. A quick look at a map of New Testament Israel will clarify the picture for us. If one wanted to travel from Judea to Galilee, the most direct route and the route that kept one out of the Decapolis[2] required a trip through the district of Samaria.

Because of the social and political history associated with Samaria, this meant a trip through territory occupied by people with whom conservative Jews had ongoing issues. The region of Samaria was part of the land promised to Abraham and ruled by Saul, David, and Solomon as part of the United Kingdom. When Solomon's kingdom divided, the future district of Samaria became part of the Northern Kingdom of Israel. Following the days of Solomon, the Northern Kingdom lived at odds with the Mosaic Covenant. The Lord took note of this apostasy. Because the Northern Kingdom shunned both their mission and passion for God's rescue plan, God allowed the nation of Assyria to defeat this Northern Kingdom and deport the people from the land (2 Kings 17:1–23). Then the king of Assyria resettled this region, replacing the former Israelites with people from other nations who did not know anything about the Lord. The false worship that these new residents brought to the land angered the Lord so much that God sent wild animals on a killing spree. This motivated the king of Assyria to send a Jewish priest back into the region of Samaria to instruct the people in the worship of the Lord so that this crisis might come to a close (2 Kings 17:24–28). The net result was an admixture of various religions and bloodlines in the region. The narrator of 2 Kings summarizes the situation in this way: "They [those living in Samaria] would not listen, however, but they continued to practice their former custom. So these nations worshiped the LORD, but also served their carved images; to this day their children and their children's children continue to do as their ancestors did" (2 Kings 17:40–41).

These events from the eighth century B.C.E. continued to impact the culture of Samaria in the Intertestimental Period. When the Jewish people gained independence and their own kings again controlled events in the region, John Hyrcanus sought to conquer the ideology of this region for the Lord by destroying the temple of the Samaritans on Mount Gerizim (128 B.C.E.). This act more than any other seems to have caused the rift between Jews and Samaritans that surfaces in the stories of the New Testament.

With this knowledge of Samaria and the Samaritans in hand, the reader can see how not just the physical setting but also the social setting for this story comes into play. The woman at the well gives voice to this social dynamic as she responds to Jesus' request for a drink of water: "How is it that you, a Jew, ask a drink of me, a woman of Samaria?" (4:9a). Should the listener miss the references to Samaria thus far, the narrator adds, "(Jews do not share things in common with Samaritans)" (4:9b). The Samaritan woman also makes reference to the social distinction between Jews and Samaritans when she points to the ongoing issue of where it would be best for God's people to worship: "Our ancestors worshiped on this mountain [Mount Gerizim], but you say that the place where people must worship is in Jerusalem" (4:20).

So we see that the physical setting points to a social setting that is a key player in ramping up the tension associated with the crisis. Knowledge of the true identity of Jesus is at stake. But who would imagine that this crisis would find any sort of resolution in this social context? Because this setting carries with it a rather negative connotation for the conservative Jew of the first century, it lowers our expectations, deepening the crisis of the plot. During his earthly ministry, Jesus met many people who sought his true identity. Among all these, who would think that a woman of Samaria and Samaritans in Sychar would get it right?

Narrative Geography

This is not the last we will hear of geography in this story. Three important segments of this story beg for the closer inquiry of a narrative-geographical investigation. First we will note that the setting is a refined well. Then in the process of their conversation, Jesus uses metaphoric language that imports hydrology into his message, talking about water and water sources. Third, in his conversation with the disciples, Jesus deploys an agricultural metaphor related to the appearance of the grain fields around them. We will now review the details and contribution of each.

JACOB'S WELL IN SYCHAR

The mention of Samaria carries with it important social connotations that inform the reading of the story, but note that the storyteller does not stop here in the exposition: "So he came to a Samaritan city called Sychar, near the plot of ground that Jacob had given to his son Joseph. Jacob's well was there" (4:5–6a). This language transports us to a time in Israel's history well before the events that incubated the social stress between Jews and Samaritans of the first century. By turning the pages in our Bible even farther back in time, we will learn more about the importance of Sychar and Jacob's well.

The New Testament city of Sychar lies at the base of Mount Gerizim and Mount Ebal, very close to the Old Testament city of Shechem. When we consider what happened at Shechem in Israel's history, we find that this location is particularly rich in history associated with the coming Messiah. When God summoned Abram to leave his homeland and travel to a new land, his first stop in the promised land is Shechem. On this very spot, the Lord reviewed his intentions. Abram's family would become a great nation. That nation would occupy this land. From that nation on this land, the messiah would be born (Gen. 12:1–3). Because of the significance of this theophany, Abram marked this spot with a memorial altar. In the years that followed, Abram's family would travel to this important crossroads at the base of Mount Gerizim and Mount Ebal again and again. They came to worship and to remember that the messianic hope lived through their family in this land (Gen. 12:6–7). Jacob, Abraham's grandson, was one of those visitors. He was so moved by the location that he purchased land in the area and dug a well there to sustain those who traveled to this spot (Gen. 33:18–20), apparently the very well that that provides the setting for the conversation between Jesus and the Samaritan woman. Thus this spot had a very important connection to the messianic promises given to Abraham and his family.

Not just the memory of the Abrahamic Covenant lived in this location. The messianic hope associated with the Mosaic Covenant also had strong connections here. The close of Genesis found Abraham's family in Egypt, where they would remain for an extended period of time. When they returned to the promised land under the leadership of Joshua, Moses was long dead; but the agreement God made with him on behalf of the Israelites lived on, governing the people in all their social and religious lifestyle. This set them apart as a people who were unique among all the nations, with a unique responsibility to bring the messiah into the world. Shortly after the initial victories of Joshua's conquest, we learn that he brought the people to the area of Shechem. This was a very dangerous undertaking. The major opponents in the land were far from defeated, and yet Joshua halted the campaign and took this detour into the heart of the promised land. Here Joshua built a memorial altar on Mount Ebal. Using the natural amphitheater of the valley lying between the two mountains, he reviewed the Law of Moses, calling for the people to rededicate themselves to the cause (Josh. 8:30–35). Later Joshua brought the Israelites back to this same spot following further conquests to once again seek the people's allegiance to the covenant God made with Moses and the hope of the coming messiah (Josh. 24:1–27). Certainly the natural amphitheater made this a choice setting for both events. But it was more than that. Shechem carried with it an important connection to Israel's history in this land and informed their mission as God's covenant people.

When we note what has happened on this spot before, it changes the way we hear Jesus' declaration in this narrative. The gospel writers rarely mention an instance when Jesus formally declares himself to be the Messiah. The fact that John does so here in a setting that is so carefully emphasized by the storyteller calls attention to the power this setting adds to the words of Jesus. Any place that Jesus would have declared himself to be the Messiah promised in the Old Testament would have had power. But this is the very spot where God first appeared to Abraham in the promised land to affirm the role of this land in the plan of rescue. This is where Jacob purchased land to guarantee access to the memorial altar. This is where Joshua, not once but twice, brought the people to recommit themselves to the Mosaic Covenant. One can hardly imagine a more powerful location for a Messianic declaration than the one that Jesus selected. By observing the detailed geographical information provided by the storyteller and by noting what happened on this very spot previously, we are able to appreciate the full depth and power that this setting gave to Jesus' statement, "I am he, the one who is speaking to you" (4:26).

WATER AND WATER SOURCES AS METAPHORS FOR THE GOSPEL

The second way in which narrative-geographical analysis can help us in this story is through decoding the metaphors Jesus uses that involve water and water sources. When the Samaritan woman hesitates to give Jesus a drink of water, he says to her, "If you knew the gift of God, and who it is that is saying to you, 'Give me a drink,' you would have asked him, and he would have given you living water" (4:10). After the woman's doubtful response, Jesus continues, "Everyone who drinks of this water will be thirsty again, but those who drink of the water that I will give them will never be thirsty. The water that I will give will become in them a spring of water gushing up to eternal life" (4:13–14). We will consider why water in general is an apt metaphor for the gospel and how the reference to two different water sources illuminates Jesus' language here.

When the woman hesitates to give Jesus a physical drink from Jacob's well, he begins to use water as a metaphor for the gospel message, the forgiveness of sins, that he has to offer. While water is more fundamental to human life than food, those of us who live with a consistent supply of fresh water as close as our kitchen faucet may fail to fully appreciate Jesus' use of water here. As noted above the average citizen in the United States will think about fresh water very differently than did the people of Jesus' day. Today per capita, we enjoy an amount of fresh water that is twenty times greater than the water available to those looking for a drink in ancient Israel.[3] It is no exaggeration to say that a considerable part of the day of the biblical characters would have been spent in identifying water resources, developing those resources, defending those resources, and transporting water from those resources. Fresh water was extremely precious. That makes it an apt metaphor for describing the forgiveness of sins Jesus offered to the world.

When Jesus begins to speak to the Samaritan woman about giving her this kind of water, a line of conversation opens that includes reference to two different water sources. Those sources are part of the larger picture of ancient hydrology. In Israel, people do not depend on lakes and rivers for their supply of fresh water. They count on rainfall. Since significant rainfall occurs only three months of the year, those living in ancient Israel had to save the rainwater that fell or reclaim that water from the ground for use during the months when little or no rain fell.

This meant getting water from springs, wells, or cisterns. Following a rainfall event, the water that did not evaporate or run off on the surface would percolate down through the upper layers of the soil, collecting at the level of the water table. Where the level of the water table touched the surface, a pool of water would form a natural spring. This kind of spring meant the least amount of work for the one seeking fresh water, as typically no excavation or improvement was necessary. But because springs were rare, particularly in the higher elevations of the promised land, people living there had to resort to an alternative water source. Either they would dig a well—a shaft excavated down to the water table; or they would dig a cistern—an underground chamber designed to capture and hold runoff water. Both required considerable labor and maintenance. The well not only had to be dug but lined with fieldstones to prevent collapse. The cistern had to be dug, lined with fieldstones, and then plastered to prevent water from seeping through the walls and floor.[4]

Given these water realities, we can now place the conversation of Jesus and the Samaritan woman into this context and note the shifting language each uses. After Jesus offers her "water," the woman objects. Jesus does not have the implements to draw water from the "well." The particular word she uses here indicates that she is thinking of a well that acts more like a cistern (4:11, 12). The flow of water into this kind of well is so slow that the water is of lower quality and may dry up all together. Jesus responds by offering her "water" from a different kind of "well." He offers her water that completely eliminates "thirst" and becomes a gushing spring of water (4:14). This is not the poor water resource the woman described but a springlike well that recharges regularly, making it so much more desirable than ordinary well water. By shifting the vocabulary, Jesus shows that he is not talking about the same kind of water she is—water drawn from an ordinary well. The water he is offering is unique and special.

Thus the lack of fresh water in the region and the various terms used for the water resources play an important role in decoding the metaphor of Jesus here. He is telling the woman that he can offer her something much more precious than the water from this old well, which flows poorly at best. He is offering her water that completely eliminates thirst, living water that promises the blessing of eternal life.

AGRICULTURE AS A METAPHOR

The third example of narrative geography appears in the agricultural metaphor Jesus uses in his conversation with the disciples. After the Samaritan woman has rushed back into the city, Jesus converses with the disciples at the well. During this conversation, Jesus points to the grain fields around them and says, "Do you not say, 'Four months more, then comes the harvest?' But I tell you, look around you, and see how the fields are ripe for harvesting" (4:35).

Agricultural metaphors like this one were clearly live metaphors for those living in the Israel of Jesus' day. But they are less likely to remain living metaphors for English readers in America for a couple of reasons. First of all, only about 2 percent of Americans are directly involved in agriculture today, in contrast to 85 percent of families who were directly involved in agriculture in Jesus' day.[5] Second, even those who are involved in agriculture today may misunderstand the metaphor Jesus used here, since the annual time of planting and harvesting are different for American farmers than the ancient farmers in Israel.

The best way to decode this metaphor is to set it within the context of the agricultural cycle in Israel. To grow grain in this water-starved region means to carefully design the planting and harvesting tasks around the annual rain cycle. Since it does not rain for months in Israel during the summer season, it is only with the arrival of the early rains (October to early November) that the planting of grain can begin. The early rain showers of October loosen the soil that has been baked hard by the summer sun. This allows the farmer to plow furrows in the field into which the grain seed can be dispersed. Once that seed is in the ground and covered, the sprouting grain eagerly awaits the arrival of the middle rains (December through February) when significant rainfall allows the grain crops to mature. As the rainfall again becomes lighter during the season of the late rains (March through early April), the grain crops ripen, turning golden in late April or early May when the grain harvest takes place.

With this agricultural cycle in mind, we can return to Jesus' words. As they look over the grain fields outside the city of Sychar, Jesus notes that most people would look at the condition of the field crops and say it would be four more months until the harvest (4:35a). Four months before the harvest would place the actual time of the conversation sometime between mid-January and mid-February. At this time of the year, the grain fields are green and immature. Jesus continues, "Yet I tell you, look around you, and see how the fields are ripe for harvesting" (4:35b).

No one looking at the physical scene before Jesus and the disciples could possibly think that the immature grain fields before them were ready for harvest. However, Jesus is not talking about literal grain fields but about people, people who were ready to hear about him. Although the disciples' quiet thoughts about the Samaritans are unspoken, they are not unheard by Jesus. He knows that they are astonished that Jesus would be spending time with this Samaritan woman (4:27). They urge Jesus to eat, to regain his strength, undoubtedly with the plan that they move on quickly to speak with people who really matter up in Galilee. That is where the disciples think the mission opportunities are the greatest. But Jesus addresses a grave misunderstanding that they are carrying both about who he is and who deserved his time. This Samaritan woman, not the leaders in Jerusalem or the people of his hometown in Galilee, had expressed this desire: "I know that Messiah is coming" (who is called Christ). "When he comes, he will proclaim all things to us" (4:25). If this is not a grain field ready for the spiritual harvest, what is? The disciples are blinded by their own social bias and their lack of understanding. Consequently, Jesus uses this agricultural metaphor to show that his ministry and mission extend to all people. Priority time will be given to those who express the longing and desire to know the Messiah no matter what their social standing or origins.

The Patterning Play of Words

With the contribution of narrative geography in view, we will return to the details of the story one more time in order to examine the artful use of language—the patterning play of words—the storyteller employs to shape our experience with this event. In this regard, we will be speaking about repetition of a word, the use of metaphor by Jesus, and the use of questions that advance the cause of the story.

REPETITION

As we observed in the story of David and Goliath, repetition is a very common form of word play exploited by the divine storyteller. This story is no exception. In fact, it contains an important key-word repetition that focuses and refocuses the listener's attention on the crisis of understanding that lies at the heart of this story. Five times throughout this story, one piece of vocabulary surfaces over and over again. That word is the one for "to know." Jesus is the first to use the word as he points up the crisis: "If you knew the gift of God, and who it is that is saying to you..." (4:10). With one deft language stroke, Jesus has placed the major issue of the story on the table. People fail to "know" what they need to know about him.

In just a few verses, we find this same word surfacing again, delivered even more bluntly and with increasing power. When the Samaritan woman says she is confused by the claims and counterclaims of Jews and Samaritans with regards to where one ought to worship, the word for "know" makes three appearances. Jesus says, "You worship what you do not know; we worship what we know, for salvation is from the Jews" (4:22). The Samaritan woman responds defensively. Tacitly acknowledging the many things she does not know, she emphasizes one thing she does know. Picking up the same word Jesus has used three times, she asserts, "I know that Messiah is coming" (4:25). After Jesus says, "I am he, the one who is speaking to you," (4:26) and the disciples return, she leaves to speak with the citizens of Sychar. Once again the disciples' failure to understand is emphasized with this piece of vocabulary. When the disciples urge Jesus to eat, he says, "I have food to eat that you do not know about" (4:32). Now they have joined the growing group of people who lack clarity on his identity and mission. In one instance after another, the repetition of this root points up the problem of understanding that is rampant among those interacting with Jesus.

When that crisis of knowledge comes to resolution, the word for "know" is right there, indicating a dramatic reversal in this situation. After Jesus has spent two days in Sychar, the people in that city confess, "We know what that this is truly the Savior of the world" (4:42). By listening carefully to the storyteller's language, we have discovered the repetition of a verb root that helps link the various scenes of the story together and keeps them focused on the crisis of knowledge. When that crisis comes to resolution, a final use of that word signals the close of the story for us.

METAPHOR

Apart from word repetition, the storyteller also puts metaphor to work in this story. When Jesus speaks about the gospel with the woman at the well, he identifies that good news with "water" that becomes a "spring of water gushing up to eternal life" (4:10, 14). When the disciples challenge Jesus to eat, he says that he has "food" to eat they know nothing about (4:32). Here food is being used as a metaphor for his work and mission. Finally, Jesus uses an agricultural metaphor, "See how the fields are ripe for harvesting" (4:35). This metaphor defines his mission and the mission of the disciples in taking the gospel message to the people of Sychar.

We have spoken about the decoding of each of these metaphors above. But here we pause again to note their cumulative weight. In a story that highlights a lack of understanding, the storyteller keeps distinguishing Jesus from all the other characters in the story both through what he says and how he says it. When we look at all the direct speech in this story, only Jesus' language rises above the mundane to speak in this more refined way. This elegant form of language, used only by Jesus, helps set him apart. He not only says he is the Messiah, he sounds like the Messiah as well.

QUESTIONS

While the use of metaphor marks the language of Jesus in this story, we find the speech of the Samaritan woman characterized by questions. In fact, her very first words take the form of a rhetorical question. In response to Jesus' request for a drink of water, she asks, "How is that you, a Jew, ask a drink of me, a woman of Samaria?" (4:9). She is not seeking an explanation but offering social commentary. All she sees before her is a Jewish man. Experience has taught her that it is inappropriate for a Jewish man to ask for anything from a Samaritan woman. In a mild but pointed rebuke, she tells Jesus that his request is out of bounds. Yet at the same time, her question puts the identity of Jesus into play.

Undaunted by her rebuke, Jesus offers to give her something to drink. Once again, she responds with a pair of rhetorical questions. "Sir, you have no bucket, and the well is deep. Where do you get that living water? Are you greater than our ancestor Jacob, who gave us the well, and with his sons and his flocks drank from it?" (4:11–12). Taken out of context, the first question might be regarded as a legitimate request for information. Jesus has offered her a drink yet has no physical means to provide it. Does he have knowledge of an alternate water source in the area? But in context, these questions must be read as rhetorical questions with a sarcastic twist. She is the local, and Jesus is the outsider. If there were another water resource in the area, she would know about it. That makes the first question another rebuke designed to put Jesus in his place: "You do not have the ability to give me water." The second rhetorical question is also meant to put Jesus in his place. But it contains a twist of irony. The woman ponders aloud if Jesus could be greater than her ancestor Jacob who had dug this well. The answer is obvious to her. Jesus might be a Jewish man but he is no Jacob. In an ironic twist, she has spoken a greater truth than she knows. Yes, the man before her is even greater than Jacob who had dug the well. How much greater she has yet to learn. But with this rhetorical question, she has unwittingly advanced a step closer toward the ultimate realization of Jesus' true identity.

The final words we hear from the Samaritan woman are also cast as a question. This time, however, the sarcasm is gone as she asks the question of a true seeker. After spending the time she had with Jesus at Jacob's well, she encourages the people in Sychar to explore the matter further with her asking, "He cannot be the Messiah, can he?" (4:29). Her question gets the people of Sychar thinking. They invite Jesus to stay the night and then another so that they can find the answer to the question the woman has posed. This question is the last word we hear from the woman. Yet it sets the stage for a remarkable story of conversion, for it sets the residents of Sychar on a quest that ultimately brings us to the climax and conclusion of the story. Could this man by the well really be the Messiah? The people of Sychar know the answer: "It is no longer because of what you [the woman] said that we believe, for we have heard for ourselves, and we know that this is truly the Savior of the world" (4:42).

Conclusion

If we believe that a divine voice lies behind the pages of our Bible, then we must acknowledge that the God who speaks there is a storyteller, for the Bible is a book filled with captivating and memorable stories. Far from a cold rehearsal of the historical facts, each narrative is an engaging composition that invites the reader to follow, to watch, and to learn as the drama unfolds. We trust that those words that opened this book will have new meaning for our readers as they close the book. We have seen how God has used the conventions of storytelling–from characterization to word play–to turn an event from the past into a story with a message for the present. God bless you as you seek the message that the divine storyteller has for you.

Notes

[1]Marianne Meye Thompson, "John," in *A Complete Literary Guide to the Bible,* ed. Leland Ryken and Tremper Longman III (Grand Rapids: Zondervan, 1993), 418.

[2]While orthodox Jews would have liked to avoid travel through Samaria, travel through the pagan region of the Decapolis was even more loathsome.

[3]John A. Beck, *The Land of Milk and Honey: An Introduction to the Geography of Israel* (St. Louis, Concordia Publishing House, 2006), 148.

[4]Ibid., 151–52.

[5]K.C. Hanson and Douglas E. Oakman, *Palestine in the Time of Jesus: Social Structures and Social Conflicts* (Minneapolis: Fortress Press, 1998), 104.

Bibliography

Narrative Criticism and the Bible

Alter, Robert. *The Art of Biblical Narrative*. New York: Basic Books, 1981.
_____. *The World of Biblical Literature*. New York: Basic Books, 1992.
Alter, Robert, and Frank Kermode, ed. *The Literary Guide to the Bible*. Cambridge: Harvard University Press, 1987.
Amit, Yairah. *Reading Biblical Narratives, Literary Criticism and the Hebrew Bible*. Minneapolis: Fortress Press, 2001.
Bar-Efrat, Shimon. *Narrative Art in the Bible*. Journal for the Study of the Old Testament Supplement Series 70. Sheffield: The Almond Press, 1989.
Berlin, Adele. *Poetics and Interpretation of Biblical Narrative*. Winona Lake, Ind.: Eisenbrauns, 1994.
Bullinger, E. W. *Figures of Speech Used in the Bible Explained and Illustrated*. Grand Rapids: Baker Book House, 1968.
Chisholm, Robert B. Jr. "History or Story? The Literary Dimension in Narrative Texts." In *Giving the Sense: Understanding and Using Old Testament Historical Texts*. Edited by David M. Howard Jr. and Michael A. Grisanti. Grand Rapids: Kregel, 2003.
Culpepper, R. Alan. *Anatomy of the Fourth Gospel: A Study in Literary Design*. Foundations and Facets, New Testament. Philadelphia: Fortress Press, 1983.
Exum, J. Cheryl, and David J. A. Clines, eds. *The New Literary Criticism and the Hebrew Bible*. Journal for the Study of the Old Testament Supplements 143. Sheffield: Sheffield Academic Press, 1993.
Fokkelman, J.P. *Reading Biblical Narrative: An Introductory Guide*. Louisville: Westminster John Knox Press, 1999.
Gerhart, Mary. "A Theory of Narrative: The Restoration of Biblical Narrative." *Semeia* 46 (1989): 13–29.
Gordon, Robert P. "Simplicity of the Highest Cunning: Narrative Art in the Old Testament." *Scottish Bulletin of Evangelical Theology* 6 (1988): 69–80.
Gros Louis, Kenneth R.R., James S. Ackerman, and Thayer S. Warshaw, eds. *Literary Interpretations of Biblical Narratives*. 2 Vols. Nashville: Abingdon Press, 1974.
Gunn, David M., and Danna Nolan Fewell. *Narrative in the Hebrew Bible*. The Oxford Bible Series. Oxford: Oxford University Press,1993.
Henry, Carl F.H. "Narrative Theology: An Evangelical Appraisal." *Trinity Journal* 8 (1987): 3–19.

House, Paul R. *Beyond Form Criticism: Essays in Old Testament Literary Criticism.* Sources for Biblical and Theological Study 2. Winona Lake, Ind.: Eisenbrauns, 1992.

Long, V. Philips. *The Art of Biblical History.* Foundation of Contemporary Interpretation 5. Grand Rapids: Zondervan, 1994.

Longman, Tremper III. *Literary Approaches to Biblical Interpretation.* Foundation of Contemporary Interpretation 3. Grand Rapids: Zondervan, 1987.

_____. "The Literary Approach to the Study of the Old Testament: Promise and Pitfalls." *Journal of the Evangelical Theological Society* 28 (1984): 385–98.

Malbon, Elizabeth S., and Adele Berlin, eds. *Characterization in Biblical Literature.* Semeia 63. Atlanta: Scholars Press, 1993.

Merenlahti, Petri. *Poetics for the Gospels? Rethinking Narrative Criticism.* London: T and T Clark, 2002.

Noble, Paul R. "Synchronic and Diachronic Approaches to Biblical Interpretation." *Literature and Theology* 7 (1993): 131–48.

Powell, Mark Allan. *What Is Narrative Criticism?* Guides to Biblical Scholarship. Minneapolis: Fortress Press, 1990.

Preminger, Alex, and Edward L. Greenstein, eds. *The Hebrew Bible in Literary Criticism.* New York: Ungar Publishing Co., 1986.

Provan, Iain, V. Philips Long, and Tremper Longman III. "Narrative and History: Stories About the Past." In *A Biblical History of Israel.* Louisville: Westminster John Knox Press, 2003.

de Regt, L.J., Jan de Waard, and J.P. Fokkelman. *Literary Structures and Rhetorical Strategies in the Hebrew Bible.* Winona Lake, Ind.: Eisenbrauns, 1996.

Resseguie, James L. *Narrative Criticism of the New Testament: an Introduction.* Grand Rapids: Baker Academic, 2005.

Rhoads, David, and Donald Michie. *Mark as Story: An Introduction to the Narrative of a Gospel.* Philadelphia: Fortress Press, 1982.

Rhoads, David, and Kari Syreeni. *Characterization in the Gospels: Reconceiving Narrative Criticism.* Sheffield: Sheffield Academic Press, 1999.

Ryken, Leland. *How to Read the Bible as Literature and Get More Out of It.* Grand Rapids: Zondervan, 1984.

_____. *Word of Delight: A Literary Introduction to the Bible.* Grand Rapids: Baker Books, 1987.

Ryken, Leland, and Tremper Longman III. *A Complete Literary Guide to the Bible.* Grand Rapids: Zondervan, 1993.

Sailhamer, John. *The Pentateuch as Narrative.* Grand Rapids: Zondervan, 1992.

Savran, George. *Telling and Retelling: Quotation in Biblical Narrative.* Indiana Studies in Biblical Literature. Bloomington: Indiana University Press, 1988.

Sternberg, Meir. *The Poetics of Biblical Narrative: Ideological Literature and the Drama of Reading.* Bloomington: Indiana University Press, 1985.

Bible Geography and Archaeology

Aharoni, Yohanan. *The Land of the Bible: A Historical Geography.* Translated by A.F. Rainey. Philadelphia: Westminster Press, 1979.

Aharoni, Yohanan, Michael Avi-Yonah, Anson F. Rainey, and Ze'ev Safrai. *The Macmillan Bible Atlas.* 3d ed. New York: Macmillan Publishing Company, 1993.

Avi-Yonah, Michael, ed. *Encyclopedia of Archaeological Investigation.* 4 Vols. Englewood Cliffs, N.J.: Prentice-Hall, Inc., 1976.

Baly, Dennis. *The Geography of the Bible.* New York: Harper and Row, 1974.

Beitzel, Barry J. *The Moody Atlas of Bible Lands.* Chicago: Moody Press, 1985.

Borowski, Oded. *Agriculture in Iron Age Israel.* Winona Lake, Ind.: Eisenbrauns, 1987.

Bright, John. *A History of Israel.* 3d ed. Philadelphia: Westminster Press, 1981.

Brisco, Thomas V. *Holman Bible Atlas.* Nashville: Holman Reference, 1998.

Cleave, Richard. *The Holy Land Satellite Atlas.* Nicosia, Cyprus: Rohr Productions, 1994.

Cornfeld, Gaalyah, and David Noel Freedman. *Archaeology of the Bible, Book by Book.* San Francisco: Harper and Row, 1982.

Dorsey, David A. *The Roads and Highways of Ancient Israel.* Baltimore: The Johns Hopkins University Press, 1991.

Elitsur, Yoel. *Ancient Place Names in the Holy Land: Preservation and History.* Winona Lake: Ind.: Eisenbrauns, 2004.

Finegan, Jack. *The Archeology of the New Testament: The Life of Jesus and the Beginning of the Early Church..* Princeton: Princeton University Press, 1992.

Free, Joseph P., and Howard F. Vos. *Archaeology and Bible History.* Grand Rapids: Zondervan, 1992.

Freeman-Grenville, G.S.P., Rupert L. Chapman III, and Joan E. Taylor. *The Onomasticon by Eusebius of Caesarea.* Jerusalem: Carta, 2003.

Frescobaldi, Gucci and Sigoli, *Visit to the Holy Places of Egypt: Sinai, Palestine and Syria in 1384 by Frescobaldi, Gucci and Sigoli.* Edited by B. Basggati. Jerusalem: Franciscan Press, 1948.

Glueck, Nelson. *The River Jordan.* New York: McGraw Hill Book Company, 1968.

_____. *Rivers in the Desert: A History of the Negev.* New York: Farrar, Straus and Cudahy, 1959.

Hareuveni, Nogah. *Tree and Shrub in Our Biblical Heritage.* Kiryat Ono, Israel: Neot Kedumim, 1984.

Harff, Arnold Ritter von. *The Pilgrimage of Arnold von Harff in the Years 1496–1499.* Translated by Malcolm Letts. Nendeln, Liechtenstein: Kraus Reprint, 1967.

Hoerth, Alfred J. *Archaeology and the Old Testament.* Grand Rapids: Baker Books, 1998.

Issar, Arie. *Water Shall Flow from the Rock: Hydrology and Climate in the Lands of the Bible.* New York: Springer–Verlag, 1990.

King, Philip J., and Lawrence Stager. *Life in Biblical Israel.* Library of Ancient Israel. Louisville: Westminster John Knox Press, 2001.

Lynch, W.F. *Narrative of the United States' Expedition to the Jordan River and the Dead Sea.* Philadelphia: Lea and Blanchard, 1849.

Mazar, Amihai. *Archaeology of the Land of the Bible 10,000–586 B.C.E.* The Anchor Bible Reference Library. New York: Doubleday, 1992.

Meyers, Eric M., ed. *The Oxford Encyclopedia of Archaeology in the Near East.* New York: Oxford University Press, 1997.

Nebenzahl, Kenneth. *Maps of the Holy Land: Images of Terra Sancta Through Two Millenia.* New York: Abbeville Press, 1986.

Nicolo of Poggibonsi. *A Voyage Beyond the Seas.* Jerusalem: Franciscan Press, 1945.

Orni, Efraim, and Elisha Efrat. *Geography of Israel.* 3d ed. Jerusalem: The Jewish Publication Society of America, 1973.

Palestine Pilgrims' Text Society. 13 Vols. New York: AMS Press, 1971.

Pfeiffer, Charles, and Howard Vos. *The Wycliffe Historical Geography of Bible Lands.* Chicago: Moody Press, 1967.

Prescott, Hilda Frances Margaret. *Friar Felix at Large; a Fifteenth-Century Pilgrimage to the Holy Land.* New Haven: Yale University Press, 1950.

Rainey, Anson, and Steven Notley. *The Sacred Bridge: Carta's Atlas of the Biblical World.* Jerusalem: Carta, 2006.

Randall, David Austin. *The Handwriting of God in Egypt, Sinai and the Holy Land.* Philadelphia: John E. Potter and Company, 1862.

Rasmussen, Carl. *The NIV Atlas of the Bible.* Grand Rapids: Zondervan, 1989.

Ritter, Carl. *The Comparative Geography of Palestine and the Sinaitic Peninsula.* 4 Vols. New York: Greenwood Press, 1968.

Robinson, Edward. *Biblical Researches in Palestine and the Adjacent Regions 1838 and 1852.* 3 Vols. Jerusalem: Universitas Booksellers, 1970.

Schur, Nathan. *Twenty Centuries of Christian Pilgrimage to the Holy Land.* Tel Aviv: Dvir Publishing House, 1992.

Scott, R.B.Y. "Meteorological Phenomena and Terminology in the Old Testament." *Zeitschrift Für Alttestamentliche Wissenschaft* 64 (1952): 11–25.

Simons, J. *The Geographical and Topographical Texts of the Old Testament.* Leiden: : E. J. Brill, 1959.

Smith, George A. *The Historical Geography of the Holy Land.* New York: Harper and Row, 1966.

Stern, Ephraim, ed. *The New Encyclopedia of Archaeological Investigation of the Holy Land.* 4 Vols. New York: Simon and Schuster, 1993.

_____. *Archaeology and the Land of the Bible, Vol. 2. The Assyrian, Babylonian, and Persian Periods (732-332 BCE).* The Anchor Bible Reference Library. New York: Doubleday, 2001.

Suriano, Francesco. *Treatise on the Holy Land.* Jerusalem: Franciscan Press, 1949.

Thompson, John Arthur. *The Bible and Archaeology.* Grand Rapids: William B. Eerdmans Publishing Company, 1972.

Thompson, William M. *The Land and the Book.* 3 Vols. London: T. Nelson and Sons, 1881.

Turner, George. *Historical Geography of the Holy Land.* Grand Rapids: Baker Book House, 1973.

Wilkinson, J., ed. *Jerusalem Pilgrims before the Crusades.* Jerusalem: Ariel, 1977.

_____. *Egeria's Travels.* Warminster, England: Airs and Phillips, 1999.

Wright, G. Ernest. *Biblical Archaeology.* Philadelphia: Westminster Press, 1962.

Wright, Thomas, ed. *Early Travels in Palestine.* London: Bohn, 1848.

Zohary, Michael. *Plants of the Bible.* Cambridge: Cambridge University Press, 1982.

Scripture Index